Academic Reading
A Content-Based Approach

Academic Reading
A Content-Based Approach

LOUIS W. HOLSCHUH
The Ohio State University

J. PATRICK KELLEY
Data Processing Educational Corporation

St. Martin's Press   New York

Acquiring Editor: Susan Anker
Senior Project Editor: Patricia Mansfield
Production Supervisor: Christine Pearson
Text Design: Barbara Bert/North 7 Atelier Ltd.
Cover Design: Ben Santora
Graphics: G&H Soho

Library of Congress Catalog Card Number: 87-060512
Copyright © 1988 by St. Martin's Press, Inc.
All rights reserved.
Manufactured in the United States of America.
21098
fedcba

For information, write:
St. Martin's Press, Inc.
175 Fifth Avenue
New York, NY 10010

ISBN: 0-312-00297-1
Instructor's Edition ISBN: 0-312-01284-5

Acknowledgments

"Vision: Your Human Camera" from *Psychology: An Introduction*, portions of pp. 104–108. Benjamin Lahey. © 1983 Wm. C. Brown Publishers, Dubuque, Iowa. All rights reserved. Reprinted by permission.

Figure 1: Adaptation of illustration in *Eye and Camera*, p. 33. Eric Mose. Appeared in *Scientific American*, August 1950. Reprinted by permission.

Figure 2: From *Psychology: An Introduction* by Benjamin Lahey © 1983 Wm. C. Brown Publishers, Dubuque, Iowa. Reprinted by permission.

"Consumer Behavior: Basic Concepts" from *Marketing* by David L. Kurtz and Louis E. Boone. Copyright © 1981 by the Dryden Press. Reprinted by permission of CBS College Publishing.

Figure 1-1 from *Human Behavior in Marketing*. John Douglas, George A. Field, and Lawrence X. Tarpey. © 1967 Charles E. Merrill Publishing Co. Reprinted by permission.

Figure 1-2 from *How We Think*. John Dewey. © D.C. Heath and Co.

Figure 1-3 adapted from *Consumer Behavior: An Integrated Framework*, p. 14. C. Glenn Walters and Gordon W. Paul. © 1970 Richard D. Irwin, Inc. Reprinted by permission.

Figure 1-4 from A. H. Maslow, "A Theory of Human Motivation." As printed in *Psychological Review*, July 1943.

Figure 1-5 adapted from *Attitude Organization and Change*, p. 3. M. J. Rosenberg and C. I. Hovland. © 1960 Yale University Press. Reprinted by permission of Yale University Press.

Figure 1-6 from William A. Mindak, "Fitting the Semantic Differential to the Marketing Problem." As printed in *Journal of Marketing*, April 1961. Reprinted by permission of the American Marketing Association.

Table 1-1 from Mason Haire, "Projective Techniques in Marketing Research." As printed in *Journal of Marketing*, April 1950. Reprinted by permission of the American Marketing Association.

"Key Business Decisions" from *Modern Market Management*, revised edition, by Burton H. Marcus, et al. Copyright © 1980 by Random House, Inc. Reprinted by permission of the publisher.

Table 2-1 from *Consumer Behavior*, 2d ed., by James F. Engel, David T. Kollat, and Roger D. Blackwell. Copyright © 1968, 1973 by Holt, Rinehart and Winston, Inc. Reprinted by permission of CBS College Publishing.

"Market Targeting" from Philip Kolter, *Marketing Essentials*, © 1984, pp. 176–180. Reprinted by permission of Prentice-Hall, Inc., Englewood Cliffs, NJ.

"Thought, Creativity, and the Computer," David D. Thornburg. In M. Edelhart and D. Garr *The Complete Computer Compendium*. © 1984 Addison-Wesley. Reprinted by permission of the author.

Acknowledgments and copyrights are continued at the back of the book on page 321, which constitutes an extension of the copyright page.

To
Linda
and
Mary Ann

Preface

In many ways, the ability to read academic prose efficiently and with adequate understanding is a hidden skill for college or university students. They are evaluated on their production, on what they say and write, but their reading skills are not directly observed or graded. Yet reading constitutes the primary means by which students gather information and concepts. The inability to read well clearly places students at a distinct disadvantage.

Academic Reading: A Content-Based Approach provides guided practice in the reading of unsimplified academic texts for either native speakers or advanced-level nonnative speakers in a college or university setting. It is structured so students first learn how and when to apply appropriate reading strategies and skills, and then are presented tasks that promote the higher-order language skills of content evaluation and integration.

The approach of *Academic Reading* is both process-oriented and content-based. The discrete reading skills are not taught and practiced in isolation, but rather practiced as required by the reading task. Exercise material always focuses on the content of the text being read instead of the type of strategy or skill employed. And the opportunities provided to integrate and evaluate content from various sources further direct students to attend to meaning.

The book begins with an introduction that presents an overview of the reading process and suggests a number of strategies for successful critical reading. The remainder of the text is divided into six units, each containing three reading selections that focus on the same topic but from different perspectives. The themes covered are population growth, computers, marketing and consumer behavior, social psychology, language, and fiber optics. The readings have been taken from representative college-level textbooks and related academic and professional sources. The initial selection in each unit is a fairly long introduction to the topic (3,000 to 4,000 words), while the second and third are shorter, corollary readings (800 to 1,500 words) that extend the ideas of the first.

Reading selections are preceded by (1) Warmup Questions to aid students in identifying their existing understanding of the topic and (2) Preview Questions designed to promote good previewing habits. Following each reading are extensive Study Questions that focus on comprehension strategies. These Study Questions are arranged to guide students through a reading selection in a more or less linear fashion, thus allowing them to practice reading skills in a realistic context as needed. Following the study questions are exercises to check comprehension. At the end of the corollary readings are Integration Questions for Writing and Discussion. These exercises require students to relate information from the three selections in a unit and to evaluate the information and apply it in meaningful ways. This process simulates what is demanded of students in regular academic coursework.

The following reviewers offered helpful comments and questions at various stages in the development of this book: Cathy Day, Eastern Michigan University; Joanne Devine, Skidmore College; Patricia L. Carrell, Southern Illinois University; Elsa Auerbach, University of Massachusetts, Harbor; Jann Huizenga, LaGuardia Community College, CUNY; Kay Westerfield, University of Oregon; Margaret S. Steffensen, Illinois State University; and Amy Sales, Boston University. We thank them for their insight and honesty.

Our appreciation also goes to Patricia Mansfield of St. Martin's Press, managing editor; Christine Pearson, production supervisor; and especially to Susan Anker, our acquiring editor. We would also like to acknowledge the staff and students of the American Language Program at The Ohio State University for field-testing several units. Finally, we thank our families for their patience and encouragement.

Louis W. Holschuh
J. Patrick Kelley

Contents

Preface   vii

Introduction   1
    WHAT HAPPENS WHEN YOU READ?   1
    STRATEGIES FOR READING   2
VISION: YOUR HUMAN CAMERA / Benjamin B. Lahey   5
    AFTER YOU READ   17
    USING THIS TEXTBOOK   18

UNIT I   Marketing   19

1   Consumer Behavior: Basic Concepts   21
    WARMUP QUESTIONS   21
    PREVIEWING   22
CONSUMER BEHAVIOR: BASIC CONCEPTS / David L. Kurtz and Louis E. Boone   25
    Part 1: STUDY QUESTIONS   37
    Part 2: STUDY QUESTIONS   38
    Part 2: COMPREHENSION EXERCISES   44
    Part 3: STUDY QUESTIONS   45
    Part 3: COMPREHENSION EXERCISES   50

2   Key Business Decisions: Branding   53
    WARMUP QUESTIONS   53
KEY BUSINESS DECISIONS / Burton Marcus et al.   55
    STUDY QUESTIONS   59
    INTEGRATION QUESTIONS FOR DISCUSSION AND WRITING   62

3   Market Targeting   64
    WARMUP QUESTIONS   65
MARKET TARGETING / Philip Kolter   67
    STUDY QUESTIONS   71
    INTEGRATION QUESTIONS FOR DISCUSSION AND WRITING   74

UNIT II   Computers   75

4   Computer Programming   77
    WARMUP QUESTIONS   77
    PREVIEWING   78

COMPUTERS, PROGRAMS, AND PROGRAMMING LANGUAGES / J. Patrick Kelley   81
    Part 1: STUDY QUESTIONS   89
    Part 1: COMPREHENSION EXERCISES   91
    Part 2: STUDY QUESTIONS   92
    Part 2: COMPREHENSION EXERCISES   98
    Part 3: STUDY QUESTIONS   99
    Part 3: COMPREHENSION EXERCISES   103

5 Thought, Creativity, and the Computer   105
WARMUP QUESTIONS   105
THOUGHT, CREATIVITY, AND THE COMPUTER / David D. Thornburg   107
    STUDY QUESTIONS   109
    INTEGRATION QUESTIONS FOR DISCUSSION AND WRITING   111

6 Controversies over Artificial Intelligence   112
WARMUP QUESTIONS   112
CONTROVERSIES OVER ARTIFICIAL INTELLIGENCE / Nancy B. Stern   115
    STUDY QUESTIONS   119
    INTEGRATION QUESTIONS FOR DISCUSSION AND WRITING   121

UNIT III   Population Growth   123

7 Populations, the Environment, and Humans   125
WARMUP QUESTIONS   125
PREVIEWING   126
POPULATIONS, THE ENVIRONMENT, AND HUMANS
William H. Mason and Norton L. Marshall / 129
    Part 1: STUDY QUESTIONS   139
    Part 2: STUDY QUESTIONS   140
    Part 2: COMPREHENSION EXERCISES   146
    Part 3: STUDY QUESTIONS   148
    Part 3: COMPREHENSION EXERCISES   153

8 Factors Limiting Growth   155
WARMUP QUESTIONS   155
FACTORS LIMITING GROWTH / David L. Kirk   157
    STUDY QUESTIONS   161
    INTEGRATION QUESTIONS FOR DISCUSSION AND WRITING   164

9 Population and Natural Resources   166
WARMUP QUESTIONS   166
POPULATION AND NATURAL RESOURCES / Andrew C. Varga   167
    STUDY QUESTIONS   169
    INTEGRATION QUESTIONS FOR DISCUSSION AND WRITING   171

UNIT IV   Social Psychology   173

10 Social Relations   175

WARMUP QUESTIONS 175
PREVIEWING 176
SOCIAL RELATIONS / Arno F. Wittig and Gurney Williams III 179
Part 1: STUDY QUESTIONS 187
Part 1: COMPREHENSION EXERCISES 192
Part 2: STUDY QUESTIONS 193
Part 2: COMPREHENSION EXERCISES 196
Parts 1 and 2: COMPREHENSION EXERCISE 197
Part 3: STUDY QUESTIONS 197
Part 3: COMPREHENSION EXERCISES 204

11 Some Conditions of Obedience and Disobedience to Authority 206
WARMUP QUESTIONS 206
SOME CONDITIONS OF OBEDIENCE AND DISOBEDIENCE TO AUTHORITY / Louis Penner 209
STUDY QUESTIONS 211
INTEGRATION QUESTIONS FOR DISCUSSION AND WRITING 214

12 Experiments in Conformity 216
WARMUP QUESTIONS 216
DIRECTIONS FOR READING 216
EXPERIMENTS IN CONFORMITY / Richard R. Bootzin, Elizabeth F. Loftus, Robert B. Zajonc, and Jay Braun 217
STUDY QUESTIONS 221
INTEGRATION QUESTIONS FOR DISCUSSION AND WRITING 224

UNIT V Language 227

13 What Is Language? 229
WARMUP QUESTIONS 229
PREVIEWING 230
WHAT IS LANGUAGE? / Victoria Fromkin and Robert Rodman 233
Part 1: STUDY QUESTIONS 241
Part 2: STUDY QUESTIONS 241
Part 2: COMPREHENSION EXERCISES 246
Part 3: STUDY QUESTIONS 248
Part 3: COMPREHENSION EXERCISES 251

14 Acquisition and Learning 253
WARMUP QUESTIONS 253
ACQUISITION AND LEARNING / Steven Krashen and Tracy Terrell 255
STUDY QUESTIONS 257
INTEGRATION QUESTIONS FOR DISCUSSION AND WRITING 259

15 Child Language Acquisition 260
WARMUP QUESTIONS 260
CHILD LANGUAGE ACQUISITION / E. Marvis Hetherington and Ross D. Parke 263
STUDY QUESTIONS 267
INTEGRATION QUESTIONS FOR DISCUSSION AND WRITING 269

UNIT VI Fiber Optics 271

16 The Global Telecommunications Revolution 273
WARMUP QUESTIONS 273
THE GLOBAL TELECOMMUNICATIONS REVOLUTION / Robert Jastrow 275
STUDY QUESTIONS 279

17 Laser Communication 282
WARMUP QUESTIONS 282
PREVIEWING 283
LASER COMMUNICATION: TOWARD THE FIBERED SOCIETY
Jeff Hecht and Dick Teresi / 285
Part 1: STUDY QUESTIONS 293
Part 2: STUDY QUESTIONS 294
Parts 1 and 2: COMPREHENSION EXERCISES 299
Part 3: STUDY QUESTIONS 301
Part 3: COMPREHENSION EXERCISES 307
INTEGRATION QUESTIONS FOR DISCUSSION AND WRITING 309
QUESTIONS FOR FURTHER RESEARCH 309

18 Fiber-Optics Applications 311
WARMUP QUESTIONS 311
FIBER-OPTICS APPLICATIONS / Jeff Hecht and Dick Teresi 313
STUDY QUESTIONS 317
INTEGRATION QUESTIONS FOR DISCUSSION AND WRITING 319

Index 323

Introduction

In this book, you will be reading a number of challenging selections that have been taken from university-level texts and other sources. These selections have not been simplified to make them easier for you to understand. Instead, extensive material has been provided to guide you through the readings and to help you check your comprehension.

As you work with unsimplified college texts, you will find that employing a number of strategies will aid your understanding of what you read. You may already use some of these strategies, either consciously or unconsciously, when you read English text. This section presents an overview of reading strategies that you should be aware of and that you should try to apply whenever you read. Using these strategies should help you become a better and more successful reader.

WHAT HAPPENS WHEN YOU READ?

According to research, successful readers do several important things when they read. Even before beginning a selection, they have some idea about the topic from their previous experience and knowledge. They also have some general idea about how the material will be organized and presented. For example, a student reading a novel will expect a story and a description of thoughts and feelings, while the same student reading a biology textbook will anticipate a totally different kind of language, content, and structure.

Good readers use what they already know about a topic and the probable organization of a selection to help them understand new material more efficiently. Rather than simply beginning with the first sentence on the first page, trying blindly to figure out what the reading is about, good readers preview the selection and consider its purpose as they read. By having a notion of the overall structure of the text, successful readers have a context, or framework, into which they can fit new information as it comes along.

Think of the part of a picture you might find on a single piece of a jigsaw puzzle. Without the larger framework of the entire picture, you cannot know what the small piece represents. Only when you fit the piece into the total picture does its meaning become clear.

Poor readers often read word by word, making sure that they understand each small detail. Successful readers, however, read for overall meaning. They first try to understand the most important general ideas within a paragraph or section. They also continually check to see how those general ideas fit into their understanding of the main point of the reading. For example, suppose you are reading an article about the use of nuclear energy. As you read the first few pages, you assume that the author intended to give both sides of the issue.

Toward the end of the selection, however, you realize that only pro–nuclear energy arguments are presented. At this point, good readers would go back and revise their understanding of the main idea and purpose of the article and then continue reading with this new understanding of the total framework.

In the final analysis, successful readers are *critical readers*. They use the new material in a reading to build and reshape their understanding of the topic. They are not passive receivers of information; they think about, react to, and evaluate what they read as they read.

STRATEGIES FOR READING

You can become a more successful reader by consciously adopting the characteristics of good readers that were outlined in the preceding section. This section examines in detail the strategies used by successful readers. It has been divided into three parts, outlining the strategies to be used (1) before you begin to read, (2) while you are reading, and (3) after you read. You probably already use a number of these techniques. However, if you work carefully through this discussion and the examples that accompany it, you will get a better idea of how these strategies can work together to make you a better reader.

Before You Read

As noted, you should not just sit down with a textbook and begin to read. It is important first to examine and think about your material for a few minutes—that is, to *preview* the reading. For this discussion of the necessary elements of previewing, refer to the brief selection that begins on page 5, titled "Vision: Your Human Camera."

STRATEGY 1

Before you read, consider what you already know about the topic. Spend some time remembering what you have already read and heard. Think about your attitudes, if any, toward the topic. Formulate questions about it.

For the selection about vision, you should ask yourself what you already know about vision. Have you studied this topic previously? What can you recall about it? What do you know about the properties of light? What do you know about the physiology of the human eye and how it translates light into vision? Why do you think vision might be compared to a camera, as the title suggests? By asking such questions and trying to answer them, you can read for new information within a known framework and thus anticipate the type of information that will be presented.

STRATEGY 2A

Before you read, preview the selection page by page. Leaf through the material you will read.

How many pages are there? How long do you think it will take to read? In the case of "Vision: Your Human Camera," how many printed pages do you find? How many minutes will you need to read this selection? Being aware of the length of a selection will help you to be realistic about reading time and will also provide a sense of where you are in the selection as you read.

STRATEGY 2B

Before you read, scan the material quickly. First, look at the headings and subheadings that are provided.

What do the headings and subheadings mean? What will each section probably discuss? How do the headings and subheadings relate to one another? Do they give you an idea about the organization of the entire selection? Write down the headings and subheadings in outline form, so that you can refer to them as you read.

Turn to the reading "Vision: Your Human Camera." How many subheadings are there? What are they, and what do you think is discussed under each one? Do the subheadings give you a sense of the organization of the selection? Why has the author organized the information in this manner? By scanning the material for headings and subheadings, you can preview the organization of the information presented. Then, when you begin to read, you can anticipate what is coming and place it more easily into the overall framework of the reading.

STRATEGY 2C

Before you read, scan the material again. This time, look for words or phrases that are highlighted, either in boldface or in *italics*.

Why are these words and phrases highlighted? Why are they important? Do you know these words? Do they give you a better sense of the type of information presented in each section?

Turn once again to the reading "Vision: Your Human Camera." Note the words that are printed in boldface type. How do they relate to the subheadings? Do you know these words? Now do the same for the words and phrases printed in italics. Don't worry if you do not know all of these terms. In many cases, highlighted words will be defined by the author. You will probably know some of them, however, and they will give you an even better idea of what the selection is about and how it is organized.

STRATEGY 2D

Before you read, scan the reading once more, this time to examine any illustrations, such as pictures, charts, and figures.

As you do this, ask yourself what type of information each illustration provides. How do you think the illustrations are related to the section headings and subheadings? How are they related to the words and phrases that are highlighted?

Turn for one last time to the reading "Vision: Your Human Camera." How many illustrations are included? What does Figure 1 illustrate? How does it relate to the title of this selection? Under which subheading do you think this information is explained? Now examine Figure 2, the horizontal illustration on which the words *blind* and *spot* are printed. Do you know what this figure is intended to illustrate? If not, you might want to read the explanation under the illustration. Examining the illustrations in this manner will provide further information about what you will be reading and enable you to read more quickly and accurately.

STRATEGY 3

Before you read, consider again what you know about the topic.

After you have previewed the reading by scanning for headings and subheadings, for highlighted words and phrases, and for illustrations, think once more about what you already know about the subject. You will probably be able to recall more information about the topic from your previous knowledge, and you will probably have more questions about it. In the case of the reading about vision, you might remember having studied some of the terms that are highlighted. You may recall in more detail how a camera works and how it is similar to the human eye. You might even remember having performed the "blind spot" experiment at some earlier time.

Vision: Your Human Camera
Benjamin B. Lahey

In 1950 psychologist George Wald wrote an important paper comparing the eye to a camera. This is still a good analogy today. Both are instruments that use a lens to focus light onto a light-sensitive surface on which the visual image is registered. The gross anatomy of the human eye shown in Figure 1 makes the resemblance to a camera very apparent. This intricate and efficient instrument transduces the physical properties of light into elaborately coded neural messages.

LIGHT: WHAT IS IT?

We need to have some knowledge of the nature of light to understand vision. Light is one small part of the form of energy known as **electromagnetic radiation** that also includes radio waves and X rays. Only a small portion of this radiation is visible—that is, our senses can only transduce a small part of it. Like sound, we can best think of light as being composed of *waves* that have *frequency* and *amplitude*. These two properties of light waves provide us with most of our information in vision.

The *amplitude* of the light wave largely determines the *brightness* of the visual sensation. The light reflected by an apple that is lighted by a single candle would be low in amplitude, so we would see the red of the apple as a dim rather than a bright sensation. The frequency of the light wave (the term **wavelength** is generally used instead of frequency when referring to light waves) largely determines the *color*, or *hue*, that we see—that is, light waves of different wavelengths are seen as different colors. But most light waves are not made up of a single wavelength and so are not seen as a pure color. Rather, they are made up of light waves of more than one wavelength. The more a color is composed of multiple wavelengths, the more *saturated* it's said to be. Like sound, however, the relationship between the physical properties of light and what is seen is not always simple and direct.

THE EYE: HOW DOES IT WORK?

The eye is an almost perfect sphere composed of two fluid-filled chambers. Light passes through the clear **cornea** into the first chamber. At the back of this chamber, the colored **iris** opens and closes to regulate how much light will pass through the **pupil** into the **lens**. The **ciliary muscle** focuses images by stretching the lens thin or letting it go thick so that a clear image falls on the light-sensitive **retina** at the back of the second chamber (see Figure 1).

The real business of transducing light waves is carried out by two types of receptor cells in the retina named the **rods** and the **cones** because of their shapes. The brightness of the light is coded in terms of the number of receptor neurons of both types that fire and the frequency with which they fire. Both types of receptors respond to light and dark, but only the cones can code information about color.

The cones are far less numerous than the rods—6 million cones compared to 100 million rods in each eye. Cones are concentrated in the center of the

FIGURE 1 Optical similarities of eye and camera are apparent in their cross sections. Both utilize a lens to focus an inverted image on a light-sensitive surface. Both possess an iris to adjust to various intensities of light. The single lens of the eye, however, cannot bring light of all colors to a focus at the same point. The compound lens of the camera is better corrected for color because it is composed of two kinds of glass.

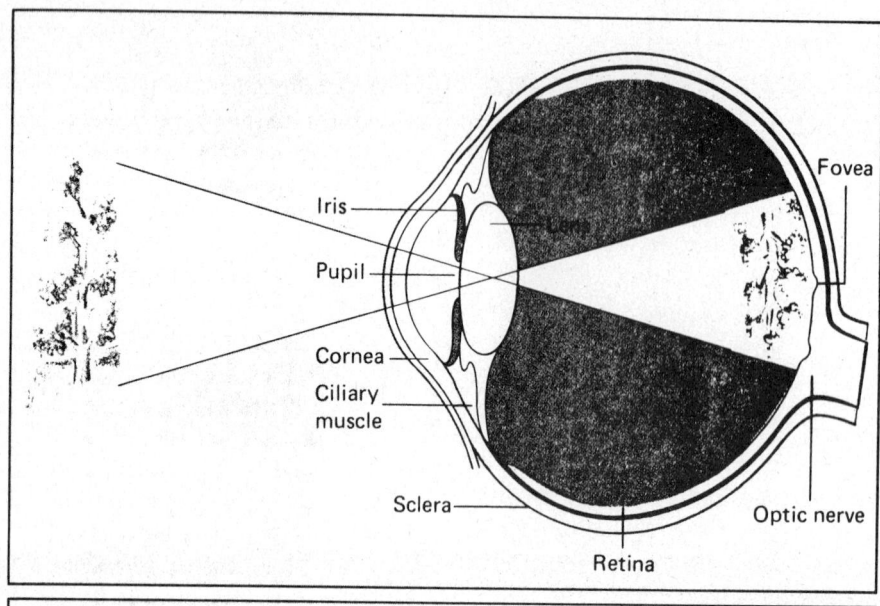

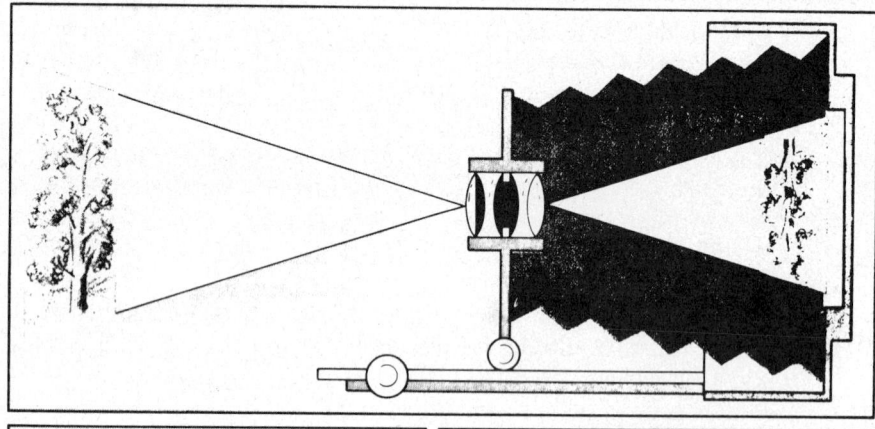

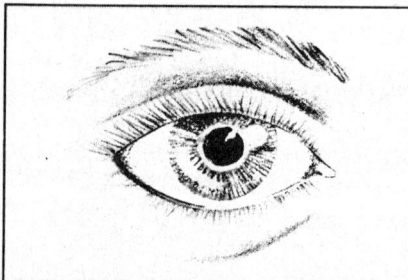

SOURCE: From *Eye and Camera* by George Wald. Copyright © 1950 by Scientific American, Inc. All rights reserved.

retina, with the greatest concentration being at a central spot called the **fovea**. In good light, **visual acuity** (the clearness and sharpness of vision) is best for images that are focused directly on the fovea, largely because of the high concentration of cones.

The rods are primarily located around the sides of the retina. They are responsible for peripheral vision and play a special role in vision in dim light.

FIGURE 2 Demonstration of the Blind Spot. You can demonstrate to yourself the existence of the "blind spot" in the following way. Hold your book at about arm's length with the word *spot* in front of your eyes. Close your right eye and stare at the word *spot*. Move the book in slowly until the word *blind* disappears. At this point, its image is falling on the spot in the retina where the optic nerve is attached and there are no receptors. We are not normally aware of the existence of this blind spot because we "fill in" a perception to compensate for the missing information. In this case, we see the dotted line as continuous after the word *blind* disappears.

Because rods are more sensitive than cones in dim light, we rely mostly on them for seeing at night. Also visual acuity is better for images focused away from the fovea on the more sensitive rods at night. Because the rods do not detect color, and because the cones can only respond in bright light, we can only see indistinct forms of black and gray in an almost totally dark room. Light of different wavelengths is still present in the room during near darkness, but the rods have no way of sending messages about them to the brain, so colors "disappear" from view.

It's also important to note that rods are less directly connected than cones to the **optic nerve**, the nerve that carries messages to the brain. Because messages from the rods take longer to reach the brain, reflexes to visual stimuli are less good at night. That is why it's harder to drive cars and catch frisbees in semidarkness.

Would you be surprised to learn that you are partially blind in each eye? The spot near the center of the retina where the optic nerve is attached contains no rods or cones. Because there is no visual reception at this point, it is known as the **blind spot**. We are not normally aware of the existence of this blind spot because we "fill in" the missing information during the process of seeing by using information coming in from the other parts of the retina. However, look at Figure 2 for a demonstration of its existence.

DARK AND LIGHT ADAPTATION

When you walk into a dark movie theatre from the daylight, you are "blind" at first; your eyes can pick up very little visual information. Within about five minutes, however, your vision in the darkened room has improved considerably, and very slowly it improves over the next twenty-five minutes until you can see fairly well. When you step out of the theatre from the matinee performance, you have the opposite experience. At first the intense light "blinds" you. You squint and block out the painful light, but in a little while you can see normally again. What is going on? How can you be sighted one moment and blind the next just because the intensity of light has suddenly changed?

What is happening is called *dark adaptation* and *light adaptation*. Be careful not to confuse these terms with the term *sensory adaptation*. ... Sensory adaptation refers to the gradual *loss* of sensitivity of a receptor to a specific stimulus that has been repeatedly presented or presented for a long time. Dark and light adaptation refers to the *regaining* of sensitivity of the eyes following a loss of sensitivity caused by an abrupt change in overall illumination.

Here is what happens in the retina during **dark adaptation**. During vision in high intensity light, the rods and cones are being used frequently, so they are "tired" and are not very sensitive. When we enter darkness, the rods and cones are not sensitive enough to be stimulated by the low intensity light and they stop firing almost completely. This gives the receptors a rest before they begin to regain their sensitivity by making a fresh supply of the chemicals used in light reception that have been literally "bleached out" by the intense light.

At first, both the rods and the cones are recovering their sensitivity, so there is fairly rapid improvement. But the cones become as sensitive as they can (remember they are not very sensitive in weak light) within about five minutes, so the rate of improvement slows after that. The rods continue to improve in sensitivity slowly, reaching maximum sensitivity after about thirty minutes in the dark.

In **light adaptation**, eyes that have been in the dark for a while have built up a full supply of the chemicals used in light reception and are very responsive to light. When we are suddenly exposed to intense light, a barrage of rods and cones fires almost at once and, in essence, "overloads" the visual circuits. It's not until the intense light has had a chance to bleach out some of the receptor chemicals and reduce the sensitivity of the receptors to a normal level that we can see comfortably again. Fortunately, this process takes place in about a minute.

By the way, your mother was right about carrots and good vision. The chemical involved in light reception in the rods is largely made up of vitamin A. This is why a deficiency of vitamin A can lead to "night blindness." And yes, there is a lot of vitamin A in carrots.

As You Read

There are a number of strategies that you should use as you read. With practice, you will be able to apply these strategies automatically and unconsciously.

STRATEGY 4

As you read, be willing to tolerate some amount of ambiguity, especially when reading a selection for the first time.

The first time that you read an academic text, you will not be able to understand every word, nor will you be able to understand every concept or idea presented. Do not stop reading or slow down in an attempt to understand every detail. If you do, you will be forcing yourself to read so slowly that you will not comprehend the total picture. The first time that you read a selection, be satisfied with understanding the main ideas and concepts.

For example, read the following paragraph about crime prevention.

> We know that sticking our fingers into live electric sockets will have shocking consequences, so we are careful to avoid the experience. Some criminologists apply similar logic to explaining criminal behavior—or the lack of it. As control theorists, they assume that crime is tempting and that individuals must be diverted from it. But unlike Reckless, Matza, and Hirschi, who seek general explanations of criminal behavior, *deterrence theorists* concentrate on the effects of a single aspect of social control, namely *punishment*. They contend that humans are rational creatures who calculate the costs and rewards of behavior. If the cost of crime (punishment) is or is perceived to be greater than the rewards, then offenses are less likely to occur.[1]

There may be some vocabulary in this paragraph that is unfamiliar to you, and you probably do not know the names *Reckless*, *Matza*, and *Hirschi*. You may not completely understand

[1] Charles H. McCaghy. *Crime in American Society*. New York: Macmillan, 1980, p. 78.

what the author means by *control theorists*. But you most likely do understand the central idea that *deterrence theorists* emphasize punishment as a means of social control. You are able to derive meaning from the paragraph even though you do not understand it completely.

STRATEGY 5
Be prepared to read the selection more than once.

If you have not understood the selection easily or completely the first time through, you may be able to understand it upon the second reading. For many readers, it is better to read a selection quickly more than once rather than to try to read it for complete understanding the first time.

STRATEGY 6
As you read each paragraph or short section, continually consider the meaning, and relate this information to what you already know about the topic and to what you have just read.

Force yourself to work with meaning rather than with isolated words or sentences. Suppose, for example, that you are reading a selection about environmental pollution and its effects upon people. The selection suggests that chemical fertilizers used by farmers can run into rivers and streams during heavy rains. Suppose also that you are already aware that some environmental agencies propose decreased use of chemical fertilizers and greater use of natural means of fertilization. You should be able to relate the new information to what you already know.

Suppose that the next paragraph you read discusses the ill effects to humans of certain chemicals found in drinking water. You should consider what you have just read about fertilizer runoff and realize that it is related to the new information about hazardous drinking water.

STRATEGY 7A
As you read, realize that some vocabulary is not essential to understanding the basic ideas and concepts presented.

You do not have to know the meaning of each word. For example, read the following paragraph about the insecticide DDT.

> About 100 years ago an obscure German chemist, Othmar Zeidler, synthesized dichloro-diphenyl-trichloroethane, or DDT. It lay on the shelf until 1930, when a Swiss entomologist, Paul Muller, tested it for its killing properties on insects and found it most effective. In 1942 DDT came to the United States, where its usefulness as a potent insecticide was quickly recognized. In many countries around the world, spraying DDT eliminated the diseases typhus, malaria, yellow fever, and plague—all of which are transmitted by insects. Since World War II the use of DDT has saved many millions of lives and prevented untold human suffering.[2]

Do you know the word *potent* or the disease names *typhus, malaria, yellow fever,* and *plague*? Even if you do not, you can still understand the author's message.

[2] Irwin W. Sherman and Vilia G. Sherman. *Biology: A Human Approach*, 2d ed. New York: Oxford University Press, 1979, p. 535.

Introduction

STRATEGY 7B

As you read, notice if words and phrases you do not know are defined by the author.

Words and phrases are especially likely to be defined in introductory academic texts, where one of the primary goals is to introduce the reader to key terms and concepts of the field being discussed. Often, these terms are highlighted in some way.

Read the following from a psychology textbook.

> The aftereffects of emotional arousal sometimes cause profound and long-lasting bodily harm. Various disorders such as peptic ulcer, colitis, asthma, and hypertension can often be traced back to emotional patterns in the patient's life and are then considered *psychosomatic* ailments in which a psychological cause produces a bodily, a somatic, effect.[3]

What does *psychosomatic* mean? Since the paragraph tells you, you should be able to provide a definition.

Now another paragraph, this one from a management textbook.

> At the beginning of the twentieth century, industries were becoming larger and more complex. Haphazard management, previously sufficient, was now inefficient. Managers were no longer involved with the production process; they had to spend more of their time on administrative planning, scheduling, and staffing problems. Managers also had difficulty in keeping abreast of the technical methods of production and, therefore, no longer had a basis for judging a fair day's work from the increased number of employees. *Scientific management*, one approach to the solution of these problems, emphasizes the one best way to perform a task through the use of time and motion studies.[4]

The paragraph defines the term *scientific management*. Can you define it in your own words?

STRATEGY 7C

As you read, use the context surrounding an unknown word or phrase to give you a general understanding of the word.

The context around an unknown word or phrase may provide enough information so that you can continue reading with comprehension. Knowing the part of speech can also help you to narrow the meaning. Be satisfied with a general understanding of an unknown word in a situation such as this. Do not consult a dictionary if it is not necessary.

Consider the following paragraph about memory.

> Certain lesions on the human temporal cortex (specifically in the *hippocampus* and other structures near the base of the brain) produce a memory disorder called *anterograde amnesia* (anterograde, "in a forward direction"). The patient often has little trouble in remembering whatever he had learned prior to the injury; his difficulty is learning anything new thereafter.[5]

Do you know the meaning of the terms *temporal cortex* and *hippocampus*? Probably not, but you can determine that they are nouns, and the context indicates that both concern areas of

---

[3] Henry Gleitman. *Psychology*. New York: W. W. Norton, 1981, p. 72.
[4] Don Hellreigel and John W. Slocum, Jr. *Management*, 3d ed. Reading, Maine: Addison-Wesley, 1982, p. 52.
[5] Gleitman, *Psychology*, p. 281.

the human brain. How about the term *anterograde amnesia*? The paragraph explains that *anterograde* means "in a forward direction," and the second sentence suggests that amnesia has something to do with remembering. From the context, you can derive a general understanding of these terms that should be adequate for comprehending the main idea.

Here is another paragraph, this one from a criminology textbook.

> Never underestimate the inventiveness of those who steal. Whereas homicide and rape have changed little, if at all, for centuries, forms of theft have altered significantly. For example, train robbery did not exist until trains did (obviously), and until the trains began carrying currency, gold, and wealthy passengers. But trains have changed and no one holds them up anymore. Today's thieves surreptitiously hijack cargo from boxcars, and occasionally they take the boxcars as well. Thieves have always adjusted their strategies to the technologies and opportunities of the times: when postal service was devised, fraud by mail was not far behind. One of the latest wrinkles is theft by computer.[6]

Are you familiar with the term "to hold up" in the fourth sentence? The context leads you to understand that it means "to steal." Now look at the word *hijack* in the fifth sentence. You should be able to determine that it acts as a verb. This, together with the context, suggests that "to hijack" has the general meaning of "to steal," and this should be enough information to allow you to continue reading. There is no need to stop and consult a dictionary.

STRATEGY 7D

As you read, look for familiar affixes and roots in unknown vocabulary.

Sometimes, analyzing an unknown word for familiar affixes and roots can provide enough information to enable you to grasp the general meaning, although you may not be able to determine an exact definition. Suppose, for example, that you come across the word *scribble* as you are reading. First, you realize that it acts as a verb in the sentence. Next, you recall that words containing the root *-scrib-* or *-script-*, such as *description* and *inscription*, generally have something to do with writing. These clues are adequate; you know that *scribble* is a verb that indicates some type of writing.

Another example of using word analysis might involve the prefix *micro-*. You know a number of words that begin with this prefix, such as *microscope* and *microphone*, and you realize that *micro-* usually indicates small size or volume. If you find the word *microorganism* as you read, you immediately understand that the term refers to organisms of extremely small size.

It is important to understand that analysis of affixes and roots to determine the meaning of unknown words is helpful only occasionally. In most cases, it is impossible to analyze words for meaning in this manner.

STRATEGY 8A

Read paragraph by paragraph (or read groups of related paragraphs), and ask yourself what the main idea or purpose of each one is.

Identifying the main idea in a paragraph is often simply a matter of deciding what general concept all (or most) of the sentences in the paragraph develop, refer to, or support. For example, look at the following paragraph from an accounting textbook. As you read, think about what main idea all the sentences in the paragraph support or develop.

---

[6]McCaghy, *Crime in American Society*, p. 257.

> Just as a firm may add a new department in an effort to increase its sales and income, it also may open new stores (branches) in different locations with the same objective in mind. Among the types of retail businesses in which branch operations were first successfully developed on a major scale were variety, grocery, and drugstores. There are a number of large corporations with hundreds of thousands of retail branches distributed over a large area. In addition to the national chain store organizations, there are many of a regional or local nature. The growth of suburban shopping centers in recent years has added materially to the number of firms, especially department stores, that have expanded through the opening of branches.[7]

The first sentence of this paragraph introduces the idea that branch stores can increase income and sales. The rest of the sentences further explain the concept of branch stores; therefore, you would probably conclude that the purpose of this paragraph is to explain the advantages and characteristics of branch stores.

Now consider another example from a developmental psychology textbook. Once again, as you read, think about the paragraph's main idea.

> It was clear that the Caucasian mothers sought their babies' attention with verve and excitement, even as their babies tended to react to the stimulation with what can be described as ambivalence. The Caucasian infants turned both toward and away from the mother with far greater frequency than did the Navaho infants. The Navaho mothers and their infants engaged in relatively stoical, quiet, and steady encounters. On viewing the films, we had the feeling that we were watching bicultural differences in the making.[8]

This paragraph begins with some details that support its main idea—the "bicultural differences" mentioned in the last sentence.

STRATEGY 8B

As you read a paragraph or section, ask yourself how the main idea or purpose relates to the previous paragraph.

Often, one paragraph introduces a topic or idea that is then developed or explained in succeeding paragraphs. As an example, consider the following three paragraphs from a book of sociology readings.

> Finally, something needs to be said about the much-discussed political "passivity" of Mexican-Americans. Here intergroup comparisons are necessary.
>
> First of all, below-median levels of political activity are not surprising insofar as first-generation immigrants are concerned. It is known from their income figures that their energies are directed toward the all-consuming task of earning a living. A good many are not citizens, and, of these, some undetermined number may not be lawfully in the country.
>
> Second, we know that levels of political activity among ethnic groups vary widely by generation. Many descendants of European immigrants vote at

---

[7] C. E. Niswonger and P. E. Fess. *Accounting Principles*, 11th ed. Cincinnati: Southwestern Publishing, 1973, p. 488.

[8] D. G. Freedman. "Ethnic Differences in Babies." In J. K. Gardner, ed. *Readings in Developmental Psychology.* Boston: Little, Brown, 1982, p. 116.

above-median levels, but this is uneven by ethnic group. For some, it peaks in the second generation and trails off later; for others, there is a slower, linear, rather than curvilinear, relationship.[9]

In the text from which this is taken, two additional paragraphs present a third and fourth point about the topic introduced in the initial paragraph. In other words, one topic was introduced and developed over the course of five paragraphs, almost a page and a half of text—quite a bit different from the one-paragraph, one-topic examples discussed under Strategy 8A above.

It is important therefore to make a preliminary guess about the relationship between the paragraph you have just read and the paragraph you are currently reading. Does the paragraph you are reading continue the previous idea, or does it introduce something new?

Look at the following two paragraphs from a geology textbook. As you read, think about the relationship between the ideas in the two paragraphs.

> If the solid earth condensed directly from cooling solar gases, then its ocean and atmosphere might have had a similar origin and be merely a residue of the most volatile elements that persisted as liquids or gases after the solidification of the crust. If, on the other hand, the earth accreted from a homogeneous mixture of solid particles, then its ocean and atmosphere must have a secondary source—from volatile elements subsequently released from its solid materials by internal heating. Regardless of the origin of the core, mantle, and crust, there is strong evidence that its covering fluids *did* have such a secondary origin from within the solid earth.
>
> This evidence comes from the relative abundance of rare gaseous elements, particularly neon, argon, krypton, and xenon. These extremely stable gases never form natural compounds with other elements and are, in addition, too heavy to escape the earth's gravitation attraction and be lost in space. As a result, any present in the earth's earliest atmosphere should still be present, for there is no known way that they could be removed, either physically or chemically. They are, however, about a million times less abundant in the earth's atmosphere than in the sun and other stars. It is therefore most probable that the earth's gaseous atmosphere is not merely a residue of solar gases, but accumulated instead from heating and "outgassing" of volatile materials originally present in materials of the solid earth.[10]

In this example, the first paragraph begins with two theories about the formation of the earth. The last sentence of the first paragraph makes a hypothesis about the formation of the earth's water and air, and the second paragraph presents evidence to support this theory. Thus, the purpose of the entire second paragraph is to support and develop a main idea that was stated in the last sentence of the previous paragraph.

STRATEGY 9

Try to determine the relationship between the main idea of a paragraph and its supporting details. How is the main idea explained—through several examples, one extended example, analogy, comparison or contrast, or explanation of a process or chronology?

---

[9]Horowitz, D. L. "Conflict and Accommodation: Mexican Americans in the Cosmopolis." In W. Connor, ed. *Mexican Americans in Comparative Perspective.* Washington D.C.: Urban Institute Press, 1985, pp. 91–92.

[10]A. L. McAlester. *The Earth: An Introduction to Geological and Geophysical Sciences.* Englewood Cliffs, NJ: Prentice-Hall, 1973, p. 377.

Introduction

One way to grasp the meaning of a paragraph quickly is to try to determine its organization—the logical arrangement of the ideas used to explain or develop the topic of the paragraph or group of paragraphs.

Many times, there will be words such as *for example* and *on the other hand* to help you determine the relationships between sentences and between paragraphs. More often, however, these words will not be present. Nevertheless, the sentences still have some logical relationship to each other, and discovering that relationship is an important part of understanding the meaning of the passage.

The following passage is taken from a textbook in business administration.

> Individuals differ in their abilities to perform different tasks, and these differences must be considered when staffing decisions are made. In verbal and intellectual capacities, you must assume no differences between men and women, younger and older workers, and people of all geographical and racial backgrounds. Of course, people have varying educational backgrounds, skill and experience levels, and personalities, and you should take these into account when you hire people for specific jobs. It's also a good idea to consider age distribution, so that when some workers retire, others have been trained to take their places.[11]

As the first sentence of the paragraph states, the purpose of this passage is to discuss some of the personal characteristics that should be considered when hiring employees. The rest of the paragraph gives *examples* that develop this idea—both in terms of what *should* and *should not* be considered.

Here is another example, from a textbook about human physiology. This paragraph is part of a longer passage that explains how enzymes work. (Enzymes promote certain important chemical changes in the body by bringing two chemicals together and causing them to react.) As you read the paragraph, think about how the topic of the paragraph is developed; consider the logical relationship among the sentences.

> You might think of an enzyme as a container capable of trapping molecules. As the molecules become trapped within the enzyme mold, the chances of molecular collision are increased. Thus, enzymes and heat achieve the same result (both bring about chemical reactions through molecular collisions) but operate in different ways. Heat increases the likelihood of molecular collision by stimulating the movement of molecules. Enzymes have no direct effect on the movement of molecules except to keep them confined in a mold. In other words, a relatively small number of molecules confined in a small area are as likely to collide as are a vast number of molecules moving in a large area.[12]

In this example, two different comparisons are used to explain the main idea of how an enzyme works. First, enzyme action is compared to a container. Next, the paragraph describes the ways in which the effect of enzymes on molecules is similar to that of heat, and the ways in which it is different. In other words, the ideas in this paragraph were developed through the use of comparison and contrast.

Here is another example to consider, taken from a book by historian Daniel J. Boorstin. Once again, as you read, consider the logical relationship among the sentences.

---

[11]E. E. Adams Jr. and R. J. Ebert. *Production and Operations Management.* Englewood Cliffs, NJ: Prentice-Hall, 1982, p. 283.

[12]A. M. Schnieder and B. Tarshis. *Introduction to Physiological Psychology.* New York: Random House, 1986, p. 50.

We do not know how Nicolo and Maffeo Polo spent their time at the court of the Khan, except that, at the end of the seventeen years, they had "acquired great wealth in jewels and gold." Every year Kublai Khan became more reluctant to lose Marco's services. But in 1292 an escort was required for a Tartar princess who was to become the bride of the Ilkhan of Persia. Envoys of the Ilkhan had already failed in their efforts to deliver the seventeen-year-old bride overland. Returned to the court of Kublai Khan, they hoped to secure sea passage. Just then Marco had come back from an assignment that had taken him on a long sea voyage to India. The Persian envoys, who knew the seafaring reputation of the Venetians, persuaded Kublai Khan to allow the Polos to accompany them and the bride by sea. After a treacherous sea voyage through the South China Sea to Sumatra and through the Sea of India from which only eighteen of the six hundred survived, the Tartar princess was safely delivered to the Persian court. She had become so attached to the Venetians that she wept at the parting.[13]

It is not difficult to see that the details in this paragraph are arranged according to time order. The purpose of the sentences is chiefly to tell a story—to describe a series of events.

These examples represent only a few of the many ways of developing a main idea within a paragraph.

STRATEGY 10

When a paragraph or section presents an argument, procedure, or related sequence of ideas, try to reconstruct it and to explain it in your own words.

The essence of this strategy lies in the fact that a complex argument or procedure can be difficult to understand or remember until you have done something to "make it your own."

If an argument is lengthy or complicated, you might try to outline it, paraphrasing the main points in your own words. When a complex procedure is being described, it is often a good strategy to try to make a diagram of the procedure. Taking the time to put something into visual form helps you not only to understand it better but also to remember it better.

Consider the following example. Read the paragraph carefully, and then look at the suggested activities that follow.

> The spread of acid rain can be prevented either by removing sulfur from the coal before it is burned or by catching the sulfur oxides before they reach the atmosphere. Conventional chemical techniques for cutting sulfur pollution from coal add about $15 a ton to its cost, but this might be halved if bacteria were called in to do the job. Several types of bacteria, especially those that inhabit hot-water springs, have a great appetite for sulfur compounds, from which they derive energy. Their activities would separate much of the sulfur from high-sulfur coal, producing a much cleaner and more valuable fuel. A small-scale plant in Ohio has shown that this process works, and in a few years time the first industrial-scale operations may commence.[14]

This passage presents both an argument (stated in the form of a problem and its proposed solution) and a procedure (the solution itself). The final sentence of the paragraph returns to the argument by giving an evaluation of the proposed solution.

---

[13]D. J. Boorstin. *The Discoverers*. New York: Vintage Books (Random House), 1985, p. 137.
[14]S. Prentis. *Biotechnology*. New York: George Braziller, 1984, p. 170.

Introduction

FIGURE 3

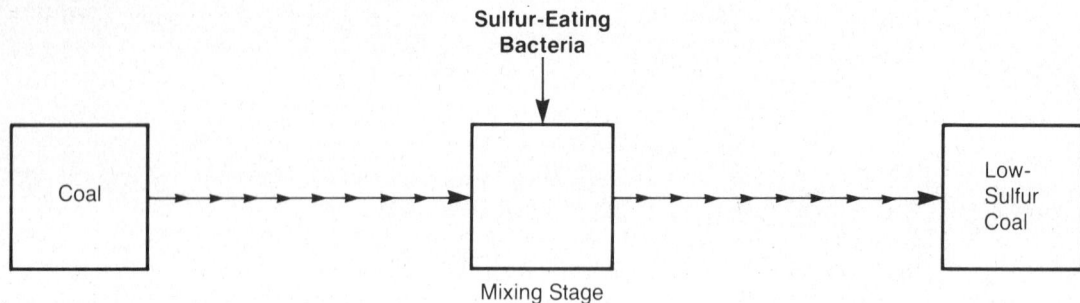

You might summarize the argument with a simple outline of the main points:

Problem: acid rain
Solution: remove sulfur
Problem: sulfur removal very expensive
Solution: use special bacteria to remove sulfur
    Evaluation: already being done on a small scale
    Evaluation: will probably be successful on a large scale

As for the process itself, you might find it easier to understand and remember if you make a simple diagram such as that shown in Figure 3.

Sometimes a procedure or other series of ideas is so complex that it cannot be easily understood just by reading the words. If a diagram or chart has not been provided to assist your understanding, you may have to provide one yourself.

The following paragraph describes one process for converting solar energy into electricity. As you read the description, try to make a diagram of the process on a separate piece of paper.

> One scheme for the conversion of solar energy into electricity which has attracted a great deal of attention has been proposed by a husband-and-wife team from the University of Arizona, Aden and Marjorie Meinel. Lenses focus the sun's rays on pipes carrying molten sodium or potassium, and raise the temperature of the sodium or potassium to about 560 degrees centigrade. This fluid is then pumped to a heat exchanger, and the heat is stored in an insulated chamber filled with a mixture of sodium and potassium chlorides which serve as a heat reservoir. Heat from this chamber is used, via a heat exchanger, to produce steam at 540 degrees centigrade, which then drives a conventional steam-electric power plant to produce electricity.[15]

Although the individual parts of this procedure are not complex, it is easier to visualize and understand the whole process once you have reconstructed it—in either diagram or outline form—in a way that makes sense to you. You will then understand the process in more detail and remember it better as well.

STRATEGY 11

When reading about a concept, try to apply it to a situation that you know and understand—one that is not described in the text. If examples are given to illustrate the concept, try to think of further examples from your own experience and knowledge.

[15] J. F. Mulligan. *Practical Physics*. New York: McGraw-Hill, 1980, p. 338.

An interesting feature of the American academic system is that students are often asked to apply principles or rules they have learned to new situations. Research has shown that good readers often do something similar: as they read, they try to apply new concepts to things they are already familiar with. (This relates back to the idea that good readers interact with the text rather than simply receive information passively.)

Suppose, for example, that you are reading an economics text that explains the concept of supply and demand in abstract terms. The textbook refers to a fictitious "Company X," which manufactures make-believe products called "widgets." Unfortunately, Company X and its widgets mean little to you, and they also do little to help you understand the concept of supply and demand. You do, however, know a little bit about practical economics because your uncle (or mother or cousin) owns a business. As you begin to think more about how the laws of supply and demand apply to your uncle's business, you begin to get a better grasp of the concept.

Even when textbooks do give useful examples, you can increase your understanding of the concept (and remember it better) by thinking of examples of your own. Suppose once again that you are reading an economics textbook, and you come to a description of the concept of inelastic demand. (This refers to the fact that consumers will continue to buy certain essential products even when the price goes up.) As examples, the textbook lists certain types of foods and household items. These examples make sense to you, but in order to understand the concept better, you try to think of something from a student's life that might be subject to inelastic demand—notebooks and pens, for example. In this way, you have made the concept more real and more accessible.

STRATEGY 12

As you finish one section of your reading selection, take a moment to summarize it before you begin the next section. As you read the next section, try to relate new information to what you have already read.

Sometimes, readers are unsuccessful because they forget to think about the meaning of what they have read in a way that goes beyond the meaning of the word, sentence, or paragraph. Therefore, when you finish a major section in a reading, it is a good idea to remind yourself about the main points of what you have just read. As with Strategies 2, 3, and 6, this will help you to understand better what you are going to read next.

Then, as you continue to read, make sure that the logical relationship between the section you have just finished and the section you are currently reading is clear to you. This will make it easier to put the new information into the larger, more complex picture that emerges as you read.

AFTER YOU READ

Perhaps the biggest mistake that many people make when reading academic material is closing the book after they have finished reading and going on to something else. Instead, good readers sit back for a few minutes and consider what they have read.

STRATEGY 13

After you have finished reading, summarize the main ideas and concepts. It may be helpful to write down this information if you did not take notes while reading. If you did take notes, read them over several times to make sure that you understand them.

Successful students often make an outline or a list of the most important ideas in their assigned readings. They can then refer to these notes when studying or doing further reading.

While useful as a study tool, this technique is also important as a reading strategy. Making notes (e.g., outlines, summary charts, diagrams) based on what you have read ensures that you have not missed any important ideas. It also ensures that you understand the relationship of the ideas to each other and to the topic as a whole.

Perhaps you have been in the situation of having to explain a difficult concept to a classmate or someone unfamiliar with your major. In such cases, having to explain the concept to someone else often helps you to understand it better. In a similar way, the act of taking notes on what you have read helps you to increase your understanding of the material.

STRATEGY 14

Think about the new information you have gained from reading. Ask yourself how it relates to what you knew about the topic previously.

As has been mentioned, good readers are not just passive receivers of information. Rather, they are actively engaged in a kind of internal dialogue with the material, constantly relating what they are reading to their own knowledge, to what they know about the structure of the reading, and, of course, to what they have just read.

This process of interaction continues to be important even after you have finished reading. This is because a successful reader is also a critical reader. When you have finished reading, you should consider your attitudes and feelings about the topic. Has the new information changed your thinking in any way? Does it confirm what you already thought? Does any of the new information surprise you?

Also, think back to the questions you asked about the topic before you began to read. Are you able to answer any of those questions now? Has the new information raised any new questions?

USING THIS TEXTBOOK

This textbook provides guided practice in using all the reading strategies that have just been discussed. As you learn to apply these strategies effectively, you will become a better reader.

Each unit contains three reading selections about a major topic. Reading several selections on the same theme will give you the opportunity to broaden your knowledge of the topic and to read critically.

Each chapter begins with exercises that help you think about the topic and preview the reading selection. After reading the selection quickly for general understanding, you will read it again paragraph by paragraph and answer study questions requiring you to apply appropriate reading strategies. These study questions are designed to give you practice in asking the kinds of questions that will make you a successful reader.

The longer readings are divided into smaller sections, with comprehension questions to check your understanding of each part. The shorter readings are followed by integration questions that ask you to relate information from the various selections on the same topic, just as students are required to do in academic coursework.

The exercises throughout this textbook focus on the content of the readings in a manner that will teach you how to use reading strategies effectively and when to use them. Do not worry if you find yourself thinking primarily about the unit topics rather than about applying specific reading strategies. Focusing on meaning rather than on skills is what successful reading is all about.

UNIT I

Marketing

CHAPTER 1

Consumer Behavior: Basic Concepts

WARMUP QUESTIONS

Chapters 1 through 3 contain readings about marketing, specifically, about consumer behavior. You probably have definite ideas about how people behave when they buy a product. After all, you are a consumer yourself, and you know what types of products and what types of advertising are attractive to you. But professional marketers must study the behavior of consumers scientifically; they cannot rely upon their personal intuition.

How can we define consumer behavior? What decision process do consumers go through when choosing a product? What types of factors influence consumers' buying decisions? How can the marketer predict the success of a new product?

Before you begin to read the first reading, "Consumer Behavior: Basic Concepts," examine the following statements, and indicate whether you *agree* or *disagree* with each one. Answer from your own knowledge only. Then discuss your opinions with your classmates.

1. _____ If a product is more effective or of higher quality than its competitors, it will always be the most successful.
2. _____ People buy certain products in order to influence what other people will think of them.
3. _____ Different people may have very different motives for buying the same product.
4. _____ Marketers do not want their advertisements to be very different from those of their competitors because consumers generally do not like the unusual.
5. _____ A consumer is more likely to be influenced by a $20 price reduction for a $100 camera than by a $500 price reduction for a $15,000 car.
6. _____ Consumers who are satisfied with a particular product are less likely to pay attention to advertisements for competing products.

Marketing

7. _____ It is generally easier to change consumers' attitudes toward a product than it is to change the product itself.

8. _____ It is important for marketers to realize that consumers' attitudes toward products may change over time, and thus advertising, and sometimes the products themselves, must also be changed.

Write three questions you have about consumer behavior and marketing. Share your questions with your classmates, and discuss possible answers.

_____

_____

_____

_____

PREVIEWING

1. Briefly look through the excerpt from the textbook *Marketing* that begins on page 25.

   How many paragraphs does the reading contain? _____

   How many pages does it have? _____

2. How many figures do you find in the reading? _____

   How many tables do you find? _____

   Which figure corresponds to each of the following topics?

   analysis of what an attitude is: _____

   how a buyer chooses a product: _____

   how we perceive certain products: _____

   how we see ourselves: _____

   what constitutes buyer behavior: _____

   how we order our needs: _____

   Examine the two shopping lists in Table 1-1. What is the difference between them?

   _____

3. Before you read the selection, you should get a sense of its organization. The major topics in this selection can be identified by the boldface section titles to the left of the text. List the major topic titles and the paragraphs that are included in each:

   _____ (paragraphs 6 –)

   _____ (paragraphs –)

   _____ (paragraphs –)

   _____ (paragraphs –)

   What do you think the function of paragraphs 1–5 is? _____

   _____

4. Several of the major topics that you listed in question 3 contain several sections, or major subtopics. Some of those major subtopics themselves contain several sections, or minor subtopics. Try to list the headings for these major and minor subtopics in the skeleton outline that follows. List the major subtopics by the capital letters and the minor subtopics by the Arabic numerals.

    I. Introduction
   II. Understanding Consumer Behavior
  III. Self-concept Theory
  IV. Consumer Behavior: A Definition
       A. _____
   V. Individual Influences on Consumer Behavior
       A. _____
          1. _____
          2. _____
          3. _____
          4. _____
          5. _____
       B. Perception _____
          1. _____
          2. _____
       C. _____
          1. _____
          2. _____
          3. _____
          4. _____

5. Look at the heading titles that you listed in the outline in question 4. Which words and phrases are familiar to you? Which are new to you? Discuss with your classmates the meanings of these words and phrases.

Known	Unknown
_____	_____
_____	_____
_____	_____
_____	_____
_____	_____
_____	_____

DIRECTIONS FOR READING

The selection for this chapter, "Consumer Behavior: Basic Concepts," comes from *Marketing* by David L. Kurtz and Louis W. Boone. This textbook is used in introductory college marketing courses.

In the previewing section you have just completed, you briefly examined the selection for an overview of its content and organization. You are now ready to read it carefully.

The selection has been divided into three parts. You will first read each section quickly for general understanding, and then examine each part more closely as you complete the study questions.

Consumer Behavior: Basic Concepts

David L. Kurtz and Louis E. Boone

1   The marketing concept, briefly stated, is: Find a need and fill it. The key to marketing success lies in locating unsatisfied consumers. These people may not be purchasing goods because the goods are currently unavailable, or they may be buying products that provide them with only limited satisfaction. In the latter case, they are likely to switch to new products that provide more satisfaction. Unsatisfied consumers should comprise the market targets for consumer-oriented firms.

2   Extensive consumer research on the burgeoning headache-remedy and antacid market led one major U.S. pharmaceutical firm to develop a new pill with the virtues of aspirin, Alka-Seltzer, Bufferin, Excedrin, and similar tablets gulped down daily by tension-ridden people. The firm's product development department created the product with one advantage no other competitor had—it could be taken without water.

3   The product, a cherry-flavored combination painkiller and stomach sweetener called Analoze, was tested for consumer acceptance. Samples were given to a panel of potential buyers, who compared it with competing products. They chose Analoze overwhelmingly.

4   Ads were then developed around the theme "works without water." The price was competitive, and the package design was eye-catching. Confident of success, the marketing vice-president gave Analoze its first real market test in four cities—Denver, Omaha, Phoenix, and Memphis—and sat back to await the positive results . . . and waited . . . and waited. Sales were virtually nil, and a few months later Analoze was withdrawn from the market.

5   What went wrong? In-depth research with headache sufferers revealed a ritual associated with pain relief. They swallowed (or dissolved) a pill and drank a glass of water. These people somehow associated water consumption with obtaining relief, and they were unwilling to spend money on a remedy that dissolved in the mouth.[1]

UNDERSTANDING CONSUMER BEHAVIOR

6   The failure of Analoze did not result from a lack of marketing planning; a declining or otherwise inadequate market; or from a lack of consumer income, education, or any of the other variables commonly used in analyzing markets. The product failed because the marketer did not take into account the psychology of the market.

7   Successful marketers attempt to understand the motivations of the individual consumers. Unfortunately, this task is perhaps the most difficult one in marketing. Marketing research studies can provide data that answers the following questions about consumer buying habits:

   1. *Who* are the buyers?
   2. *When* do they buy (time of day, seasonality of product sales)?

[1] Burt Schorr, "The Mistakes: Many New Products Fail Despite Careful Planning, Publicity," *Wall Street Journal*, April 5, 1961, pp. 1, 22.

Marketing

3. *Where* do they buy?
4. *What* do they buy?
5. *How* do they buy (how much and what type of sales—cash or credit)?

But answers to the question "*Why* do they buy (or not buy)?" are much more difficult to ascertain.

SELF-CONCEPT THEORY

8 Individuals are physical and mental entities possessing multifaceted pictures of themselves. One young man, for example, may view himself as intellectual, self-assured, moderately talented, and a rising young business executive. People's actions, including their purchase decisions, are related to their mental conception of self—their *self-concept*. And the response to direct questions like "Why do you buy Jovan cologne?" is likely to reflect this desired self-image.[2]

9 As Figure 1-1 indicates, the self has four components: real self, self-image, looking-glass self, and ideal self. The real self is an objective view of the total person. The self-image, the way individuals view themselves, may distort the objective view. The looking-glass self, the way individuals think others see them, may also be quite different from self-image, since people often choose to project a different image to others. The ideal self serves as a personal set of objectives, since it is the image to which the individual aspires.

FIGURE 1-1 Components of Self-Image

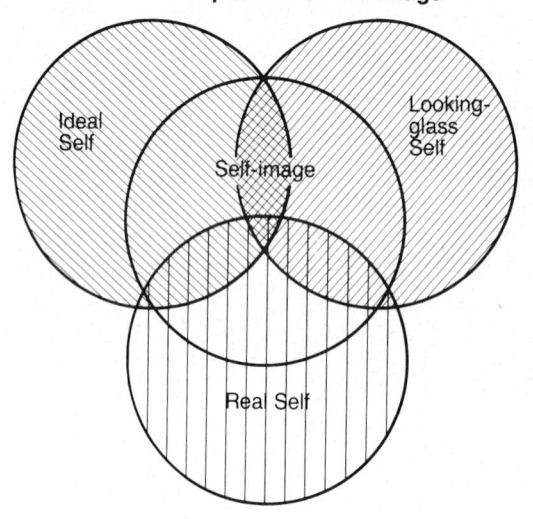

Ideal self—the way you'd like to be
Real self—you as you are
Self-image—the way you see yourself
Looking-glass self—the way you think others see you.

SOURCE: John Douglas, George A. Field, and Lawrence X. Tarpey, *Human Behavior in Marketing* (Columbus, Ohio: Charles E. Merrill Publishing, 1967), p. 65. Reprinted by permission.

[2]See Corbett Gaulden, "Self and Ideal Self-images and Purchase Intentions," in *Proceedings of the Southern Marketing Association*, ed. Robert S. Franz, Robert M. Hopkins, and Alfred G. Toma, New Orleans, La., November 1978; and Terrence V. O'Brien, Humberto S. Tapia, and Thomas L. Brown, "The Self-concept in Buyer Behavior," *Business Horizons*, October 1977, pp. 65–74.

Consumer Behavior: Basic Concepts

10   In purchasing goods and services, people are likely to choose products that will move them closer to their ideal self-image. Those who see themselves as scholars are more likely than others to join literary book clubs. The young woman who views herself as a budding tennis star may become engrossed in evaluating the merits of graphite versus steel rackets and may view with disdain any cheaply made imports. The college graduate on the way up the organization ladder at a bank may hide a love for bowling and instead take up golf—having determined that golf is the sport for bankers. One writer used the self-concept idea to explain the failure of the Edsel. He claimed that potential Edsel purchasers were unsure of the car's image and faced the risk of moving away from their self-concept.[3]

CONSUMER BEHAVIOR: A DEFINITION

11   *Consumer behavior* consists of the acts of individuals in obtaining and using goods and services, including the decision processes that precede and determine these acts.[4] This definition includes both the ultimate consumer and the purchaser of industrial products. A major difference in the purchasing behavior of industrial consumers and ultimate consumers is that additional influences from within the organization may be exerted on the industrial purchasing agent.

Consumer Behavior as a Decision Process

12   The above definition recognizes that consumer behavior may be viewed as a decision process and that the act of purchasing is merely one point in the process. To understand consumer behavior, the events that precede and follow the purchase act must be examined. Figure 1-2 identifies the steps involved in the consumer decision process.

13   As Figure 1-2 indicates, the decision process is utilized by the consumer in

FIGURE 1-2 Steps in the Consumer Decision Process

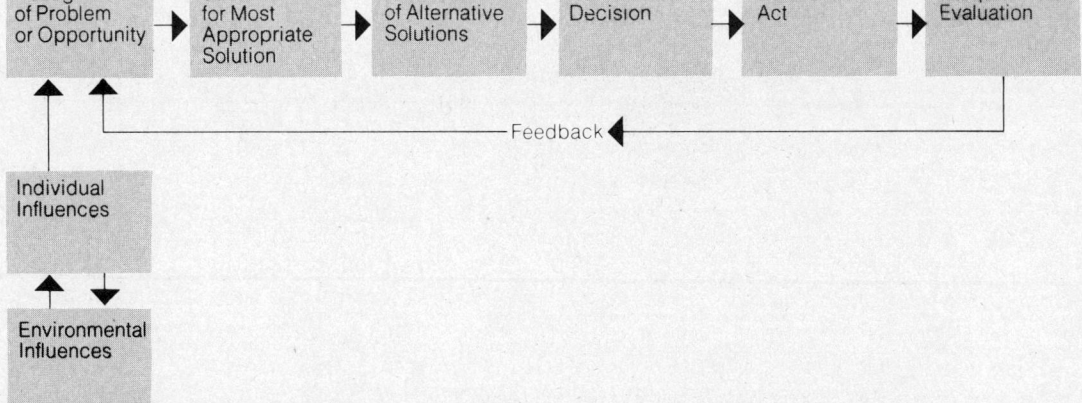

Recognition of Problem or Opportunity → Search for Most Appropriate Solution → Evaluation of Alternative Solutions → Purchase Decision → Purchase Act → Postpurchase Evaluation

Feedback

Individual Influences

Environmental Influences

SOURCE: Adapted from John Dewey, *How We Think* (Boston, Mass.: D.C. Heath, 1910), pp. 101–5. These steps are also discussed in Kenneth E. Runyon, *Consumer Behavior* (Columbus, Ohio: Charles E. Merrill, 1980), pp. 346–54.

[3] Richard H. Buskirk, *Principles of Marketing*, 3rd ed. (Hinsdale, Ill.: Dryden Press, 1970), pp. 139–40.

[4] James F. Engel, Roger D. Blackwell, and David T. Kollat, *Consumer Behavior*, 3rd ed. (Hinsdale, Ill.: Dryden Press, 1978), p. 8.

Marketing

solving problems and in taking advantage of opportunities that arise. Such decisions permit consumers to correct differences between their actual and desired states. Feedback from each decision serves as additional experience to rely upon in subsequent decisions.

14 Consumer behavior results from individual and environmental influences. Consumers often purchase goods and services to achieve their ideal self-image and to project the self-image they want others to accept. Behavior is therefore determined by the individual's psychological makeup and the influences of others. This dual influence can be summarized as:

$$B = f(P, E)$$

Consumer behavior (*B*) is a function (*f*) of the interaction of consumers' *personal influences (P)* and the pressures exerted upon them by outside forces in the *environment (E).*[5] Understanding consumer behavior requires an understanding of the nature of these influences.

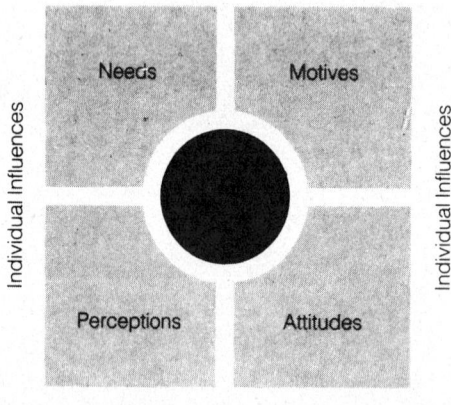

INDIVIDUAL INFLUENCES ON CONSUMER BEHAVIOR

15 The basic determinants of consumer behavior include the individual's *needs, motives, perceptions, and attitudes*. The interaction of these factors with influences from the environment causes the consumer to act. Figure 1-3 presents a graphic picture of these interactions.

Needs and Motives

16 The starting point in the purchase decision process is the recognition of a felt need. A *need* is simply the lack of something useful. The consumer is typi-

FIGURE 1-3 Basic Determinants of Consumer Behavior

SOURCE: C. Glenn Walters and Gordon W. Paul, *Consumer Behavior: An Integrated Framework* (Homewood, Ill.: Richard D. Irwin, 1970), p. 14. © 1970 by Richard D. Irwin, Inc. Reprinted by permission.

---

[5]See Kurt Lewin, *Field Theory in Social Science* (New York: Harper & Row, 1951), p. 62. See also C. Glenn Walters, "Consumer Behavior: An Appraisal," *Journal of the Academy of Marketing Science*, Fall 1979, pp. 273–84.

FIGURE 1-4 Hierarchy of Needs

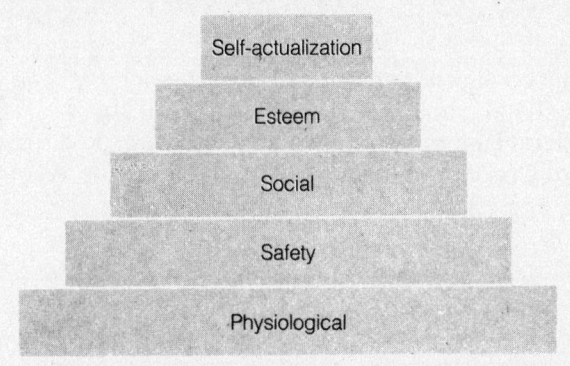

Pyramid from bottom to top: Physiological, Safety, Social, Esteem, Self-actualization

SOURCE: Adapted from A. H. Maslow, "A Theory of Human Motivation," *Psychological Review*, July 1943, pp. 370–96.

cally confronted with numerous unsatisfied needs, but a need must be sufficiently aroused before it can serve as a motive to buy something.

Motives are inner states that direct people toward the goal of satisfying a felt need. The individual is moved to take action to reduce a state of tension and to return to a condition of equilibrium.

Although psychologists disagree on specific classifications, a useful theory of the hierarchy of needs has been developed by A. H. Maslow. Maslow's hierarchy is shown in Figure 1-4. His list is based on two important assumptions:

1. People are wanting animals, whose needs depend on what they already possess. A satisfied need is not a motivator; only those needs that have not been satisfied can influence behavior.
2. People's needs are arranged in a hierarchy of importance. Once one need has been at least partially satisfied, another emerges and demands satisfaction.[6]

Physiological Needs The primary needs for food, shelter, and clothing that are present in all humans and must be satisfied before the individual can consider higher-order needs are physiological needs. A hungry person, possessed by the need to obtain food, ignores other needs. Once the physiological needs are at least partially satisfied, other needs enter the picture.

Safety Needs The second-level safety needs include security, protection from physical harm, and avoidance of the unexpected. Gratification of these needs may take the form of a savings account, life insurance, the purchase of radial tires, or membership in a local health club.

Social Needs Satisfaction of physiological and safety needs leads to the third level—the desire to be accepted by members of the family and other individuals and groups—the social needs. The individual may be motivated to join various groups, to conform to their standards of dress and behavior, and to become interested in obtaining status as means of fulfilling these needs.

Esteem Needs The higher-order needs are more prevalent in developed countries, where a sufficiently high per capita income has allowed most consumers to satisfy the basic needs and to concentrate on the desire for status, esteem, and self-actualization. These needs, which are near the top of the ladder, are more difficult to satisfy. At the esteem level is the need to feel a sense of accomplishment, achievement, and respect from others. The competi-

[6]A. H. Maslow, *Motivation and Personality* (New York: Harper & Row, 1954).

tive need to excel—to better the performance of others—is almost a universal human trait.

23 The esteem need is closely related to social needs. At this level, however, the individual desires not just acceptance but also recognition and respect. The person has a desire to stand out from the crowd in some way.

24 **Self-actualization Needs** The top rung on the ladder of human needs is self-actualization—the need for fulfillment, for realizing one's own potential, for using one's talents and capabilities totally. Maslow defines self-actualization this way: "The healthy man is primarily motivated by his needs to develop and actualize his fullest potentialities and capacities. What man can be, he must be."[7]

25 Maslow points out that a satisfied need is no longer a motivator. Once the physiological needs are satiated, the individual moves on to higher-order needs. Consumers are periodically motivated by the need to relieve thirst or hunger, but their interests are most often directed toward satisfaction of safety, social, and other needs in the hierarchy.

Perception

26 Individual behavior resulting from motivation is affected by how stimuli are perceived. *Perception* is the meaning that each person attributes to incoming stimuli received through the five senses.

$$\text{To perceive is} \begin{cases} \text{to see} \\ \text{to hear} \\ \text{to touch} \\ \text{to taste} \\ \text{to smell} \end{cases} \text{some} \begin{cases} \text{thing} \\ \text{event} \\ \text{idea} \end{cases}[8]$$

Psychologists once assumed that perception was an objective phenomenon, that the individual perceived only what was there to be perceived. Only recently have researchers come to recognize that what people perceive is as much a result of what they want to perceive as of what is actually there. This does not mean that dogs may be viewed as pigeons or shopping centers as churches. But a retail store stocked with well-known brand names and staffed with helpful, knowledgeable sales personnel is perceived differently from a largely self-service discount store. The Honda Civic and the Datsun 280-ZX are both automobile imports, but they carry quite different images.

27 The perception of an object or event is the result of the interaction of two types of factors:

1. *Stimulus factors*—characteristics of the physical object, such as size, color, weight, or shape.
2. *Individual factors*—characteristics of the individual, including not only sensory processes but also past experiences with similar items and basic motivations and expectations.

The individual is continually bombarded with many stimuli, but most are ignored. In order to have time to function, people must respond selectively. The determination of which stimuli they do respond to is the problem of all mar-

---

[7]Ibid., p. 382. See also George Brooker, "The Self-actualizing Socially Conscious Consumer," *Journal of Consumer Research*, September 1976, pp. 107–12.

[8]Adapted from Paul T. Young, *Motivation and Emotion* (New York: Wiley, 1961), pp. 280–99.

keters. How can the consumer's attention be gained so he or she will read the advertisement, listen to the sales representative, react to the point-of-purchase display?

28   Even though studies have shown that the average consumer is exposed to more than a thousand ads daily, most of these ads never break through people's perceptual screens. Sometimes breakthroughs are accomplished in the printed media through large-sized ads. Doubling the size of an ad increases its attention value by about 50 percent. Using color in newspaper ads—in contrast to the usual black and white ads—is another effective way of breaking through the reader's perceptual screen. However, the color ad must reach enough additional readers to justify the extra cost. Other methods using contrast include the use of a large amount of white space around the printed area or using white type on a black background.

29   In general, the marketer seeks to make the message stand out, to make it sufficiently different from other messages that it will gain the attention of the prospective customer. Menley & James Laboratories followed the practice of running hay-fever radio commercials for their Contac capsules only on days when the pollen count was above certain minimum levels. Each commercial was preceded by a live announcement of the local pollen count.

30   Analysis of audience reaction to television commercials shows either a sharp drop or a sharp rise in interest during the first five seconds. After that point, the audience will become only less interested, never more. The attention-grabbing opening of commercials for American Express Travelers Cheques is, "You are about to witness a crime!" Viewers then watch a pickpocket at work. The campaign showing the dangers of carrying cash reportedly helped American Express increase sales 28 percent.[9]

31   The relationship between the actual physical stimulus—such as size, loudness, or texture—and the corresponding sensation produced in the individual is known as psychophysics. It can be expressed as a mathematical equation:

$$\frac{\Delta I}{I} = k.$$

where: ΔI = the smallest increase in stimulus that will be noticeably different from the previous intensity
I = the intensity of the stimulus at the point where the increase takes place
k = a constant (that varies from one sense to the next)

The higher the initial intensity of a stimulus, the greater the amount of the change in intensity that is necessary in order for a difference to be noticed. This relationship, known as *Weber's law*, has some obvious implications in marketing. A price increase of $300 for a $5,000 Mazda GLC is readily apparent to prospective buyers; the same $300 increase on a $25,000 Mercedes-Benz seems insignificant. A large package requires a much greater increase in size for the change to be noticeable than does a small package. People perceive by exception, and the change in stimuli must be sufficiently great to gain their attention.[10]

32   **Selective Perception** Considerable light is shed by *selective perception* on the problem of getting consumers to try a product for the first time. The manufacturer bombards people with television and magazine advertising, sales

---

[9]Kenneth Roman and Jane Maas, *How to Advertise* (New York: St. Martin's Press, 1976), pp. 15–16.

[10]Steuart Henderson Britt, "How Weber's Law Can Be Applied to Marketing," *Business Horizons*, February 1975, pp. 21–29.

promotion discounts and premiums, and point-of-purchase displays—often with little change in sales. Follow-up research shows that many consumers have no knowledge of the product or promotion. Why? Because this information simply never penetrated their perceptual filters. Consumers perceive incoming stimuli on a selective basis. To a large extent they are consciously aware of only those incoming stimuli they wish to perceive.

33   With such selectivity at work, it is easy to see the importance of the marketer's efforts to obtain a "consumer franchise" in the form of brand loyalty to a product. Satisfied customers are less likely to seek information about competing products. And even when it is forced on them, they are not as likely as others to allow it to pass through their perceptual filters. They simply tune out information that is not in accord with their existing beliefs and expectations.

34   **Subliminal Perception**   It is possible to communicate with persons without their being aware of the communication? In 1957, the words "Eat popcorn" and "Drink Coca-Cola" were flashed on the screen of a New Jersey movie theater every five seconds at 1/300th of a second. Researchers reported that these messages, though too short to be recognizable at the conscious level, resulted in a 58 percent increase in popcorn sales and an 18 percent increase in Coca-Cola sales. After the findings were published, advertising agencies and consumer protection groups became intensely interested in *subliminal perception*—the receipt of incoming information at a subconscious level.

35   Subliminal advertising is aimed at the subconscious level of awareness to avoid viewers' perceptual screens. The goal of the original research was to induce consumer purchasing while keeping consumers unaware of the source of their motivation to buy. Further attempts to duplicate the test findings, however, have invariably been unsuccessful.

36   Although subliminal advertising has been universally condemned (and declared illegal in California and Canada), it is exceedingly unlikely that it can induce purchasing except in those instances where the person is already inclined to buy. The reasons for this are:

1. Strong stimulus factors are required to even gain attention.
2. Only a very short message can be transmitted.
3. Individuals vary greatly in their thresholds of consciousness.[11] Messages transmitted at the threshold of consciousness for one person will not be perceived at all by some people and will be all too apparent to others. The subliminally exposed message "Drink Coca-Cola" may go unseen by some viewers, while others may read it as "Drink Pepsi-Cola," "Drink Cocoa," or even "Drive Slowly."

Despite early fears, research has shown that subliminal messages cannot force the receiver to purchase goods that he or she would not consciously want.

Attitudes

37   Perception of incoming stimuli is greatly affected by attitudes about them. In fact, the decision to purchase a product is based on currently held attitudes about the product, the store, or the salesperson.

---

[11]See James H. Myers and William H. Reynolds, *Consumer Behavior and Marketing Management* (Boston: Houghton Mifflin, 1967), p. 14; J. Steven Kelly and Barbara M. Kessler, "Subliminal Seduction: Fact or Fantasy?" in *Proceedings of the Southern Marketing Association*, November 1978, pp. 112–14; and Joel Saegert, "Another Look at Subliminal Perception," *Journal of Advertising Research*, February 1979, pp. 55–57.

FIGURE 1-5 Three Components of an Attitude

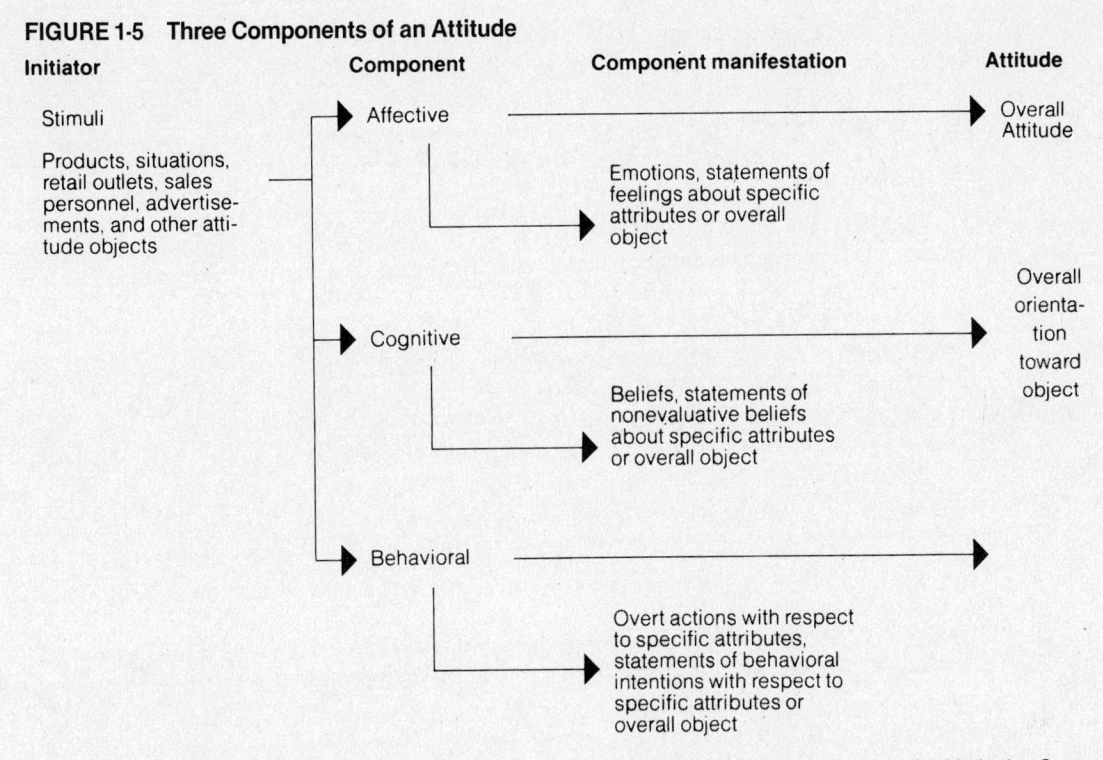

Initiator	Component	Component manifestation	Attitude
Stimuli Products, situations, retail outlets, sales personnel, advertisements, and other attitude objects	Affective	Emotions, statements of feelings about specific attributes or overall object	Overall Attitude
	Cognitive	Beliefs, statements of nonevaluative beliefs about specific attributes or overall object	Overall orientation toward object
	Behavioral	Overt actions with respect to specific attributes, statements of behavioral intentions with respect to specific attributes or overall object	

SOURCE: Del I. Hawkins, Kenneth A. Coney, and Roger J. Best, *Consumer Behavior: Implications for Marketing Strategy* (Dallas, Tex.: Business Publications, Inc., 1980), p. 334. The figure is adapted from M. J. Rosenberg and C. I. Hovland, *Attitude Organization and Change* (New Haven, Conn.: Yale University Press, 1960), p. 3. Reprinted by permission.

38 *Attitudes* are a person's enduring favorable or unfavorable evaluations, emotional feelings, or pro or con action tendencies in regard to some object or idea. They are formed over a period of time through individual experiences and group contacts and are highly resistant to change.

39 **Components of an Attitude** Attitudes consist of three related components: cognitive, affective, and behavioral. The *cognitive* component refers to the individual's information and knowledge about an object or concept. The *affective* component deals with feelings or emotional reactions. The *behavioral* component has to do with tendencies to act or to behave in a certain manner. In considering the decision to shop at a warehouse-type food store, the individual would obtain information from advertising, trial visits, and input from family, friends, and associates (cognitive). The consumer would also receive inputs from others about their acceptance of shopping at this new type of store, as well as information about the type of people who shop there (affective). The shopper may ultimately decide to make some purchases of canned goods, cereal, and bakery products there, but continue to rely upon a regular supermarket for major food purchases (behavioral).

40 All three components exist in a relatively stable and balanced relationship to one another and combine to form an overall attitude about an object or idea. Figure 1-5 illustrates the three components.

41 **Measuring Consumer Attitudes** Since favorable attitudes are likely to be conducive to brand preferences, marketers are interested in determining consumer attitudes toward their products. Numerous attitude scaling devices have been developed, but the semantic differential is probably the most commonly

FIGURE 1-6 Product Images of Brands X, Y, and Z

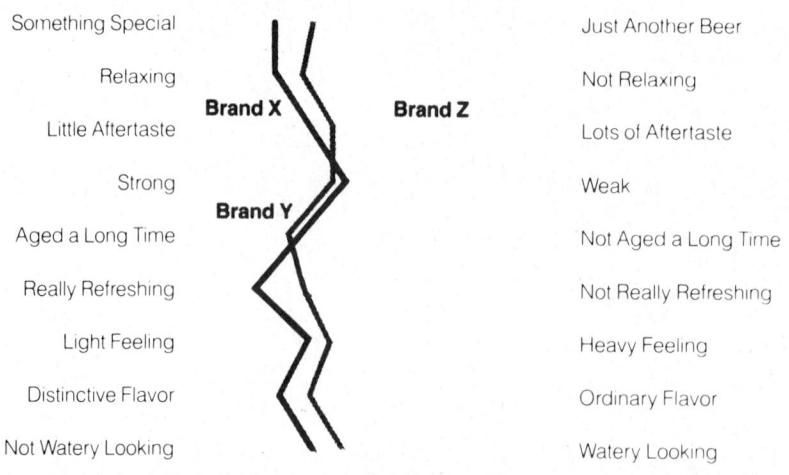

Something Special	Just Another Beer
Relaxing	Not Relaxing
Little Aftertaste	Lots of Aftertaste
Strong	Weak
Aged a Long Time	Not Aged a Long Time
Really Refreshing	Not Really Refreshing
Light Feeling	Heavy Feeling
Distinctive Flavor	Ordinary Flavor
Not Watery Looking	Watery Looking

SOURCE: Adapted from William A. Mindak, "Fitting the Semantic Differential to the Marketing Problem," *Journal of Marketing*, April 1961, pp. 28–33. Reprinted from the *Journal of Marketing* published by the American Marketing Association.

used technique.[12] The *semantic differential* involves the use of a number of bipolar adjectives—such as new-old, reliable-unreliable, sharp-bland—on a seven-point scale. The respondent evaluates the product by checking a point on the scale between the extremes. The average rankings of all respondents then become a profile of the product.

42 A test comparing three unidentified brands of beer produced the profiles illustrated in Figure 1-6. Brands X and Y dominated the local market and enjoyed generally favorable ratings. Brand Z, a newly introduced beer, was less well-known and was reacted to neutrally.

43 Using the information provided by the profiles, weak areas in the image of any of the brands can be noted for remedial action. The semantic differential scale thus provides management with a more detailed picture of both the direction and the intensity of opinions and attitudes about a product than can be obtained through a typical research questionnaire. It supplies a comprehensive multidimensional portrait of brand images.

44 **How Attitudes Change** Given that a favorable consumer attitude is a prerequisite to marketing success, how can a firm lead prospective buyers to adopt this kind of attitude toward its products? The marketer has two choices: to attempt to change consumer attitudes, making them consonant with the product; or to first determine consumer attitudes and then change the product to match them.[13]

45 If consumers view the product unfavorably, the firm may choose to redesign it to better conform with their desires. It may make styling changes, vary ingredients, change package size, or switch retail stores.

46 The other course of action—changing consumer attitudes—is much more difficult. A famous study of coffee drinkers revealed surprisingly negative attitudes toward those who serve instant coffee. Two imaginary shopping lists,

---

[12] C. E. Osgood, G. J. Suci, and P. H. Tannenbaum, *The Measurement of Meaning* (Urbana: University of Illinois Press, 1957). For a comparison of the semantic differential with the Likert Scale and the Stapel Scale—two other widely used attitude scaling formats—see Dennis Menezies and Norbert F. Elbert, "Alternative Semantic Scaling Formats for Measuring Store Image: An Evaluation," *Journal of Marketing Research*, February 1979, pp. 80–87.

[13] See Robert A. Westbrook and Joseph W. Newman, "An Analysis of Shopper Dissatisfaction for Major Household Appliances," *Journal of Marketing Research*, August 1978, pp. 450–66.

Consumer Behavior: Basic Concepts

35

TABLE 1-1 Shopping Lists Used in the Haire Study

Shopping List 1	Shopping List 2
1½ lbs. of hamburger	1½ lbs. of hamburger
2 loaves of Wonder Bread	2 loaves of Wonder Bread
Bunch of carrots	Bunch of carrots
1 can Rumford's Baking Powder	1 can Rumford's Baking Powder
Nescafé Instant Coffee	1 lb. Maxwell House coffee (drip grind)
2 cans Del Monte peaches	2 cans Del Monte peaches
5 lbs. potatoes	5 lbs. potatoes

SOURCE: Mason Haire, "Projective Techniques in Marketing Research." *Journal of Marketing*, April 1950, pp. 649–56. Reprinted from the *Journal of Marketing* published by the American Marketing Association.

shown in Table 1-1, were shown to a sample of one hundred homemakers. Half were shown List 1 and half List 2. Each respondent was then asked to describe the hypothetical shopper who purchased the groceries. The only difference in the lists was the instant versus the regular coffee.

The woman who bought instant coffee was described as lazy by 48 percent of the women evaluating List 1; but only 24 percent of those evaluating List 2 described the woman who bought regular coffee as lazy. Forty-eight percent described the instant coffee purchaser as failing to plan household purchases and schedules well; only 12 percent described the purchaser of regular coffee this way.

But consumer attitudes often change with time. The shopping list study was repeated twenty years later, and the new study revealed that much of the stigma attached to buying instant coffee had disappeared. Instead of describing the instant coffee purchaser as lazy and a poor planner, most respondents felt she was a working wife.[14] Nonetheless, General Foods took no chances when it introduced its new freeze-dried Maxim as a coffee that "tastes like *regular* and has the convenience of *instant*."

Producing Attitude Change Since the individual must maintain consistency among the three attitudinal components, attitude change frequently occurs when inconsistencies are introduced. The most common example of such inconsistencies are changes to the cognitive component of an attitude as a result of new information. The development of convection cooking ovens and the advantages they possess over conventional ovens may lead to product trial by homebuilders. The development of smaller, more effective sterilizer kits for soft contact lenses may increase the probability of acceptance by wearers of hard contact lenses.

The affective component may be attacked through relating the use of the new product or service to desirable consequences for the user. The attractive, healthy appearance of a deep sun-tan and the convenience of acquiring it are primary appeals of the thousands of tanning salons that have diffused rapidly throughout North America.

The third alternative in attempting to change attitudes is to focus upon the behavioral component by inducing the person to engage in attitude-discrepant behavior. Such behavior is contradictory to currently held attitudes. Attitude-discrepant behavior may occur if the consumer is given a free sample of a product. Such trials may led to attitude change.

[14] Frederick E. Webster, Jr., and Frederick Von Pechmann, "A Replication of the 'Shopping List' Study," *Journal of Marketing*, April 1970, pp. 61–63. See also George S. Lane and Gayne L. Watson, "A Canadian Replication of Mason Haire's 'Shopping List' Study," *Journal of the Academy of Marketing Science*, Winter 1975, pp. 48–59.

Consumer Behavior: Basic Concepts

37

PART 1: STUDY QUESTIONS
(Paragraphs 1–5)

Directions: Read paragraphs 1–5 quickly for general understanding. Then refer to the selection to answer the following study questions.

1. Read paragraph 1 carefully.
   A. In your own words, what do the authors mean when they write that the marketer should "find a need and fill it"?

   _____

   _____

   B. What are the two types of "unsatisfied customers" mentioned in this paragraph?

   1. _____

   2. _____

   C. Which of the following has the same meaning as the word *comprise* in the last sentence?
      a. consist of
      b. make up
      c. recognize

2. Skim paragraphs 2–5 quickly. These paragraphs provide one extended example.
   A. What is the topic of this extended example?
      a. the introduction of a new medicine called Analoze
      b. the relative effectiveness of different headache remedies
      c. the ignorance of people who buy pain relief medicines
   B. Why do you think the authors present an extended example so early in the chapter?

   _____

   _____

3. Read paragraph 2 carefully.
   A. What do you think is the meaning of "pharmaceutical firm" in the first sentence?
      a. a company that does consumer research
      b. a hospital
      c. a company that makes medicines
   B. For what types of illnesses would people take the new product described in this paragraph?

   _____

   C. How was this new product better than other, similar products?

   _____

4. Read paragraph 3 carefully.
   A. What was the name of the new product? _____
   B. When the company tested the new product with a panel of potential buyers, how did it compare with competing products?

   _____

Marketing

5. Read paragraph 4 carefully.
   A. What three factors mentioned in this paragraph indicated that Analoze would become a successful product?
      a. _____
      b. _____
      c. _____
   B. Did many people buy Analoze when it was test marketed? _____
   C. What does the word *nil* mean in the last sentence?
      a. average
      b. below average
      c. zero

6. Read paragraph 5 carefully.
   A. In your own words, why did Analoze fail?
      _____
      _____
      _____

   B. In the second sentence, what does the word *ritual* mean?
      a. a type of pain that headache sufferers experience
      b. an unwillingness to spend money
      c. an activity always performed in the same way
   C. What is the ritual described in this paragraph?
      _____
      _____

PART 2: STUDY QUESTIONS
(Paragraphs 6–25)

Directions: Part 2 of this selection covers paragraphs 6–25. Quickly look over these paragraphs. Below is the outline of the entire selection that you completed in the previewing exercises. Circle the portion of the outline that corresponds to the section you will read in Part 2.

I. Introduction
II. Understanding Consumer Behavior
III. Self-Concept Theory
IV. Consumer Behavior: A Definition
   A. Consumer Behavior as a Decision Process
V. Individual Influences on Consumer Behavior
   A. Needs and Motives
      1. Physiological Needs
      2. Safety Needs
      3. Social Needs
      4. Esteem Needs
      5. Self-Actualization Needs
   B. Perception
      1. Selective Perception
      2. Subliminal Perception

Consumer Behavior: Basic Concepts

39

      C. Attitudes
          1. Components of an Attitude
          2. Measuring Consumer Attitudes
          3. How Attitudes Change
          4. Producing Attitude Change

Read paragraphs 6–25 quickly for general understanding. Then refer to the selection to answer the following study questions.

1. Paragraphs 6 and 7 discuss consumer behavior. Read both paragraphs carefully.
    A. Does paragraph 6 introduce a new topic, or continue to discuss a previous one?

___

    According to paragraph 6, which of the following contributed to the failure of the new product, Analoze?
      a. a poor understanding of the pharmaceutical market
      b. an inadequate understanding of how consumers think and behave
      c. a lack of understanding, on the part of the consumer, of the effectiveness of Analoze

    B. According to paragraph 7, what is the most difficult task in marketing?

___

    Refer again to paragraph 7. According to the authors, if you understand _____ people buy or do not buy products, you then understand consumer behavior.

2. Paragraphs 8–10 discuss a new major topic. What is it?

___

3. Read paragraph 8 carefully.
    A. How would you define the term *self-concept* as it is explained in this paragraph?

___

    B. What does the word *multifaceted* mean in the first sentence? (Look for clues in the example in the second sentence.)

___

    Can you analyze the word *multifaceted*? What does *multi-* mean? What does *faceted* mean?

___

    From the information conveyed in this paragraph, fill in the blanks in the following sentences:

        The various pictures that people have of themselves comprise their _____

        _____. When people buy products, they often choose those that _____

        _____ how they see themselves.

4. Read paragraph 9 carefully.
    A. Which of the following is the purpose of this paragraph?
      a. to describe the parts that make up the self
      b. to explain how the real self is different from self-image
      c. to explain why the ideal self is the most important component of the self

Marketing

B. Identify each of the following descriptions as *the real self, the self-image, the looking-glass self,* or *the ideal self*:

    a. John believes that his friends view him as assured and confident. _____

    b. John thinks of himself as shy and unsure. _____

    c. John would like to be daring and unconventional. _____

C. Examine Figure 1-1. Why do you think "Self-image" is placed in the center circle?

_____

_____

5. Read paragraph 10 carefully.
   A. Which sentence contains the main idea of this paragraph?
       a. sentence 1
       b. sentence 2
       c. the last sentence
       d. the last two sentences
   B. Try to apply the concepts explained in this paragraph. What kind of car do you think the following people might tend to purchase?
       a. a middle-aged man who thinks of himself as young and swinging

   _____

       b. a recent college graduate who aspires to become very successful in banking

   _____

6. Paragraphs 11–14 discuss a new topic. What is it?

   _____

7. Read paragraph 11 carefully.
   A. Paraphrase the definition of *consumer behavior* given in this paragraph. Be sure to use your own words.

   _____

   _____

   _____

   B. What do you think an "ultimate" consumer is?

   _____

   What do you think an "industrial" consumer is?

   _____

8. Read paragraphs 12 and 13 carefully.
   A. According to paragraph 12, in order to understand consumer behavior, what must be examined in addition to the act of purchasing?

   _____

   _____

   B. Examine Figure 1-2 carefully. It describes four steps that precede the act of purchasing, and one that follows it. Which step from Figure 1-2 does each of the following situations represent?

a. Dena decides that she is happy she bought the house on Lakeview Avenue because the neighborhood is friendly and she has ample space for her family.

b. Dena realizes that she is not satisfied with her apartment. It is too small, and the neighbors are unfriendly.

c. Dena makes a list of the good and bad aspects of the five houses she is considering buying.

d. Dena decides that the house on Lakeview Avenue is her best choice.

e. Dena looks at five houses that are for sale in an area where she would like to live.

C. Which of the following is a paraphrase of the last sentence in paragraph 13?
   a. Consumers need more experience upon which to rely when they make purchasing decisions.
   b. When consumers evaluate a purchase they have made, they often realize that they understood the problem or opportunity incorrectly in the beginning.
   c. Consumers use what they have learned from making one decision when they make another decision.

9. Read paragraph 14 carefully.
   A. According to this paragraph, what two types of factors influence buyer behavior?

   B. Which type of factor is the ideal self-image?

   Which type of factor is the looking-glass self?

   C. Can you think of other examples of individual, or personal, influences on consumer behavior?

   Can you think of examples of influences that come from the environment?

10. Read paragraph 15 carefully.
    A. The previous paragraph stated that a buyer's behavior is a function of personal influences and outside environmental influences. According to paragraph 15 and Figure 1-3, what are the individual influences upon buyer behavior?

    B. Quickly skim paragraphs 16–25. Specifically, what personal influences are examined?

Marketing

11. Read paragraphs 16 and 17 carefully.
   A. In your own words, define the term *need*.

   _____

   B. In your own words, define the term *motive*.

   _____

   C. According to these paragraphs, do all needs become motives?

   _____

   D. How does paragraph 17 relate to the following situation? Your math instructor has said that you should have a calculator for the course, but you have not been able to afford one. Eventually, you realize that you will not do well in the class without a calculator. You finally find the money to buy one.
   At what point does the need arise?

   _____

   At what point does the motivation to buy arise?

   _____

   In what way does the purchase of the calculator reduce the "state of tension"?

   _____

12. Read paragraph 18 carefully and examine Figure 1-4.
   A. What is meant by a "hierarchy of needs"?
      a. grouping needs by similarity
      b. ordering needs by their importance
      c. reducing needs by satisfying them
   B. Paragraph 18 presents two assumptions upon which Maslow's hierarchy of needs is based. Which of the following is a paraphrase of the first assumption?
      a. People are motivated to obtain only what they do not already possess.
      b. Only satisfied needs can motivate behavior.
      c. People are like animals; they want what they cannot have and are motivated to get it.
   Which of the following is a paraphrase of the second assumption?
      a. When a need has been partially satisfied, it can never again motivate behavior.
      b. The most important needs become motives, and when they are satisfied, other (less important) needs take their place.
      c. Needs emerge unexpectedly, and there is no way to predict how they will be ordered or how they will be satisfied.

13. Read paragraphs 19–25 carefully.
   A. What examples of physiological needs are given?

   _____

   Why are physiological needs represented at the base of Figure 1-4?

   _____

   B. What examples of safety needs are given?

   _____

Can you think of other ways in which safety needs might be fulfilled, in addition to those given in paragraph 20?
_____
_____

C. In your own words, explain what Maslow means by social needs.
_____
_____

Explain how conforming to "standards of dress and behavior" might be a way of fulfilling a social need.
_____
_____

D. How does paragraph 22 define esteem needs?
_____
_____

How are esteem needs different from social needs?
_____
_____

Why are esteem needs more common motivators in the developed countries?
   a. The cultures of these countries emphasize these needs more than the cultures of developing countries do.
   b. Satisfying esteem needs requires more money per individual than is available in most developing countries.
   c. Only in developed countries have individuals been able to fulfill the lower-order needs.

E. In your own words, explain what is meant by self-actualization needs.
_____
_____

Can you think of specific examples of how an individual might fulfill his or her self-actualization needs?
_____
_____

F. Consider the following activities. What type of need does each one satisfy?
   a. A female college student continues studying toward an advanced degree because she feels that she has special ability in a particular area.
   _____

   b. A woman installs a smoke alarm in her apartment in case of fire.
   _____

   c. A man buys an expensive Mercedes sports car because he wants to be the first among his friends to own such a car.
   _____

   d. A mother purchases especially warm jackets for her young children because the winter is supposed to be unusually cold.
   _____

Marketing

44

    e. A teenage boy pesters his parents to let him dye his hair green, just like all his friends.

_____

PART 2: COMPREHENSION EXERCISES
(Paragraphs 6–25)

Exercise 1

The following statements are either *true* or *false* according to paragraphs 6–25 of the selection. Write either T or F in the space before each one.

1. _____ The looking-glass self can be defined as the way that others view us.
2. _____ It is the actual act of purchasing that most interests marketers when they study consumer behavior.
3. _____ The first step in the consumer decision process is recognition of a problem or opportunity.
4. _____ All motives are based upon felt needs.
5. _____ An individual would be likely to attempt to satisfy a social need before a safety need.
6. _____ An example of a physiological need is the desire to be the best in your profession.
7. _____ Understanding consumer behavior involves answering the question "Why do consumers buy or not buy products?"
8. _____ People who see themselves as thrifty would not be likely to buy products that have an expensive image.
9. _____ Environmental influences upon consumer behavior include such factors as needs, motives, perceptions, and attitudes.

Exercise 2

Complete the following summary of paragraphs 6–25 by filling in each blank with an appropriate word or phrase.

Marketers must understand the _____ of individual consumers if they wish to market their products successfully. Understanding consumer behavior means understanding _____ people buy or do not buy products.

People's mental pictures of themselves are called their _____. In reality, the self has four parts: _____, _____, _____, and _____. When people buy goods and services, they generally select those that move them _____ to their ideal self-image.

_____ can be defined as individuals' actions in obtaining and using products, including the _____ that comes before the actual purchase. This process consists of four steps that precede the purchase act: _____, _____, _____, and _____

_____. The last step in the process, after the purchase act, is _____

_____. The behavior that is displayed during the consumer decision process is a

function of _____ and _____ influences.

The individual influences on consumer behavior consist of _____,

_____, _____, and _____. A _____

_____ is the lack of something, while a _____ is an internal state that

causes an individual to attempt to fulfill a need. _____ developed a hierarchy

of needs that has proven very helpful in understanding consumer behavior. According to this

theory, needs are arranged in a hierarchy of importance. Those that are primary needs must

be satisfied before the individual will consider fulfilling higher-order ones. The most impor-

tant, basic needs are called _____, such as the need for food. Next

are the _____ needs, followed in importance by the _____

_____ needs. The fourth level of needs is called _____; in this category

falls the need for _____ and _____. The final category of needs

is _____, the need to realize one's potential. Individuals are motivated to sat-

isfy such needs only when all other levels of needs have been fulfilled.

Exercise 3

Look back at questions 1, 2, and 3 in the Warmup section on page 21. Now that you have read Part 2 of "Consumer Behavior: Basic Concepts," which of these questions might you answer differently? Which would you answer in the same way?

PART 3: STUDY QUESTIONS
(Paragraphs 26–51)

Directions: Part 2 of "Consumer Behavior: Basic Concepts" ended with a discussion of needs and motives as individual influences on buyer behavior. Part 3 of this selection examines other individual influences that are necessary to our understanding of why consumers make the choices they do: perception and attitudes.

Read paragraphs 26–51 quickly for general understanding. Then refer to the reading to answer the following study questions.

1. Skim paragraphs 26–51 quickly.

    A. Which paragraphs discuss perception by the consumer? _____
       What are the two subtopics examined in this section?

        a. _____

        b. _____

    B. Which paragraphs discuss the attitudes of the consumer? _____
       What are the four subtopics examined in this section?

        a. _____

        b. _____

Marketing

        c. _____
        d. _____

2. Read paragraph 26 carefully.
   A. In your own words, define *perception* as it is explained in this paragraph.
   _____
   _____
   _____

   B. Which of the following has the same meaning as *objective* in the third sentence?
      a. not influenced by emotion or opinion
      b. influenced by emotion or opinion
      c. goal or aim

   Do psychologists now believe that perception is an objective phenomenon? _____
   Is it possible for two people to perceive the same object or event in different ways? _____

3. Read paragraph 27 carefully.
   A. What two types of factors determine our perception of an event or object?
      a. _____
      b. _____
   Which of these types of factors would tend to make perception subjective rather than objective? _____
   B. What do the authors mean when they state that people respond "selectively" to stimuli?
      a. People respond to all stimuli.
      b. People respond to only some stimuli.
      c. People try to ignore all stimuli.
   C. If people respond selectively to stimuli, what is the marketer's main concern?
   _____
   _____

4. Read paragraph 28 carefully.
   A. What is the purpose of this paragraph?
      a. It introduces a new concept in regard to consumer perception.
      b. It explains why advertising is important for the marketer.
      c. It attempts to answer the question posed at the end of the previous paragraph.
   B. What do the authors mean in the first sentence when they state that most ads do not "break through people's perceptual screens?"
      a. Most ads do not catch people's attention.
      b. Most ads are not large enough.
      c. Most ads are too difficult to understand.
   C. The authors mention several methods for making ads more noticeable. List several of these methods.
   _____
   _____

   Which of these methods do you think is most effective?
   _____

Consumer Behavior: Basic Concepts

47

5. Read paragraph 29 carefully.
   A. What is the purpose of this paragraph?
      a. It introduces the concepts needed to understand radio advertising.
      b. It presents details that help the reader understand the general ideas presented in the previous paragraph.
      c. It acts as a transition to help the reader move from the general idea of paragraph 28 to that of paragraph 30.
   B. Do you think the methods used by Menley & James Laboratories would be effective in catching your attention if you suffered from severe hay fever? _____

6. Read paragraph 30 carefully.
   A. According to this paragraph, why are the first five seconds of a television commercial important?

   _____
   _____

   B. Why have the commercials for American Express Travelers Cheques been so successful?

   _____
   _____

7. Read paragraph 31 carefully.
   A. In your own words define *psychophysics*.

   _____
   _____

   B. It is not necessary to understand the equation given in this paragraph because its meaning is explained in the sentences that follow it. Fill in the blanks in the following paragraph so that the meaning of Weber's law is clear.

   When marketers want to make a stimulus _____ so that consumers will notice it, they must _____ the stimulus a greater amount if it was strong initially. However, if the stimulus was initially _____, it does not have to be increased as much.

   C. A company wishes to increase the sales of its laundry detergent. It can increase the size of the detergent box from four pounds to five pounds by increasing the price from $3.98 to $5.29. Do you think that the company should make these changes? Why or why not?

   _____
   _____

8. Read paragraphs 32 and 33 carefully.
   A. These paragraphs discuss selective perception, a concept introduced in paragraph 27. In your own words, briefly explain how selective perception causes many advertisements and other marketing methods to be unsuccessful.

   _____
   _____

   B. Paragraph 33 discusses brand loyalty on the part of the consumer, and how such a "consumer franchise" can work to the benefit of the marketer. According to the

Marketing

authors, if a consumer is very loyal to a particular brand, how will that person perceive advertisements for competing brands?

9. Paragraphs 34–36 discuss subliminal perception. Read these paragraphs carefully.
   A. *Sub-* means "below" or "under"; *limen* is a term in psychology that means "threshold," or "point where something becomes meaningful." Using this information and the explanation in paragraph 34, how would you define *subliminal perception*?

   Where did the first experiment in subliminal advertising take place?

   Was the experiment successful in increasing sales? _____
   B. According to paragraph 35, what is the goal of subliminal advertising?

   Can consumers be selective in perceiving subliminal messages? _____

   Do experts now believe that subliminal advertising is effective? _____
   C. Which of the following are mentioned in paragraph 36 as reasons why subliminal advertising is unlikely to cause consumers to buy products they do not really want?
      a. The messages that can be conveyed are not long enough.
      b. Consumers can screen out the messages they do not want to perceive.
      c. Subliminal messages will not be perceived in the same way by all people.
      d. Consumers buy only what meets their real needs.
      e. Subliminal messages may be too weak.

10. The remainder of the reading selection, paragraphs 37–51, discusses attitudes as a type of individual influence on buyer behavior. Read paragraphs 37 and 38 carefully.
    A. In your own words, briefly explain what is meant by the term *attitude*.

    B. What is the relationship between attitudes and perception?
       a. Attitudes about an object influence how an individual perceives it.
       b. Perception of an object and attitudes toward it are independent of each other.
       c. Perception and attitude are really the same thing.
    C. Do you think the fact that attitudes are difficult to change is helpful to the marketer? Why or why not?

11. Paragraphs 39 and 40 discuss the components of an attitude. Read these paragraphs carefully and examine Figure 1-5.
    A. Write one or two words that describe each type of attitude component.
       a. cognitive _____

Consumer Behavior: Basic Concepts

49

    b. affective _____

    c. behavioral _____

B. John has a strong attitude about personal computers. Identify each of the following as the cognitive, affective, or behavioral component of his overall attitude.

    a. John is unwilling to sit down in front of a computer; when he gets near one, his palms begin to sweat. _____

    b. John knows almost nothing about how computers work or what they can do.

_____

    c. John's friends tell him that computers are dehumanizing. In addition, John doesn't like most of the people who speak favorably of personal computers.

_____

12. Paragraphs 41–43 discuss how consumers' attitudes can be measured. Read these paragraphs carefully, and examine Figure 1-6.

    A. What is the semantic differential used for?

_____

_____

    B. Paragraph 41 states that the semantic differential uses "bipolar adjectives," such as *new-old* and *reliable-unreliable*. What does *bipolar* mean?

_____

    C. Look at Figure 1-6. For which brand of beer were consumer attitudes least favorable overall?

_____

        For which brand were they most favorable overall?

_____

        Which brand has the image of being the strongest beer?

_____

    D. Do you think the semantic differential is an accurate method of discovering consumers' attitudes toward different products? Why or why not?

_____

_____

_____

13. Paragraphs 44–48 discuss how attitudes change. Read paragraphs 44 and 45 carefully.

    A. What two choices does a marketer have if consumers have unfavorable attitudes toward a product? (Use your own words.)

        a. _____

_____

        b. _____

    B. If a marketer decides to change a product so that it will elicit more favorable consumer attitudes, what are some possible modifications that can be made?

_____

_____

_____

Marketing

14. Paragraphs 46–48 concern an experiment involving consumer attitudes toward a product. Read these paragraphs carefully, and examine Table 1-1.
    A. What product was the focus of this experiment?

    Did the attitudes that were measured concern the product itself or the people who used the product?

    B. What adjectives were used to describe the consumer of the instant coffee?

    What adjectives could be used to describe the attitude toward the consumer of regular coffee?

    C. When the experiment was repeated twenty years later, what were the results?

15. Paragraphs 49–51 discuss how consumer attitudes can be changed. Read these paragraphs carefully.
    A. According to the authors, when can attitudes most easily be changed?
        a. when the individual maintains consistency among the attitudinal components
        b. when the affective, cognitive, and behavioral components of the attitude do not agree
        c. when the marketer attempts to change the cognitive component of the attitude
    B. Which of the attitudinal components might be changed by giving consumers new information about a product?

    What examples of such a change are given?

    C. If a beer manufacturer attempts to change the image of its beer by using advertisements and commercials of young, successful people having a good time, what attitudinal component is the manufacturer trying to change?

    D. What is "attitude-discrepant behavior" as discussed in paragraph 51?

    When a newspaper or magazine offers to send you several free issues, what attitudinal component is it attempting to change?

PART 3: COMPREHENSION EXERCISES
(Paragraphs 26–51)

Exercise 1

The following statements are either *true* or *false* according to paragraphs 26–51 of the selection. Write either T or F in the space before each one.

1. _____ Perception is an objective phenomenon; people perceive only what is really there.
2. _____ Consumers do not actually notice all the advertisements they are exposed to each day.
3. _____ The last few seconds of a television commercial are the most important in catching the consumer's attention.
4. _____ According to Weber's law, the weaker the original stimulus, the smaller the amount of change that is necessary in order for a difference to be noticed.
5. _____ The goal of subliminal advertising is to make the message loud and clear so that the consumer will pay attention to it.
6. _____ Marketers find it relatively easy to change consumers' attitudes toward products.
7. _____ The fact that a consumer knows someone who has had bad luck with a product is part of the cognitive component of that consumer's attitude.
8. _____ In order to change consumer attitudes, it is often necessary to change only one attitudinal component.

Exercise 2

Complete the following summary of paragraphs 26–51 by filling in each blank with an appropriate word or phrase.

When consumers are motivated to act, their actions are influenced by how stimuli are perceived. _____ can be defined as the meaning that is given to the stimuli as they are received through the five senses. It is commonly agreed today that perception is not an _____ phenomenon, but a subjective one. Two types of factors, _____ (characteristics of the physical object) and _____ _____ (characteristics of the person receiving the stimuli), result in the perception of an object or event.

Every individual is exposed to a tremendous number of _____, but most are ignored. This ability to respond only to some stimuli is called _____ _____. It is the job of the marketer to catch the consumers' _____ so that advertisements will break through the consumers' perceptual screens.

_____ is the study of the relationship between the individual's perception of a stimulus and the physical stimulus itself. One application of this relationship, known as _____, states that a stimulus that is _____ initially must be increased to a higher degree if the difference is to be perceived by the individual.

The receipt of information at a subconscious level is known as _____ _____. Although this method was shown to be effective in influencing consumers in one experiment, many experts question whether it can be used successfully as an advertis-

Marketing

ing tool. The purpose of this method, of course, is to avoid the consumers' _____ _____ so that they cannot choose which stimuli to perceive.

Another individual influence on buyer behavior is consumers' attitudes. Attitudes consist of three components: _____, _____, and _____. A popular method to measure consumer attitudes is the _____, which asks respondents to rate an object using _____ _____ adjectives, such as *flavorful-unflavorful*.

If consumer attitudes about a product are not favorable, the firm has two options: it can try to change the consumers' _____ toward the product, or change the _____ itself so that it is more in line with what potential buyers want. However, it is much more difficult to change _____ because they are very enduring.

Exercise 3

Look back at questions 4, 5, 6, 7, and 8 in the Warmup section on page 21. Now that you have read Part 3 of "Consumer Behavior: Basic Concepts," which of these questions might you answer differently? Which would you answer in the same way?

CHAPTER 2

Key Business Decisions: Branding

WARMUP QUESTIONS

The reading in this chapter has been taken from *Modern Marketing Management* by Burton Marcus and others. This text is aimed at university-level courses in marketing, with an emphasis on managerial aspects.

"Key Business Decisions: Branding" examines the importance of establishing a special name or symbol for a particular product, such as Ivory soap or Marlboro cigarettes. Before you read, consider the following statements, and indicate whether you *agree* or *disagree* with each one. Discuss your opinions with your classmates.

1. _____ Buyers become loyal to a particular product brand because it satisfies them.
2. _____ If a certain product has no competitors, it is not necessary for the manufacturer to create a strong brand image in the minds of consumers.
3. _____ The marketer can change the way that consumers feel about a particular product brand through advertising.
4. _____ A product that does not have a good brand image among consumers is still likely to sell well if the product is of high quality.
5. _____ A well-known brand image can also work against a product in certain situations.

Answer the following questions about branding, and then discuss your opinions with your classmates.

In what ways do you think branding of particular products can be helpful to consumers?

_____

_____

Marketing

What do you think are some of the reasons consumers might want to purchase specific brands of products?
_____
_____

When you go shopping, which brand of the following products do you usually buy? Why?

laundry detergent: _____

coffee: _____

cola soft drink: _____

DIRECTIONS FOR READING

Before you read this selection, first scan it quickly, noting the section headings and the words in italics. Also examine the chart (Table 2-1) briefly. Then read the entire selection quickly for general understanding, and turn to the study questions that follow.

Key Business Decisions
Burton Marcus et al.

BRANDING

1. What sets a product apart from the others with which it competes? Appearance and quality aside, branding is probably the most direct way to distinguish an item from its peers on the market shelf. Consequently, most products sold in the United States and the Western world (and even some in the Soviet Union) carry an identification indicating a particular name, place, or organization of manufacture.

2. According to the American Marketing Association, a brand is a name, term, sign, symbol, or design—or a combination of these—intended to identify the goods or services of one seller or group of sellers and to differentiate them from those of competitors.[1] A brand name is that part of a brand that can be vocalized. A trademark is a brand, or part of a brand, given legal protection because it is capable of exclusive appropriation.

3. Branding identifies a particular manufacturer's product. By branding its products, an organization makes it possible for the customer to note easily a particular product and repeat the purchase if satisfaction resulted from the initial purchase.

4. At the same time, branding represents a dual-edged sword. If the previous purchase of that particular brand resulted in dissatisfaction, then by being able to easily identify the product or service, the customer is able to avoid repeat purchase on subsequent occasions.

5. Most important, branding offers the consumer confidence in product consistency. Assuming that the manufacturer makes a consistent product, branding helps convey the message that the item being purchased is similar in quality and performance to those products of the same brand that have previously been used.

6. For example, Maytag washing machines have, for years, been considered by many consumers to be the finest products in their field. Hence, the company's fabled "lonely repairman." This image of a smooth-running, long-lasting product was no accident. The organization attempted to build a sound product and, at the same time, ensure that servicing of the product was equally good. Consequently, consumers who owned Maytag washing machines and needed to purchase new ones more often than not would "think" Maytag when making their purchases. In essence, the consumer in such a case bets on the consistency of product and performance indicated by a brand name.[2] In the case of more frequently purchased products, such as toothpaste or detergent, brand identification facilitates continued and frequent repurchases, an indicator of consumer brand loyalty.

7. Such loyalty is a measure of the consumer's tenacity in regularly repurchasing the same product in the light of other offerings and promotional or price enticements. Those consumers who are an organization's loyal customers typically comprise the core group which accounts for a lion's share of sales and

---

[1] American Marketing Association Committee on Definitions, Ralph S. Alexander, Chairman, *Marketing Definitions: A Glossary of Marketing Terms* (Chicago: American Marketing Association, 1960).

[2] "Just What the Doctor Ordered?," *Forbes*, September 15, 1974, pp. 32–33.

contributes heavily toward profits. The six-pack-a-night Budweiser drinker would fall into this category.

8 Another benefit of branding is the psychological satisfaction it may offer the consumer. Owning a Cadillac is far more than simply possessing the comfort or performance the vehicle can offer. For many buyers, the psychological satisfaction associated with such a purchase is more important than the mechanical qualities of the car itself. Its importance is symbolic: the owner of a Cadillac often feels that he or she has arrived—both socially and economically.

9 This is similar to the sense of satisfaction some individuals derive from seeing famous labels sewn into their clothes or accouterments. For these people, carrying a Vuitton bag or briefcase is a symbol of limitless cachet. The power of the brand itself counts for as much, if not more than, the quality of the company's products. This is brand imagery in action.

BRANDING AND IMAGERY

10 According to behaviorists, learning takes place and habit is established when the experience or experiences that satisfy an individual's needs are cognitively registered and repeated whenever the need occurs. In other words, once we learn to like something, we will continue to like it until a bad experience teaches us otherwise. However, when stimuli—such as a product—are not clearly differentiable, a particular pattern of behavior is difficult to establish. Imagery, through branding, fills the differential need. As far as marketing experts are concerned, such imagery is a prerequisite for establishing a learning response toward a given product.[3]

11 Brands, as we have seen, are identifications for products. These products, in turn, conjure up images. Images are, themselves, mental representations of the product and its meaning to the purchaser. They are the sensory perceptions —conceptualizations from the product's appearance, use, place of purchase, and association that the individual draws from his or her experience with the product and its use.[4] Because brand image stands for the product's character, it represents a complex of all the attitudes purchasers hold toward the product. These attitudes are a result of the experiences individuals have with the product, its packaging, color, and shape, the place or places in which it can be purchased, the methods of use and the behavior in use, the other people who use and purchase the product, advertising and many other, lesser factors.

12 Because products and brands have interwoven sets of characteristics that are complexly evaluated by consumers, a firm's marketing efforts for a particular brand represent long-term investments that affect the brand's profitability.[5]

BRAND AWARENESS

13 As we have seen, one purpose of branding is to identify products so that consumers can select those products from among their competitors. Basically, a consumer is aware or ignorant of a brand's existence.

[3]Herbert O. Mowrer, *Learning Theory and Behavior* (New York: John Wiley and Sons, 1961), p. 14; and Thomas S. Robertson, *Consumer Behavior* (Glenview, Ill.: Scott Foresman, 1970), p. 32.

[4]Ben M. Enis, "Analytical Approach to the Concept of Image," *California Management Review* 9 (Summer 1967), 51–58.

[5]Burleigh B. Gardner and Sidney J. Levy, "The Product and the Brand," *Harvard Business Review* 33 (March–April 1955), 33–39.

Key Business Decisions: Branding

14 If a consumer is unaware of a product, there is little that the manufacturer can do to entice a purchase. One key job of the seller, therefore, is to build brand awareness. In some cases, this may also imply building awareness of the product category, particularly when only one product brand exists. This was the case when Polaroid introduced its automatic Land cameras in the decade after World War II. It was also true when Xerox introduced its dry copier to the market in the late 1950s. On the other hand, if an organization markets one of many products that consumers are aware of, a major communication task is to educate the consumer in the relative differences among brands.

15 Four levels of brand awareness may be identified: brand recognition, brand preference, brand insistence, and brand rejection.[6] *Brand recognition* usually indicates knowledge that the brand exists. It does not, however, imply [educating] the consumer in the relative differences among brands.

16 *Brand preference*, on the other hand, implies positive attitudes by the consumer toward the brand. These positive attitudes are usually demonstrated by the consumer's purchase preference for that particular brand over others, that is, a consumer's preference for General Electric appliances over those of other makers. This preference would probably reflect the consumer's experience with the product, the consumer's knowledge about the brand and product performance as well as the promotional or sales influences leading to product selection and preference.

TABLE 2-1   Matrix of Consumer Satisfaction and Purchase Pattern

	Completely Satisfied	Partially Satisfied	Completely Dissatisfied
Always Use	High loyalty No search for alternative brands 1	 2	Disloyal users Receptive to information about competitive brands 3
Sometimes Use	 4	Unstable purchase behavior 5	 6
Never Use	Nonproduct reasons for nonpurchase (price, channel facilities, and so on) 7	 8	 9

From *Consumer Behavior*, Second Edition, by James F. Engel, David T. Kollat, and Roger D. Blackwell. Copyright © 1968, 1973 by Holt, Rinehart and Winston, Inc. Reprinted by permission of Holt, Rinehart and Winston.

[6]Glenn Walters and Paul Gordon, *Consumer Behavior* (Homewood, Ill.: Irwin Dorsey, 1970), p. 509.

17   *Brand insistence* goes beyond mere preference to consumer demand for one brand and not another. It also implies extreme satisfaction or at least a desire to obtain that particular brand rather than any alternative and may also reflect fear of dissatisfaction from use of alternative brands with which the consumer is unfamiliar. The Tareyton smoker who would "rather fight than switch" is probably one of marketing's most famous—even if fictional—examples of brand insistence.

18   Finally, *brand rejection* indicates negative consumer attitudes toward a given brand. It also implies negative experiences with, or information about, the product that causes the potential purchaser to eliminate the brand from product selection lists. This recently happened to McDonald's in the South, where rumors about chopped worms in the hamburger meat resulted in a fairly widespread brand rejection.

19   A matrix of consumer purchase patterns in terms of product satisfaction is presented in Table 2-1. Those consumers who insist on particular brands are typically those consumers who are core, loyal users, as in cell 1. Those who would prefer particular brands also represent loyal users, and could be situated in cell 2. Those consumers who recognize, but do not necessarily prefer, the brand typically represent fringe purchasers at best, such as those in cell 5. Those consumers who reject the brand, of course, are nonusers, found in cells 7, 8, and 9.

Key Business Decisions: Branding

STUDY QUESTIONS

Directions: Refer to the reading to answer the following study questions.

1. Read paragraphs 1 and 2 carefully.
   A. What does the expression *set apart* mean in the first sentence of paragraph 1?
      a. to place in a different location
      b. to show that something is different
      c. to show the quality of something
   B. According to paragraph 1, what three factors are important in setting one product apart from other, similar products?

      a. _____
      b. _____
      c. _____
   C. The second paragraph provides several definitions. In your own words, briefly define each of the following terms.

      a. *brand:* _____
         _____

      b. *brand name:* _____
         _____

      c. *trademark:* _____
         _____

2. Read paragraphs 3, 4, and 5 carefully.
   A. Each of these paragraphs discusses one effect of branding. List each effect, using your own words.

      a. paragraph 3: _____
         _____

      b. paragraph 4: _____
         _____

      c. paragraph 5: _____
         _____

   B. Can you think of any types of products for which confidence in product consistency is especially important?
      _____
      _____

3. Read paragraphs 6 and 7 carefully.
   A. What is the purpose of paragraph 6?
      a. It provides an example of the notion, discussed in paragraph 4, that branding can be a "dual-edged sword."
      b. It provides information about Maytag washing machines, a popular brand.
      c. It provides an example of consumer confidence in product consistency, a notion discussed in paragraph 5.

Marketing

B. The term *brand loyalty* is introduced in paragraph 6 and further defined in paragraph 7. In your own words, what is brand loyalty?

_____

_____

C. According to paragraph 7, what type of consumers generally contribute most greatly to the sale of a particular product?

_____

What example is given?

_____

What do you think *lion's share* means in the second sentence?

_____

4. Read paragraphs 8 and 9 carefully.
   A. These paragraphs discuss the "psychological satisfaction" that branding can provide to the consumer. What example does paragraph 8 give of such psychological satisfaction?

   _____

   _____

   What other product brands can you think of that might give some consumers this type of psychological satisfaction?

   _____

   _____

   B. Paragraph 9 provides another example of psychological satisfaction. What is it?

   _____

   _____

   For the people described in paragraph 9, which is more important, the quality of the product itself or the brand name?

   _____

   Which of the following is a synonym for the word *cachet* in the second sentence of paragraph 9?
   a. prestige
   b. usefulness
   c. satisfaction

5. Paragraphs 10, 11, and 12 discuss branding and imagery (a brand's image is the way people feel about the brand, or their attitudes toward it). Read these paragraphs carefully.
   A. Which of the following is the main idea of paragraph 10?
      a. Consumers who learn to like a certain product brand will not change their preference unless they have a negative experience with it.
      b. Behaviorists define learning and habit formation as the association of certain experiences that satisfy the consumer's needs and that are repeated whenever the needs arise.
      c. In order for consumers to develop brand loyalty, it is first necessary for the brand to have a clear image to separate it from other, similar products.
   B. What does *prerequisite* mean in the last sentence in paragraph 10?
      a. something required before something else

Key Business Decisions: Branding

61

      b. something that follows as a consequence
      c. a bonus, or added reward
  C. Paragraph 11 explains the concept of brand image in more detail. What types of factors contribute to a brand's image?

_____

_____

_____

  D. Do you think that all consumers have the same image of a particular product brand? For instance, do McDonald's restaurants project the same image to all consumers? What image do they convey to you?

_____

_____

_____

_____

6. Paragraphs 13–19 discuss consumer awareness of brands. Read paragraphs 13 and 14 carefully.
  A. According to these paragraphs, why is it important for a seller to build brand awareness of a product?

_____

_____

  B. When Polaroid introduced the automatic Land cameras, did it have to establish awareness of a new brand? Explain your answer.

_____

_____

7. Read paragraphs 15–19 carefully and examine Table 2-1.
  A. These paragraphs explain four levels of brand awareness. Match each of the following levels of brand awareness with the appropriate description.

      _____ brand recognition   **a.** consumer demand

      _____ brand preference   **b.** negative consumer attitudes

      _____ brand insistence   **c.** consumer knowledge of brand

      _____ brand rejection   **d.** positive consumer attitudes

  B. Indicate if each of the following situations represents brand recognition, brand preference, brand insistence, or brand rejection.
    a. Janet loves Dannon yogurt, especially the raspberry flavor. When the grocery store is out of this product, she does not buy any yogurt at all.

_____

    b. John is planning to buy a 35mm camera. Although he does not know much about cameras, he has heard that the Japanese brands are good bargains. Friends have told him to look at the Ricoh and Minolta models.

_____

c. Dena is planning to buy a new car, but she will not look at Japanese or German imports. She has heard that it is difficult to get them repaired and that replacement parts are hard to find.

d. Whenever Joe buys typing paper, he tries to find a particular brand that he especially likes. The stationery store is usually out of this brand, however, so he buys whatever is in stock.

C. Refer to paragraph 19 and Table 2-1. The table presents a matrix of how satisfied consumers are with certain brands, and how frequently they purchase those brands.
  a. Which cell(s), or box(es), in the table would you label "brand insistence"?

  b. Which cell(s) would you label "brand rejection"?

  c. Which cell(s) would you label "brand preference"?

  d. Which cell(s) would you label "brand recognition"?

INTEGRATION QUESTIONS FOR DISCUSSION AND WRITING

Directions: These questions require you to find relationships among the ideas in the first two articles of this unit: "Consumer Behavior: Basic Concepts" and "Key Business Decisions: Branding." Discuss your answers with your classmates.

1. According to self-concept theory, as presented in "Consumer Behavior: Basic Concepts," buyers choose products that are consistent with their self-images. Keeping this theory in mind, what should marketers try to do when creating a brand image for a new product?

    Imagine that you are a marketing executive for a large manufacturing company. You are in charge of creating brand images, or personalities, for products. What type of brand image might you create for each of the following situations? (Keep in mind the likely self-image of the consumer group.)

	Consumer Group	Product	Brand Image
a.	young male college students	coffee	
		watches	
b.	successful working women	coffee	
		watches	

2. Consumers' images of many products are influenced in large part by television advertising. Think of several brand images conveyed by television commercials. Do the images

seem designed to satisfy the lower-order or higher-order needs, as defined by Maslow's hierarchy (see "Consumer Behavior: Basic Concepts")?
   a. What brand image might a marketer create for an automobile in order to appeal to consumers' safety needs?
   b. What brand image might a marketer create for a mouthwash in order to appeal to consumers' social needs?
   c. What brand image might a marketer create for a news magazine in order to appeal to consumers' self-actualization needs?
3. A marketer attempts to create a brand image that will differentiate the product from other, similar products, and that will appeal to consumers. The best way to measure the success of a brand image is to measure consumer attitudes toward the product. Often, the semantic differential technique is used (see "Consumer Behavior: Basic Concepts").

   With one or two classmates, conduct a simple consumer attitude test using the semantic differential. Choose a product that is familiar to most of your classmates, and then choose appropriate bipolar adjectives to describe the product. Use a chart similar to the following one. Average the responses, and present your results to the class.

Product: _____

(adjective)   (adjective)

_____ 1 2 3 4 5 6 7 _____

_____ 1 2 3 4 5 6 7 _____

_____ 1 2 3 4 5 6 7 _____

_____ 1 2 3 4 5 6 7 _____

CHAPTER 3

Market Targeting

WARMUP QUESTIONS

The selection in this last chapter of the unit on marketing and consumer behavior has been taken from *Marketing Essentials* by Philip Kolter, another textbook intended for use in university-level marketing courses.

"Market Targeting" discusses the strategies that may be used by firms to sell their products effectively. A *market* can be defined as a group of people who have the ability and the willingness to buy goods. For example, we might speak of all the people who are potential car buyers as the car market. Of course, this group of people is not homogeneous; individuals look for different features when they shop for cars. So we can say that the car market is *segmented*; that is, the car market is composed of separate groups of people, with one group or segment interested in small economical automobiles, another segment interested in sports cars, and another in large luxury cars. "Market Targeting" examines the different strategies available to a firm in approaching its market.

Before you read this selection, consider the following statements, and indicate whether you *agree* or *disagree* with each one. Discuss your opinions with your classmates.

1. _____ It is better for a manufacturer to make only one type or brand of a particular product than to manufacture several different brands of the same general product.

2. _____ A company will find it more profitable to aim its products at a small, specific market segment (for example, professional photographers) than at a broader, less specific market group (all camera users).

3. _____ Japanese and German car manufacturers have been very successful in selling their cars in the United States because American car companies have neglected an important car-market segment—that is, those people interested in smaller, fuel-efficient automobiles.

4. _____ When a company creates a brand image for a product, it should examine carefully the market segments that are likely to purchase the product.

Market Targeting

65

5. _____ It is more expensive for a manufacturer to produce different brands of a product for different market segments than it is to produce just one general product for all segments.

Answer the following questions about markets and market segments, and then discuss your answers with your classmates.

There is a very large market in the United States for restaurants, but obviously different people are interested in different types of restaurants for different reasons. What segments of the restaurant market can you identify?

_____
_____
_____

The soft-drink market around the world is enormous. Can you think of any smaller market segments within this large market? What brands of soft drinks might appeal to these separate segments?

_____
_____
_____

DIRECTIONS FOR READING

Before you read this selection, first scan it quickly, looking for subheadings and noting the figures and their labels. Then read the entire selection quickly for general understanding, and turn to the study questions that follow.

Market Targeting
Philip Kolter

1   Marketing segmentation reveals the market segment opportunities facing the firm. The firm now has to decide on (1) how many segments to cover and (2) how to identify the best segments. We will look at each decision in turn.

THREE MARKET-COVERAGE ALTERNATIVES

2   The firm can adopt one of three market-coverage strategies: undifferentiated marketing, differentiated marketing, and concentrated marketing. These strategies are illustrated in Figure 3-1 and discussed below.

Undifferentiated Marketing

3   The firm might decide to ignore market segment differences and go after the whole market with one market offer.[1] It focuses on what is common in the needs of consumers rather than on what is different. It designs a product and a marketing program that will appeal to the broadest number of buyers. It relies on mass distribution and mass advertising. It aims to give the product a superior image in people's minds. An example of undifferentiated marketing is the Hershey Company's marketing some years ago of only one chocolate candy bar for everyone.

4   Undifferentiated marketing is economical. Production, inventory, and transportation costs are low. The undifferentiated advertising program keeps down advertising costs. The absence of segment marketing research and planning lowers the costs of marketing research and product management.

5   The firm that uses undifferentiated marketing typically develops a product aimed at the largest segments in the market. When several firms do this, the result is intense competition for the largest segments and less satisfaction for the smaller ones. Thus the American auto industry for a long time produced only large automobiles. The result is that the larger segments may be less profitable because of heavy competition.

Differentiated Marketing

6   Here the firm decides to operate in several segments of the market and designs separate offers to each. Thus General Motors tries to produce a car for every "purse, purpose, and personality." By offering various products, it hopes to attain higher sales and a deeper position within each market segment. It hopes that obtaining a stronger position in several segments will strengthen the consumers' overall identification of the company with the product category. Furthermore, it hopes for greater repeat purchasing because the firm's product matches the customer's desire rather than the other way around.

---

[1] See Wendell R. Smith, "Product Differentiation and Market Segmentation as Alternative Marketing Strategies," *Journal of Marketing*, July 1956, pp. 3–8; and Alan A. Roberts "Applying the Strategy of Market Segmentation," *Business Horizons*, Fall 1961, pp. 65–72.

FIGURE 3-1 Three Alternative Market-Coverage Strategies

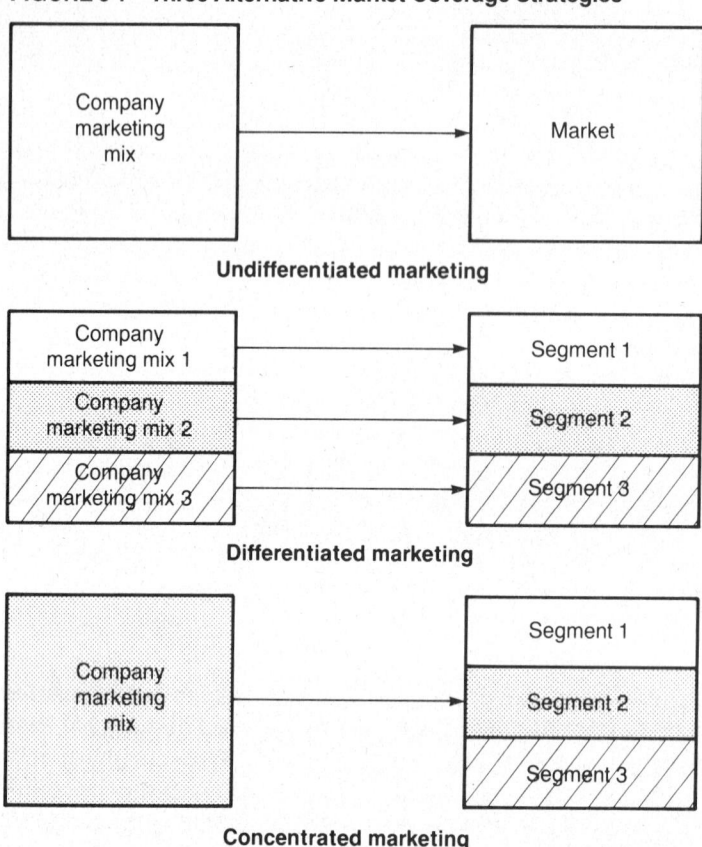

```
┌─────────────┐         ┌─────────────┐
│   Company   │         │             │
│  marketing  │────────▶│   Market    │
│     mix     │         │             │
└─────────────┘         └─────────────┘
```
Undifferentiated marketing

```
┌─────────────┐         ┌─────────────┐
│   Company   │────────▶│  Segment 1  │
│marketing mix 1│       ├─────────────┤
├─────────────┤         │             │
│   Company   │────────▶│  Segment 2  │
│marketing mix 2│       ├─────────────┤
├─────────────┤         │             │
│   Company   │────────▶│  Segment 3  │
│marketing mix 3│       │             │
└─────────────┘         └─────────────┘
```
Differentiated marketing

```
                        ┌─────────────┐
┌─────────────┐         │  Segment 1  │
│             │         ├─────────────┤
│   Company   │         │             │
│  marketing  │────────▶│  Segment 2  │
│     mix     │         ├─────────────┤
│             │         │             │
│             │         │  Segment 3  │
└─────────────┘         └─────────────┘
```
Concentrated marketing

7   A growing number of firms have adopted differentiated marketing. Here is an excellent example.[2]

> Edison Brothers operates nine hundred shoe stores that fall into four different chain categories, each appealing to a different market segment. Chandler's sells higher-priced shoes. Baker's sells moderate-priced shoes. Burt's sells shoes for budget shoppers, and Wild Pair is oriented to the shopper who wants very stylized shoes. Within three blocks on State Street in Chicago are found Burt's, Chandler's, and Baker's. Putting the stores near each other does not hurt them because they are aimed at different segments of the women's shoe market. This strategy has made Edison Brothers the country's largest retailer of women's shoes.

Concentrated Marketing

8   Many firms see a third possibility that is especially appealing when company resources are limited. Instead of going after a small share of a large market, the firm goes after a large share of one or a few submarkets.

9   Several examples of concentrated marketing can be cited. Volkswagen has concentrated on the small-car market; Hewlett-Packard on the high-priced calculator market; and Richard D. Irwin on the economics and business textbook market. Through concentrated marketing the firm achieves a strong market

---

[2]Natalie McKelvy, "Shoes Make Edison Brothers a Big Name," *Chicago Tribune*, February 23, 1979, Sec. 5, p. 9.

position in the segments it serves, because of its greater knowledge of the segments' needs and its special reputation. Furthermore, it enjoys many operating economies because of specialization in production, distribution, and promotion.

10 At the same time, concentrated marketing involves higher than normal risks. The particular market segment can turn sour; for example, when young women suddenly stopped buying sportswear, it caused Bobbie Brooks's earnings to go deeply into the red. Or a competitor may decide to enter the same segment. For these reasons, many companies prefer to diversify in several market segments.

Choosing a Market-Coverage Strategy

11 The following factors need to be considered in choosing a market-coverage strategy:[3]

- *Company resources:* When the firm's resources are limited, concentrated marketing makes the most sense.
- *Product homogeneity:* Undifferentiated marketing is more suited for homogeneous products, such as grapefruit or steel. Products that are capable of design variation, such as cameras and automobiles, are more suited to differentiated or concentrated marketing.
- *Product stage in the life cycle:* When a firm introduces a new product, it is practical to launch only one version, and undifferentiated marketing or concentrated marketing makes the most sense.
- *Market homogeneity:* If buyers have the same tastes, buy the same amounts per period, and react the same way to marketing stimuli, undifferentiated marketing is appropriate.
- *Competitive marketing strategies:* When competitors segment the market, undifferentiated marketing can be suicidal. Conversely, when competitors practice undifferentiated marketing, a firm can gain by using differentiated or concentrated marketing.

IDENTIFYING ATTRACTIVE MARKET SEGMENTS

12 Suppose the firm uses the preceding criteria for choosing a market-coverage strategy and decides on concentrated marketing. It must now identify the most attractive segment to enter. Consider the following situation:

> A successful manufacturer of snow-removal equipment is looking for a new product. Management reviews several opportunities and lands on the idea of producing snowmobiles. Management recognizes that it could manufacture any of three product types: gasoline, diesel, or electric. And it can design a snowmobile for any of three markets: consumer, industrial, or military. The nine product/market alternatives are shown in Figure 3-2. Assuming that the company wants to focus initially on a single segment, management has to decide on which one.

13 The company needs to collect data on the nine market segments. The data would include current dollar sales, projected sales-growth rates, estimated profit margins, competitive intensity, marketing channel requirements, and so

[3] R. William Kotrba, "The Strategy Selection Chart," *Journal of Marketing*, July 1966, pp. 22–25.

FIGURE 3-2 Product/Market Grid for Snowmobiles

	Consumer	Industrial	Military
Gas-driven snowmobiles			
Diesel-driven snowmobiles			
Electric-driven snowmobiles			

on. The best segment would have large current sales, a high growth rate, a high profit margin, weak competition, and simple marketing channel requirements. Usually no segment would excel in all of these dimensions, and trade-offs would have to be made.

After the company identifies the more objectively attractive segments, it must ask which segments fit its business strengths best. For example, the military market may be highly attractive, but the company may have had no experience selling to the military. On the other hand, it may have a lot of experience in selling to the consumer market. Thus the company seeks a segment that is attractive in itself and for which it has the necessary business strengths to succeed.

Market Targeting

STUDY QUESTIONS

Directions: Refer to the reading to answer the following study questions.

1. Read paragraphs 1 and 2 carefully and examine Figure 3-1.
   A. According to paragraph 1, which two of the following questions will the selection examine?
      a. How can a firm decide what type of brand image will be best?
      b. To what number of separate market segments should a firm try to sell its product?
      c. Which market segments for a particular product are the largest?
      d. In what ways can a firm discover the market segments that will be most profitable?
   B. Paragraph 2 lists three market-coverage strategies that a firm can use: undifferentiated, differentiated, and concentrated. What do you think each of these adjectives means in its general sense (not applied to marketing)?
      a. undifferentiated: _____
      b. differentiated: _____
      c. concentrated: _____
   C. Examine Figure 3-1. How many market segments are indicated for undifferentiated marketing?

   _____

   How many segments are indicated for differentiated marketing?

   _____

   How many segments are indicated for concentrated marketing?

   _____

   What difference between differentiated and concentrated marketing does the figure show?

   _____
   _____
   _____

2. Paragraphs 3, 4, and 5 discuss undifferentiated marketing. Read these paragraphs carefully.
   A. According to paragraph 3, how many brands, or types, of a particular product will a firm offer to consumers if it uses undifferentiated marketing? _____
   Which of the following should be true of a product that is offered through undifferentiated marketing?
      a. The product should be simple and common.
      b. The product should be attractive to a large number of people.
      c. The product should be superior.
   What example of undifferentiated marketing does paragraph 3 give?

   _____

   Can you think of other products that are aimed at an undifferentiated market?

   _____
   _____

   B. What is the purpose of paragraph 4?
      a. to show the advantages of undifferentiated marketing

Marketing

  b. to show the disadvantages of undifferentiated marketing
  c. to show how difficult undifferentiated marketing is
 C. Paragraph 5 describes a multiple cause-effect relationship. Place the following ideas in the correct cause-effect order.

   _____ causes _____, which causes _____
  a. Products aimed at the largest market segments do not make much profit.
  b. A number of companies decide to aim their products at the largest market segment.
  c. Few or no products are made for the smaller market segments, but there is intense competition for the larger segments.

3. Paragraphs 6 and 7 discuss differentiated marketing. Read these paragraphs carefully.
 A. In your own words, define *differentiated marketing*.

  _____

  _____

 B. What does the author mean when he states that "General Motors tries to produce a car for every 'purse, purpose, and personality' "?

  _____

 C. According to paragraph 6, which of the following are reasons that a firm might produce various products (that is, use differentiated marketing)? More than one answer may be correct.
  a. It believes that more people will buy the product again because the product fits the consumers' needs more closely.
  b. It believes that it can produce goods of a much higher quality, which consumers will then wish to buy.
  c. It believes that consumers will be more likely to think of that company when buying the product because many types of the product are offered.
  d. It believes that it is important to satisfy as many different types of consumers as possible because in that way everyone will benefit.
 D. The example given in paragraph 7 shows how Edison Brothers has used differentiated marketing successfully. To how many market segments does this company sell shoes? _____

  Using just a short phrase, how would you describe the market segments of each of the following?
  a. Chandler's: _____
  b. Wild Pair: _____
  c. Burt's: _____
  d. Baker's _____

4. Paragraphs 8, 9, and 10 discuss concentrated marketing. Read these paragraphs carefully.
 A. In your own words, define *concentrated marketing*.

  _____

  _____

  _____

Market Targeting

73

When might a company use concentrated marketing?
a. when the company is relatively small
b. when the company wants a small share of a large market
c. when the company does not have a large amount of money or other resources

B. According to paragraph 9, what are two advantages of concentrated marketing?

a. _____

b. _____

C. What are the potential disadvantages of concentrated marketing, according to paragraph 10? (More than one answer may be correct.)
a. Competition from another company for the same market segment may cause sales to drop.
b. If the company decides to diversify in several market segments, it may not have adequate resources.
c. The people who make up the particular market segment may change their tastes and no longer buy the specialized product.
d. The company takes higher than normal risks because it must create a strong reputation in the specialized market.

D. Paragraph 9 lists three examples of concentrated marketing. Can you think of any others?

_____

_____

5. Read paragraph 11 carefully.
A. What does the author mean by "market-coverage strategy" in the first sentence? What are the market-coverage strategies that have been discussed so far?

_____

_____

B. What does the term *product homogeneity* mean?
a. a product that cannot be varied
b. a product that can be varied
c. a product that is differentiated

C. What does the term *market homogeneity* mean?

_____

_____

D. Think about each of the following marketing situations. According to the information given in paragraph 11, which market-coverage strategy (undifferentiated, differentiated, or concentrated) would be best in each situation?
a. Company B wants to enter the women's clothing market. There are now many different market segments for women's clothing occupied by many different manufacturers.

_____

b. Company A is going to manufacture light bulbs. The company projects that most consumers will be satisfied with the product and hopes that its low price will attract buyers.

_____

c. Company C is a new firm with little financial backing. The company plans to enter the computer market.

_____

Marketing

6. Read paragraphs 12, 13, and 14 carefully.
   A. What is the purpose of these three paragraphs?
      a. to give the reader information about snowmobile marketing
      b. to show how a firm can identify its business strengths and become successful
      c. to show how the theory of market-coverage strategy can be applied
   B. According to paragraphs 13 and 14, what should a firm consider when choosing a new market segment?
      a. its own business strengths
      b. the attractiveness of each potential market segment
      c. both a and b

INTEGRATION QUESTIONS FOR DISCUSSION AND WRITING

Directions: These questions require you to find relationships among the ideas in the three selections in this unit: "Consumer Behavior: Basic Concepts," "Key Business Decisions: Branding," and "Market Targeting." Discuss your answers with your classmates.

1. "Market Targeting" discusses various market-coverage strategies. Should a firm that uses a differentiated strategy try to create different brand images for its products?
   Consider the example of Edison Brothers shoes, given in this reading. The company targets four different markets, so different types of advertising should probably be used for each of the shoe-store chains that the company operates. List several adjectives that would help create a successful brand image for each one.

   Chandler's: _____
   _____

   Baker's: _____
   _____

   Burt's: _____
   _____

   Wild Pair: _____
   _____

2. Do you think that it is possible for a firm to create a new market—in other words, to create a desire for a product that has never existed before?
   List three or four products sold today that were not available twenty years ago. What types of needs on Maslow's hierarchy (physiological, safety, social, esteem, self-actualization) do you think each one satisfies in the consumer?

3. Most American supermarkets carry products that are called "generic." These products are "nonbranded" items—they do not carry a brand name and are not advertised, so they can be sold at a lower price. What segment of grocery buyers do you think is attracted to generic items? What type of image do you think generic items project? Would you buy generic items? Why or why not?

UNIT II

Computers

CHAPTER 4

Computer Programming

WARMUP QUESTIONS

The readings in this unit (Chapters 4, 5, and 6) deal with computers. How are computers programmed? How "intelligent" are they? Can they be programmed to understand human language or to write a symphony? Will computers solve all our problems in the future, as some people claim? Or, as others say, will computers create more problems than they solve?

Before you begin the first reading, "Computer Programming," read the following statements, and indicate whether you *agree* or *disagree* with each one. Answer from your own knowledge only. Then discuss your opinions with your classmates.

1. _____ It is possible to build a computer that can think like a human being.
2. _____ Someday computers will be so advanced that they will control people, instead of people controlling them.
3. _____ Today's computers are so advanced that there is no problem in chemistry or medicine or physics that they cannot solve.
4. _____ Computers have made our society cold and impersonal. Everything is based on logic instead of human feelings.
5. _____ Factories of the future will contain mostly robots, controlled by computers. This will put many people out of work and cause many social and economic problems.
6. _____ Computers should be carefully controlled because they can be used to invade our privacy.
7. _____ Because computers are everywhere, it is impossible to advance in your chosen career without a knowledge of computers.

Describe a personal experience that you have had with computers. Was the experience good or bad?

_____
_____

Computers

Describe some task in your life that you now perform differently because of computers (math or banking, for example). How do you feel about this change?
_____
_____

Do you use computers on a regular basis now? For what purposes do you use them? Share your experiences with your classmates.
_____
_____

If you do not use computers now for work or school, are you curious about them? If you do use computers on a regular basis, do your friends without access to computers ask you questions about them?
_____
_____

Discuss how computers are perceived in the typical college or university.
_____
_____
_____

Do you think computers can help you to learn? If so, do you think they will be able to replace teachers one day?
_____
_____

PREVIEWING

1. Look through the reading quickly to get some idea of its length and organization. Glance at the section headings while you are doing this.

    How many pages does the reading have? _____

    How many paragraphs does it contain? _____

2. Complete the following outline with the headings and subheadings from the reading. Indicate the paragraph numbers that are included in each section.

Heading or Subheading	Paragraph Numbers
I. COMPUTERS	1–5
II. _____	_____
III. _____	_____
A. _____	_____
B. _____	_____
IV. _____	_____
A. _____	_____
B. _____	_____
C. _____	_____

3. Many of the italicized words in this reading are emphasized because they are important concepts. Words may also be italicized when they are defined for the first time. Look quickly through the reading at all the italicized words. Then list four italicized words that are defined in the reading, and include the paragraph numbers where you found the words.

_____

_____

DIRECTIONS FOR READING

The reading in this chapter was written by J. Patrick Kelley for beginning computer-science majors. A reading such as this might also be found in a programming course for nonmajors—for example, a course for graduate students in business who need some experience with computer science.

If you have completed the previewing exercises, you should have a general idea of the content and organization of the selection. You are now ready to read it carefully.

The selection has been divided into three parts. You will first read each section quickly and then examine each part more closely as you complete the study questions.

Computers, Programs, and Programming Languages

J. Patrick Kelley

COMPUTERS

1   Depending on the dictionary you use, you may find a definition of *computer* that is something like the following:

> *com-pu-ter:* a device that computes, esp. an electronic machine that performs high speed mathematical or logical calculations or assembles, stores, correlates or otherwise processes and prints information derived from coded data in accordance with a predetermined program. (American Heritage, 1980)
>
> *com-pu-ter:* a person who computes or a device used for computing; specifically, an electronic machine which, by means of stored instructions and information, performs rapid, often complex calculations or compiles, correlates, and selects data. (Webster's New Universal, 1976)

2   The fact that you are reading this textbook means that you are interested in learning more about these "electronic machines"; specifically, you are interested in learning more about the "predetermined programs" and "stored instructions" that, in the final analysis, are really what make computers function and determine their ultimate usefulness.

3   When we think of the typical computer user, we usually think of large institutions with a lot of money to spend: government, corporations, large universities. However, every day, computers are becoming more and more common, and in an increasingly diverse number of applications. In fact, because of rapid advances in miniaturization and semiconductor physics, the microprocessor (really a small computer on a square of silicon or gallium arsenide about the size of your thumbnail) has become quite ubiquitous. It can be found in everything from kitchen appliances to expensive toys to automatic welding machines. Some of the more expensive late-model cars have no fewer than seven separate microprocessors monitoring and controlling all aspects of the car's performance.

4   Not only have computers become commonplace, but they have also become indispensable: without the computer, for example, many recent advances in medical diagnosis and treatment would not have been possible.

5   And yet, without its set of predetermined and logical instructions—without its *program*—the computer is little more than a collection of useless parts. It is the programmer's job to give function and purpose to this faceless collection of wire and silicon chips; the programmer has the ability to breathe life, utility, and even personality into his or her machine. But before taking on a task of such complexity, the programmer must learn to work and think in a logical and structured way, analyzing problems in a way that will not only produce results, but will produce them with efficiency and elegance. The purpose of this book is to help you begin to develop habits of thought that will lead you toward these goals.

WHAT IS A PROGRAM?

6   To begin with a general definition of programming, we can say that it is "the planning, scheduling, or performing of a task or an event." Unfortunately, this definition lacks the specificity required in this technical context; therefore, we must refine our formulation as follows: *computer programming* is "the process of planning a sequence of instructions for a computer to follow." Following from this, the sequence of instructions that outline the steps to be performed by our computer is referred to as the *computer program*.

7   One important element of programming that should be immediately accessible to students, especially those from a math or science background, is that a program involves a series of sequenced steps that must be arranged in a logical way in order for them to work. While the definition of "logical" has itself been the subject of many philosophical debates over the centuries, and in fact may be defined differently from one culture to another, most of us will recognize—given a specific task or situation—what is logical and what is not. We become familiar with a certain kind of logic even when, as children, we are learning to explore and react to the world around us.

8   Think, for example, about the series of unconscious mental steps that are required for us to utter the simple sentence, "The book is on the table." First, we have to identify the names in our language that go with the objects "book" and "table." Then we have to decide about singular or plural (if our language even has such a thing!), and about whether to choose an article (or perhaps we need an adjective, to distinguish a red book from a blue book?). Next, we have to choose a verb that expresses the correct relationship between these two objects, and in this case we also need a preposition to complete the meaning and indicate the correct location. Obviously, in order to say this simple sentence, we don't consciously think about each step separately before we speak—it would take us too long to get any communicating done! Nevertheless, at some point in our development, we learned that this logical sequence of steps would convey the intended meaning of "The book is on the table."

9   When you think about some of the complex tasks that we would like computers to do for us—analyze large amounts of data, produce statistical models and analyses, interpret figures in graphic form, speed the preparation of books, manuscripts and reports, and generally increase our overall productivity—it should become clear that not only careful planning but logical steps in logical sequence are what is necessary. We need to learn how to tell the computer not only what we want it to do, but the exact order in which we want it done.

WHAT IS PROGRAMMING?

10   To begin with, we need to elaborate on the general definition we have been working with so far. Computer programming can be further defined as being composed of two distinct stages: the planning stage and the implementation stage.

11   During the planning stage, the task of the conscientious programmer is largely threefold: he or she must (1) understand and clearly define the problem, (2) develop an algorithm, or general plan for solution of the problem, and (3) follow the steps (not actually but in the abstract, as a kind of dry-run or test) to see if the algorithm or solution really works.

12   During the second, or implementation phase, a programmer translates the algorithm into an actual computer language (sometimes referred to as "code"),

tests the program to make sure it works correctly, and then uses the program, making whatever subsequent changes or revisions are required by the end-user. These last two parts of the implementation phase are often referred to as "debugging"; without careful planning, getting the "bugs" out of a program can be the most frustrating and time-consuming part of the entire program development process.

13   Because this is a text concerned with how to write structured programs, we will concentrate on the implementation phase by using the computer language PASCAL to solve a representative subset of example problems.[1] Another major focus of this text, however, is to stress the importance of the planning stage in the overall process of computer programming. To this end, Chapter 11 contains additional discussion and exercises concerned with how to clearly identify and define a problem.

14   Once you have defined and identified the problem, the next step is to discover an efficient solution.

Algorithms

15   In noncomputer terms, an *algorithm* is defined as "any mechanical or repetitive mathematical procedure" (American Heritage) or "in mathematics, any special method of solving a certain kind of problem; specifically, the repetitive calculations used in finding the greatest common divisor of two numbers."[2]

16   It shouldn't be surprising that this key computer concept is drawn from mathematics, since the actions that a computer performs can be ultimately reduced to the repetition of simple mathematical operations such as addition, subtraction, or the comparison of two numbers. However, the definition of an algorithm has, in the last several decades, taken on a somewhat wider meaning when applied to computer programming. For the purposes of our discussion, an *algorithm* can be defined as "a set of specific steps or procedures for solving a problem in a finite amount of time."

17   Actually, we use algorithms every day, even though we may not call them that. Any set of instructions for accomplishing a specific task can be considered an algorithm, from the verbal instructions you receive when you ask a stranger for directions in an unfamiliar part of town, to the recipe you follow when learning to cook a new dish, to the detailed book of instructions you might receive with a complex piece of machinery.

18   Calling someone on the phone is another example of a step-by-step procedure, and the algorithm, if written out, might look something like this:

1. Look up (or remember) phone number.
2. Lift receiver and listen for dial tone.
3. Dial number.
4. If phone is busy, hang up receiver, and return to step 2.
5. If phone rings ten times and there is no answer, hang up, and call again after a suitable amount of time has passed.

19   Written out in English, the logical steps that make up our computer programs will look much like this. Unfortunately, if the preceding example were a computer program, we would immediately notice that several difficulties prevent

---

[1] The computer language PASCAL is named after the nineteenth-century French mathematician Blaise Pascal, who invented the first mechanical calculator.

[2] The term *algorithm* is derived from the name of a ninth-century Arabic mathematician.

the program from running the way we expect. Can you guess what the difficulties are?

20   To begin with, look at step 4. What if the person we are calling has taken the phone off the hook? Or what if the phone is out of order? In that case, we would be caught in what programmers call an "infinite loop"; to follow the instructions exactly, we would have to stand and dial the phone number endlessly, for hours or even days—something that a reasonable person would never even consider. A computer, however, is not reasonable, and it would continue in this mindlessly repetitive loop, just as we told it to, until the power was turned off or the world came to an end.

21   Step five also has some difficulties as a computer instruction. Specifically, how much is a "suitable amount of time"? If we don't tell the computer directly how much time must go by before beginning the sequence again, then at least we must provide the program with a way of finding out that information through a data file, keyboard entry, or other means. In other words, this last instruction lacks the exactness necessary for a workable programming statement.

22   It can be said then that our definition of an algorithm contains two central concepts: (1) the set of instructions we give to the computer must be specific enough for the job we want done, and (2) the instructions must anticipate every possibility that might come up during execution of the program. Otherwise, the program will crash (i.e., it will unexpectedly stop processing data) or it will get caught in an infinite loop, endlessly repeating the same program statements over and over.

23   For a more practical example of an algorithm—one that will more likely be applied to computers—consider this set of instructions (adapted from *Introduction to PASCAL and Structured Design* by Dale and Orshalick) for computing the weekly pay for an employee of a mythical company:

1. Look up employee's hourly salary.
2. Determine the number of hours worked during the week.
3. If the number of hours worked is less than or equal to 40.0, multiply the number of hours by the pay rate to get regular wages.
4. If the number of hours worked is greater than 40.0, multiply the pay rate by 40.0 to get regular wages. Then determine overtime wages by multiplying one and a half times the pay rate by the difference between the number of hours worked and 40.0
5. Add regular wages to overtime wages (if any) to get total wages for the week.

You don't need to be an accountant or personnel clerk to realize that the procedure for computing a person's weekly salary by hand will be something similar to this set of logical steps. You shouldn't be surprised to learn that—as Dale and Orshalick point out—"the final solution done by the computer is very often the same as the solution done by hand" (p. 6).

Algorithms vs. Heuristics

24   Before we leave our discussion of general problem-solving strategies and techniques as they apply to programming, it should be pointed out that until now the examples we have examined were carefully chosen for their easy adaptability to the algorithmic method of problem solving. Unfortunately, an algorithm is not always the most efficient or effective way of approaching a task. Even though an algorithm by definition is a series of logical problem-

solving steps guaranteed to succeed, the problem may be so large that such a methodical and exhaustive approach is not practical or possible.

25 The classic example of an impractical algorithm is the well-known "British Museum algorithm," which proposes that if you put a large number of monkeys together with unabridged dictionaries and typewriters in the basement of the British Museum, eventually the monkeys will produce the complete works of William Shakespeare.

26 This example is of course somewhat frivolous, but consider the following statistics:

- A simple logic puzzle would take about 8000 years for a computer to solve, even if it examined every possible solution to the puzzle at a speed of one million operations per second.
- In order for a computer to examine all possible moves in the game of chess, the computer would need more individual memory cells than there are atoms in the universe.
- The number of all possible moves in the simple board game of checkers is 10 to the power of 40; the number of all possible moves in chess is 10 to the power of 120; whereas the age of the solar system is generally believed to be only about 10 to the power of 18 seconds.

27 It should be clear from such statistics that what is often called the "brute force" method—solving problems based simply on memory size and processing speed—comprises a totally inadequate approach when faced with computational tasks of such scope and complexity.

28 What is needed instead in order to construct, for example, a program that can play chess, is a set of general guidelines or principles that, even though they may fail to arrive at a solution a significant percentage of the time, will nevertheless cut the problem down to manageable size, and lead us in the general direction of the solution. We call this "general guidelines" approach to problem solving *the heuristic approach.*

29 For an example of how we use heuristics to help solve everyday problems, consider how you might react if you discovered your car didn't start. Instead of undertaking a detailed examination of every complicated part and system in your car, the first thing you might do is check to see if there was enough gas. In other words, you would know from past experience that this was a common cause of automobiles failing to start. The next thing you might do is check to make sure that your car battery contains a sufficient electrical charge, because this is another common cause of starting difficulty, particularly in cold weather.

30 Note, however, that this approach does not always mean that you will discover what is wrong with your car; in fact, the probability is very good that you will not discover the true cause of your trouble. Checking the gas and the battery, however, is a logical first step toward solving a potentially complex problem. The chances of getting your car to start in a reasonable amount of time are much better than if you simply started by examining the headlights of your car and worked your way systematically toward the back.

31 To summarize, then: an algorithm is a method of problem solving that is guaranteed to succeed, a step-by-step solution that will definitely work. A heuristic, on the other hand, is an inherently fallible general guideline, or rule of thumb, based on past experience and designed to help break a large problem down into smaller, more manageable parts.

32 Having looked in a general way at the basic concepts behind computer programs and how they are designed, we will now turn to a brief discussion of the physical structure of the computer itself.

WHAT IS A COMPUTER?

33   We will begin our discussion of the physical machine itself (often referred to as the computer *hardware*) by talking about computers in the abstract. After identifying the major types of components that all computers possess, the three major ways in which computers in general can be classified will be discussed. This section of the chapter concludes by examining the functional structure of microcomputers in particular, because it is assumed that most students will be working with an IBM PC implementation of Waterloo Pascal, or something similar.

Parts of a Computer

34   Computers in general can be said to have four major components: a central processing unit, an input device or channel, an output device or path, and a memory unit.

35   In our idealized computer, the component of most importance is the central processing unit, or CPU. This "heart" of the machine contains two major subunits: an arithmetic processor and a logic or control unit. The arithmetic processor is dedicated to the computer's main function, by which it accomplishes all of its much more complex tasks: the adding, subtracting, or comparing of groups of numbers. The purpose of the logic unit, on the other hand, is to retrieve information from the appropriate places in memory and to make sure that the results of the arithmetic unit's calculations get sent to the correct places in memory.

36   The parts of a computer that users come into most frequent contact with are the input and output devices. An example of a familiar *input device* is the computer keyboard, which allows the user to program and otherwise communicate with the computer itself. A familiar type of *output device* is the monitor, or cathode ray tube (CRT). Resembling a common television set, although often with only a single color such as green or amber, the monitor allows users to see the results of their data input and programming.

37   These of course are not the only methods for achieving input and output on a computer. Other common input devices, especially on large time-sharing systems where batch processing is required, are magnetic tape or punched cards. In addition, output frequently takes the form of a printout, or "hard copy," produced by the computer on a special high-speed printing device.

38   The final component of the typical computer is the *memory unit*, which stores not only the instructions for the computer's operation (the program) but also the data upon which the computer is operating. The memory is divided up into individual memory cells or compartments, and each one of these cells has its own address—a special number that the computer uses to store or retrieve information from a given memory location. These memory cells can be thought of as analogous to individual post-office boxes. Just as in a post office, each of these memory cells has an "address," which the programmer uses to control the flow and arrangement of data.

39   As an example, consider one popular low-cost computer, the Apple IIc. It has 256 x 256 x 2, or 131,072 of these individual memory cells.[3] The fact that the contents of most of these memory cells can be easily changed by the programmer is what makes it such a powerful and flexible tool.

---

[3] The significance of the number 256 is that it is derived from the binary, or base 2, number system used by computers. The computer counts using a row of eight ones and zeros:
00010111

40   Not only can the data that a computer processes be changed, even from one type of data to another, but the programmed instructions that operate on that data can be changed, even while the program is running, if that should be necessary. This provides for a data-processing tool that is at once dynamic and extremely powerful.

41   Before going on to a discussion of the major types of computers, one final concept needs to be introduced: the idea of the *interface*. In a large computer system, there are subunits whose purpose is to make sure that all the parts can work smoothly together, and transmit data back and forth easily and accurately. This kind of device, the sole purpose of which is to connect different parts of a computer together, is known as an interface.

42   To summarize, then: the typical computer system consists of four main elements: (1) the CPU, with subcomponents for math and logic; (2) some sort of input device, such as a keyboard or punched cards; (3) an output device, such as a CRT or printer; and (4) the memory unit.

Types of Computers

43   Computers can be classified into three main categories: mainframes, minicomputers, and microcomputers. After giving a brief definition of each type, some additional information about the microcomputer will be given, because it is assumed that most of you will be working with this type of computer.

44   Mainframes are the largest and most powerful kind of computer. They are designed to quickly perform a large number of complex calculations, operate on and store large amounts of data, and service a significant number of simultaneous users so that all are able to have access to the same information and facilities at the same time. The typical mainframe installation consists of (1) an air-conditioned machine room containing the central processor, core memory, and devices such as tapes and discs designed to store large amounts of data; and (2) remote terminals for accessing the computer, high-speed line printers, and other peripheral devices for input/output. Typical users of mainframe computers (which can cost anywhere from $200,000 to several million dollars) are universities, large corporations, and government agencies.

45   The category of mainframes also includes the so-called "supercomputers." By itself, this term has no real meaning, however; it simply means the fastest and most powerful mainframe computers currently in use today.

46   The second major type of computer emerged in the early 1970s in the United States partly as a response to the size and cost of mainframes, and partly as a result of advances in the fields of semiconductors and microprocessors. This type of computer, know as a minicomputer, is favored by many smaller companies not only for its size and cost but because of its ease of use and accessibility. Engineers or accountants or personnel officers can have more control over the flow of important information in their office; in addition, they do not have to work through a specialist or technician, but can access the data directly and work with it themselves.

Starting on the right, if the first digit is a zero, then it is worth zero; but if it is a one, it is worth one times two (the basis for this number system) to the power of zero (the "place" which the digit has in relation to the number as a whole). The second digit from the right is worth 2 to the power of 1, the third digit from the right is worth 2 to the power of 2, etc.

Thus, we add up the value of all the digits that are ones, and we get the number. If all of the digits in an eight-digit binary number were 1, then the total would be $(1 * 2^0) + (1 * 2^1) + (1 * 2^2) \ldots + (1 * 2^7) = 256$.

The example number above (00010111) is $(1 * 2^0) + (1 * 2^1) + (1 * 2^2) + (1 * 2^4) = 1 + 2 + 4 + 16 = 23$.

47   The minicomputer, like the mainframe, has its own "super" subcategory, the "superminis." A supermini, such as the Vax 11/780 manufactured by the Digital Equipment Corporation, is so-called because it has processing speed, processing capability, and memory size that rival those of the larger and more expensive mainframes. This is accomplished not only through technological advances but through the use of innovative designs for the internal architecture of the computer. In fact, because of such advances, the distinction between mainframes and minicomputers is beginning to blur.

Microcomputers

48   Microcomputers, the smallest of the computers (hence the name *micro*), have experienced a surprisingly rapid growth both in terms of numbers and popularity since they first were marketed on a broad scale beginning in about 1977. Microcomputers can range from large, full-featured models, with generous data-storage capacity, designed for use by business and industry, to smaller more inexpensive models designed for entertainment and general home use. This last type of micro is often referred to as a "personal" or "home" computer.

49   The typical microcomputer system consists of two main components: the system module, containing the CPU, memory, and related electronics; and the peripheral devices for input, output, mass storage of data, and other uses.

BIBLIOGRAPHY

Boden, Margaret. *Artificial Intelligence and Natural Man*. New York: Basic Books, 1977.

N. Dale and D. Orshalick, *Introduction to PASCAL and Structured Design*. Lexington, Mass.: D. C. Heath. 1983.

E. B. Koffman, *Problem Solving and Structured Programming in PASCAL*. Reading, Mass.: Addison-Wesley. 1982.

Computer Programming

89

PART 1: STUDY QUESTIONS
(Paragraphs 1–9)

Read paragraphs 1–9 quickly for general understanding. Then refer to the reading to answer the following study questions.

1. Read paragraphs 1 and 2 again carefully.
   A. Compare and contrast the two definitions in paragraph 1 (in other words, list the similarities and the differences between them). Some of the answers have been done for you.

First definition	Second definition
a device	a person or device
_____	used for computing
_____	rapid, complex calculations
assembles, stores, correlates data	_____
_____	— — — —
derived from coded data	— — — —
_____	stored instructions and information

   Are these definitions technical or nontechnical? Why have they been included here?
   _____

   B. According to paragraph 2, what is it that makes computers useful and allows them to function?
   _____

2. Read paragraphs 3 and 4 again.
   A. Complete the following sentence with a word or phrase so that it gives the main idea of paragraph 3.

       Computers are _____

   B. Without using the dictionary, make an inference about the meaning of the phrase "diverse number of applications" in the second sentence of paragraph 3. Give the reasons for your inference.
   _____

   C. What is the purpose of the phrase in parentheses in the third sentence of paragraph 3?
   _____

   D. Which of the following means the same as *ubiquitous* (paragraph 3, sentence 3)?
      a. important
      b. advanced
      c. expensive
      d. well known
      e. widely used

   E. What is the purpose of paragraph 4?
      a. to introduce a new main idea

Computers

      b. to add additional information about the previous main idea
      c. to form a link between paragraphs 3 and 5
  F. Complete the following sentence with a word or phrase so that it gives the main idea of paragraph 4.

      Computers are _____ .

3. Read paragraph 5 again carefully.
     A. Which of the following is the most important idea in this paragraph?
         a. A computer without a program is a collection of useless parts.
         b. A good programmer must learn to think logically.
         c. This book helps the reader to develop certain ways of thinking.
     B. The first sentence in paragraph 5 contains a technical term and its definition. What are they?

     C. In the second sentence of paragraph 5, the author uses the words *faceless* and *personality* to describe a machine. Why has the author used these words when referring to a computer?

     D. Why does a programmer have to think logically?

4. Paragraphs 6–9 make up the section titled "What Is a Program?" Look again at paragraph 6.
     A. How many words are defined in paragraph 6? Write these words in the following space.

     B. What is the difference between the general definition of programming and the technical definition?

5. Read paragraph 7 again carefully.
     A. Fill in the blanks to complete this definition of a program from paragraph 7.

         A program is a series of _____ steps arranged in a _____ _____ way.

     B. According to paragraph 7, does the definition of logic vary from one culture to another? How about from one individual to another?

     C. Do you agree or disagree with the statements about logic in the last two sentences of this paragraph?

Computer Programming

91

6. Read paragraph 8 again carefully.
   A. What is the *purpose* or *function* of paragraph 8? (Hint: What is the relationship between paragraphs 7 and 8?)
   _____
   _____

   B. List the steps necessary (according to paragraph 8) to say the sentence, "The book is on the table." Are there any steps in the paragraph with which you disagree? Add steps of your own if you think they are necessary.
   _____
   _____
   _____

   C. Now make a similar list of steps necessary to perform another simple, everyday action: for example, putting on a shoe and tying the laces. Make your list detailed enough so that someone who has never done this task could follow your directions.
   _____
   _____
   _____
   _____
   _____

7. Read paragraph 9 again.
   According to this paragraph, what are the two main requirements for a successful program?
   _____
   _____

PART 1: COMPREHENSION EXERCISES
(Paragraphs 1–9)

Exercise 1

The following statements are either *true* or *false* according to paragraphs 1–9 of the reading. Write either *T* or *F* in the space before each one.

_____ 1. The instructions stored inside the computer are not as important as the computer equipment (hardware).
_____ 2. The performance of most small cars is controlled by computers.
_____ 3. Governments, corporations, and large universities are really the only ones who can afford to use computers extensively.
_____ 4. Medicine is one of the few areas that still do not use computers to their full potential.
_____ 5. It is the programmer's responsibility to design and build computers using wires, transistors, and silicon chips.
_____ 6. The definition of a computer program is "the planning of a task or event."

Computers

_____ 7. People have defined logic differently, depending on when and where they have lived.

_____ 8. A computer program is a set of instructions arranged in logical order.

Exercise 2

Complete the following summary of paragraphs 1–9 by filling in each blank with an appropriate word or phrase.

A dictionary defines the word *computer* as "an _____ device that uses stored _____ and information to perform calculations and _____ _____ data."

Computers have become _____; they are found in everything from kitchen appliances to _____. They have also become very important in _____ and other areas that directly benefit human beings.

What really makes computers useful is the stored instructions, or _____. In order to write programs, the programmer must learn to think in a _____, structured way. Even though we may not realize it, we learn about a certain kind of logic even as children. Consider, for example, the series of unconscious _____ that are necessary just to _____.

The act of programming can be defined as "the process of planning a _____ _____ of instructions for a computer to _____." This process has two important aspects: careful _____ and the identification of the most _____ steps.

PART 2: STUDY QUESTIONS
(Paragraphs 10–32)

Directions: Part 2 of the reading describes in detail the act of writing a computer program. Read paragraphs 10–32 quickly for general understanding. Then refer to the reading to answer the following study questions.

1. Refresh your memory about the organization of this section.
   A. This part of the reading has two subsections. What are these sections titled? In what paragraph does each one begin?

   _____
   _____

2. Read paragraphs 10 and 11 carefully.
   A. According to paragraph 10, what are the two main steps in computer programming?
      a. _____
      b. _____

Computer Programming

93

    B. Compare the description of programming in paragraph 10 with the definition of computer programming in paragraph 6. How are the two definitions different? How are they similar?

    _____
    _____

    C. Which paragraph describes the planning stage? _____ Which paragraph describes the implementation stage? _____

    D. Use no more than two words to describe each step in the planning stage.

        a. _____

        b. _____

        c. _____

    E. According to paragraph 11, what is the definition of *algorithm*?

    _____

    F. According to paragraph 11, what is a "dry run"?

    _____

3. Read paragraph 12 carefully.

    A. Which of the following phrases means the same as *implementation*?
        a. second or secondary
        b. getting the "bugs" out
        c. careful planning
        d. putting an idea into practice

    B. Use no more than two words to describe each step in the implementation stage.

        a. _____

        b. _____

        c. _____

    C. According to paragraph 12, what is sometimes referred to as "code"?

    _____

    D. Why is the word *bugs* in quotation marks in this paragraph? What does *bug* usually mean? What does it mean here?

    _____
    _____
    _____

4. Read paragraphs 13 and 14 again carefully.

    A. The purpose of paragraph 13 is to describe:
        a. the implementation phase.
        b. the organization of the textbook.
        c. the computer language PASCAL.

    B. Which of the following represent the main focuses of the textbook from which this reading is taken? (Circle all that apply)
        a. the implementation phase
        b. how to use PASCAL
        c. structured programs
        d. how to identify and define a problem
        e. the overall process of computer programming

Computers

94

    C. Which of the following means the same as "to this end" in paragraph 13?
        a. on the other hand
        b. for example
        c. therefore
    D. What is the purpose of paragraph 14?

    E. Paragraph 14 contains a two-word phrase that means the same as *algorithm*. What is it?

5. Paragraphs 15–23 discuss algorithms. Read paragraphs 15 and 16 again.
    A. How many definitions of the term *algorithm* do paragraphs 15 and 16 contain? ____ Which of these definitions are meant for mathematics? Which are meant to be used in programming? Which are simply general-purpose definitions?

    B. According to paragraph 16, why is it not surprising that a computer concept is related to mathematics?
        a. because mathematics is logical
        b. because all computer operations require complex math
        c. because computers use numbers to represent data

6. Look again at paragraph 17.
    A. Underline the restated definition of *algorithm* in paragraph 17.
    B. What is the purpose of paragraph 17?
        a. to give some examples of algorithms
        b. to show that everyone uses algorithms
        c. to talk about different kinds of instructions
    C. Using the definition and examples given in this paragraph, what are some additional examples of algorithms?

7. Read paragraphs 18–21 carefully.
    A. What is the purpose of paragraph 18?

    B. Briefly state the main idea of paragraph 19 in your own words.

    C. According to paragraphs 20 and 21, what are the two main problems with the phone call algorithm in paragraph 18?
        a. It doesn't say what to do if you don't know the number.
        b. You must follow the instructions exactly.
        c. The steps don't anticipate possible difficulties.
        d. Some of the steps are in the wrong order.
        e. Some of the steps are not specific enough.
        f. The person has taken the phone off the hook.

D. On the basis of the information in paragraphs 19–21, rewrite the procedure in paragraph 18 so that it is a workable algorithm.
   1. Look up (or remember) phone number.
   2. Lift receiver and listen for dial tone.
   3. Dial number.
   4. _____
      _____
   5. _____
      _____

E. In your own words, define the term *infinite loop* in paragraph 20. Include in your definition an example of your own that will help explain the term.
   _____
   _____

F. According to paragraph 21, what is the function of "data files" or "keyboard entry"?
   a. gives the computer more exact instructions
   b. tells the computer when to begin and end
   c. indicates a workable programming statement
   d. causes problems with the algorithm

8. Read paragraphs 22 and 23 carefully.
   A. According to paragraph 22, computer instructions must be
      a. specific and complete.
      b. flexible and possible.
      c. modifiable and infinite.
      d. central and repeating.
   B. Which of the following means the same as *then* in the first sentence of paragraph 22?
      a. at that time
      b. after that
      c. therefore
   C. Assume that you are an employee who makes $6 an hour. This week you worked 47 hours. Follow the steps in the algorithm in paragraph 23 to compute your weekly salary.
      1. _____
      2. _____
      3. _____
         _____
      4. _____
         _____
      5. _____
   D. The author says that "you don't need to be an accountant or personnel clerk" to understand the example in paragraph 23. Do you agree or disagree? Why?
      _____
      _____

Computers

9. Paragraphs 24–32 discuss the differences between algorithms and heuristics. Read paragraphs 24 and 25 again carefully.
   A. According to paragraph 24, why are algorithms sometimes impractical?

   B. Why is the British Museum algorithm in paragraph 25 impractical? How long do you think it would take the monkeys to produce the entire works of William Shakespeare?

10. Read paragraphs 26 and 27 carefully.
    A. What is the purpose of the examples in paragraph 26? What main idea are they meant to support?
       a. The British Museum algorithm is impossible.
       b. The power of algorithms is unlimited.
       c. Future computers will need greatly expanded memory.
       d. In some cases, algorithms are impractical.
    B. Without using the dictionary, think of a synonym for the word *frivolous* in the first sentence of paragraph 26. How do you know this is a synonym?

    C. What is the "brute force" method (paragraph 27), and why is it "totally inadequate"?

11. Look again at paragraph 28.
    A. What is the main purpose of this paragraph?
       a. to give an example of a computer program
       b. to provide a set of general rules for computer programs
       c. to give the definition of an important term
    B. This paragraph uses a two-word phrase that means the same as *heuristics*. Write this phrase in the space below.

    C. What two advantages of the heuristic approach does this paragraph mention?
       a. _____
       b. _____
    D. Is the heuristic approach always able to provide a solution?

12. Read paragraphs 29 and 30 carefully.
    A. What is the purpose of these paragraphs?
       a. to give an example of the heuristic approach
       b. to give a formal definition of the heuristic approach
       c. to describe the best way to fix your car
       d. to provide information about a specific problem
    B. According to paragraph 29, which of the following is true of a heuristic?
       a. Starting a car is an example of a heuristic.
       b. A heuristic is something used to solve everyday problems.

Computer Programming

97

   c. A heuristic involves examining all the complicated parts and systems in detail.
   d. The heuristic approach to solving problems means checking for the most logical cause of the problem first.
C. According to paragraph 29, what are the first two things you might check if your car didn't start? Why?

_____

_____

_____

_____

D. According to paragraph 30, checking the gas and the battery will not always identify the problem with your car. If this approach has a good chance of failing, what are the reasons for using it?
   a. The problem is too complex.
   b. You have a better chance of solving the problem quickly.
   c. Using an algorithmic approach probably wouldn't work either.
   d. You can use your past experience with similar problems.

E. Can you think of another everyday problem that could be solved using the heuristic approach? Briefly describe the problem, the first few solutions you would try, and the consequences of using a problem-solving method other than the heuristic approach.

_____

_____

_____

_____

13. Read paragraphs 31 and 32 again carefully. These paragraphs summarize the differences between an algorithm and a heuristic, and provide a transition to the next section of the reading.
   A. Each of the following characteristics applies to one of the two problem-solving methods discussed in this reading. Label each characteristic as either H (heuristic) or A (algorithm).

   _____ may not work

   _____ best for complex problems

   _____ based on past experience

   _____ good for problems where no information on previous solutions is available

   _____ step-by-step solution

   _____ general rule

   _____ will always succeed

   B. Without using the dictionary, make an inference about the meaning of "inherently fallible" in the second sentence of paragraph 31. Give the reason for your answer.

   _____

   _____

   C. According to paragraph 32, what aspect of computers will the next section discuss?

   _____

Computers

98

PART 2: COMPREHENSION EXERCISES
(Paragraphs 10–32)

Exercise 1

The following statements are either *true* or *false* according to paragraphs 10–32 of the reading. Write either *T* or *F* in the space before each one.

_____ 1. It is a good practice to test an algorithm in some way before translating it into the actual computer language.

_____ 2. The planning stage of program development is not required if the program is a short one.

_____ 3. The purpose of the book from which this reading is taken is to teach you how to solve some problems using the PASCAL language.

_____ 4. The instruction book that comes with a new camera probably contains algorithms.

_____ 5. The word *algorithm* means the same to programmers as it does to mathematicians. This is one reason why programmers need a good math background.

_____ 6. Computer programming is difficult because the logic used to solve the problem is usually very different from the steps that would be taken to solve the problem without a computer.

_____ 7. A complicated computer program may not work correctly the first time unless all of the steps are planned very carefully ahead of time.

_____ 8. Computer instructions must be as specific and exact as possible.

_____ 9. If a problem to be solved by computer is extremely large or extremely complex, using an algorithm might take too much time or too much computer power.

_____ 10. Programmers should use the heuristic approach to problem solving because it is usually the most efficient solution, and it is always certain to succeed.

Exercise 2

Complete the following summary of paragraphs 10–32 by filling in each blank with an appropriate word or phrase.

Computer programming consists of two stages: the _____ stage and the _____ stage.

The planning stage has three parts: (1) clearly _____ the problem, (2) developing an _____ to solve the problem, and (3) _____ the algorithm with sample data to see if it works.

During the _____ phase, the programmer translates the solution into a _____, tests the program to make sure it works properly, and then makes whatever _____ are necessary. This textbook will _____ the implementation phase.

Once the problem to be solved has been identified, the next step is to discover an _____ solution.

One type of solution is an _____, or series of specific and logically _____ steps designed to solve the problem. These steps must be _____

Computer Programming

99

_____ enough so that the computer will know exactly what to do, and they must also try to _____ everything that might come up during the execution of a program.

An example of an algorithm easily _____ to computers is the method companies use to _____ the weekly paychecks of their employees.

In some cases, algorithms are not _____ because the problem is too large or too _____. In this case, the _____ approach is used.

The heuristic approach to problem solving uses a set of _____ based on past experience to reduce the _____ of the problem. Although a heuristic may not always _____, it is often the only way to arrive at a _____ in a reasonable amount of time. In some instances (such as programming a computer to _____), the heuristic approach is the only method possible.

Exercise 3

Look back at the Warmup questions at the beginning of this chapter. Which of these questions apply to Parts 1 and 2 of the reading? Now that you have read Parts 1 and 2, which of these questions would you answer differently? Which would you answer in the same way?

PART 3: STUDY QUESTIONS
(Paragraphs 33–49)

Directions: Part 3 of the reading gives an introduction to computer hardware. Read paragraphs 33–49 quickly for general understanding. Then refer to the reading to answer the following study questions.

1. Carefully read paragraph 33, which describes how the remainder of the reading will be organized.
   A. According to paragraph 33, which of the following will be discussed in this section?
      a. the best type of computer to buy
      b. parts of a typical computer
      c. major types of computers
      d. abstract computers
      e. parts of a microcomputer
      f. implementation of PASCAL
   B. According to this paragraph, what is the definition of *computer hardware*?

   _____

   _____

   C. Which two phrases mean the same as *functional structure* (sentence 3)?
      a. what the parts are
      b. what the parts are used for
      c. the structure of the parts
      d. how the parts are put together

2. Look carefully at paragraphs 34 and 35.
   A. Briefly identify each of the four parts of a computer that will be discussed in this section.

Computers

100

        a. _____

        b. _____

        c. _____

        d. _____

    B. Why is the central processing unit (CPU) discussed first?

    _____

    C. According to paragraph 35, the CPU is divided into two main subunits. Identify the name and function of each.

    _____

    _____

    _____

    _____

3. Read paragraphs 36 and 37 carefully.
    A. What parts of the computer are discussed in these two paragraphs?

    _____

    B. According to paragraph 36, what is the purpose of a keyboard?

    _____

    C. Paragraph 36 gives both the technical name and the common name for a CRT. What are they?

    _____

    D. List the additional input and output devices mentioned in paragraph 37.

    input: _____

    output: _____

4. Look again at paragraph 38.
    A. What part of the computer is discussed in this paragraph?

    _____

    B. What does the memory contain when the computer is running?
        a. output
        b. program
        c. hardware
        d. data
        e. compartment

    C. Use the information in paragraph 38 to fill in the blanks in the following paragraph.

        The computer's memory is divided into _____. Each of these has an _____ that the programmer uses to _____ and _____ information.

5. Read paragraphs 39 and 40 carefully.
    A. What is the purpose of paragraph 39?

    _____

    B. According to paragraph 39, what makes computers truly powerful?

    _____

Computer Programming

101

C. Fill in the blanks in the following paragraph.

Paragraph 39 states that the _____ in a computer's memory can be changed. Paragraph 40 explains that the _____ in a computer's memory can also be changed while the computer is running.

D. Look at the word *dynamic* in the last sentence of paragraph 40. Which of the following meanings for *dynamic* is most appropriate in this context?
   a. energetic; vigorous; forceful
   b. relating to or tending toward change

6. According to paragraph 41, what is the purpose of an interface?
   _____

7. Look again at paragraph 42.
   A. What part of the reading does this paragraph summarize?

   paragraph _____ to paragraph _____

   B. Label Figure 4-1 with the parts and subparts of a computer listed in paragraph 42.

   FIGURE 4-1

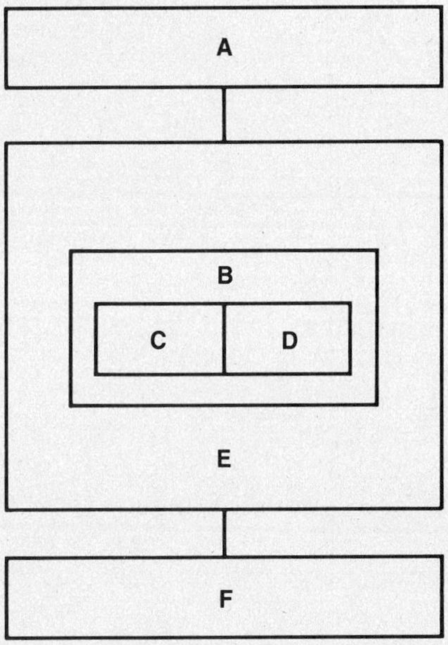

   A. _____
   B. _____
   C. _____
   D. _____
   E. _____
   F. _____

8. Paragraphs 43–49 discuss the main types of computers. Read paragraph 43 again.
   A. What is the purpose of paragraph 43?
   _____

   B. List the three types of computers that this section will discuss.
      a. _____
      b. _____
      c. _____

Computers

C. On what basis have computers been classified into these three categories? (Hint: Look at the first sentence of paragraphs 44, 46, and 48.)
  a. size
  b. use
  c. location
  d. programming

9. Read paragraphs 44 and 45 carefully.
   A. Which of the following best describes the two parts of a typical mainframe installation (paragraph 44)?
      a. machine room; terminals
      b. control units; storage units
      c. memory, storage, and central processing; input/output devices
      d. disks and tape; printers and peripherals
   B. Why are "supercomputers" mentioned in paragraph 45?
      a. They are another kind of computer.
      b. They are a type of mainframe computer.
      c. "Supercomputer" is just another name for the large multiuser computers.

10. Read paragraphs 46 and 47 again.
    A. What type of computer is discussed in these two paragraphs?
    _____

    B. Paragraph 46 gives four reasons for the popularity of minicomputers. Try to summarize the four reasons in one word each.
       a. _____
       b. _____
       c. _____
       d. _____
    C. What three factors identify a "supermini" (paragraph 47)?
       a. _____
       b. _____
       c. _____
    D. What advances have made "superminis" possible?
       a. _____
       b. _____

11. The final two paragraphs of the reading, paragraphs 48 and 49, deal with microcomputers. Read these two paragraphs carefully.
    A. Compare and contrast the two types of microcomputers mentioned in paragraph 48 in terms of data-storage capacity, price, and use.
    _____
    _____
    _____

    B. Draw a simple diagram (like the one in question 7B) of the typical microcomputer system described in paragraph 49. You do not have to draw a real picture of a computer. Simply draw some rectangles or squares, and connect them with lines, or place them on the page in a way that indicates you understand how the parts of a microcomputer system work together. (Your drawing should *not* look exactly like the one on page 101, however.)

PART 3: COMPREHENSION EXERCISES
(Paragraphs 33–49)

Exercise 1

The following statements are either *true* or *false* according to paragraphs 33–49 of the reading. Write either T or F in the space before each one.

_____ 1. This part of the reading deals mostly with IBM computers.
_____ 2. The logic unit of a computer contains a central processor and an arithmetic processor.
_____ 3. The arithmetic processor is for mathematical calculations, while the logic unit is used for letters and words.
_____ 4. Input devices are used to control or program the computer.
_____ 5. Magnetic tape and punched cards are examples of output devices.
_____ 6. CRTs and printed "hard copy" allow programmers to see the results of their data input and programming.
_____ 7. The contents of a computer's memory can be changed even while a program is running.
_____ 8. The purpose of an interface is to connect the input device to the output device.
_____ 9. The "supercomputer" is a type of mainframe.
_____ 10. The microcomputer was first invented in 1977.

Exercise 2

Complete the following summary of paragraphs 33–49 by filling in each blank with an appropriate word or phrase.

This section of the reading discusses the major _____ of a computer, and the _____ main categories of computers. The reading concludes by discussing the _____ of microcomputers.

Computers in general have four main components: a _____, an input device, an output device, and a _____ unit. The central processing unit, which is the heart of the computer, contains subunits for _____ processing and _____ or control. The input and output units allow data to flow in and out of the computer. A _____ is an example of an input device; a _____, or CRT, is an example of a familiar output device. The final _____ of the typical computer is the memory unit. The memory is divided up into _____. Each of these has an _____, or number, which the _____ uses to control the flow and arrangement of data.

Computers

An important part of large computer systems is the _____, which connects different parts of the computer together.

There are three main categories of computers: _____, _____, and _____. Mainframes are large, _____, and very expensive. They perform large tasks quickly and are typically designed to be used by _____ at the same time. Minicomputers are _____ than mainframes but still quite powerful. They are favored in applications where the _____ is not so complex or where the user wants more _____ over the data. Due to advances in _____ and technology, some minicomputers (called "superminis") have the speed and _____ of mainframes. Microcomputers can vary in size and price from large, _____ systems to small, inexpensive _____. The typical microcomputer consists of two main parts: the _____, and the _____ for input, output, and memory storage.

Exercise 3

Look back at the Warmup questions at the beginning of this chapter. Which of these questions apply to Part 3 of the reading? Now that you have read Part 3, which of these questions would you answer differently? Which would you answer in the same way?

CHAPTER 5

Thought, Creativity, and the Computer

WARMUP QUESTIONS

The following reading comes from *The Complete Computer Compendium*, edited by Michael Edelhart and Douglas Garr. The book is a collection of short, general-interest articles written for nontechnical people who want to learn more about computers.

The author of this selection, David D. Thornburg, addresses the question of whether computers will ever be able to think or reason like human beings.

Before you read the selection, consider the following statements and indicate whether you *agree* or *disagree* with each one. Discuss your opinions with your classmates.

1. _____ It is possible for computers to simulate human thought.
2. _____ It is impossible for a computer to be "alive" in the same way that a human being is.
3. _____ Humans will always be able to beat computers at games like chess.

What is your opinion about the future ability of computers? Do you think that the possibilities are limitless, or do you think that there will always be some things computers cannot do?

_____
_____

Do you think that computers will ever have the potential to harm human beings? Why or why not?

_____
_____

DIRECTIONS FOR READING

Before you read this selection, first skim it quickly. Read the first sentence of each paragraph, and note the words printed in italics. Then read the entire selection quickly for general understanding.

Thought, Creativity and the Computer
David D. Thornburg

1. In his book *Mind and Nature*, Gregory Bateson tells the following tale:

2. A man, engaging in discourse with his computer, once asked: "Do you suppose that you will ever think like a human being?" To which the machine replied (after much delay): "That reminds me of a story."

3. I suppose the reason I find this tale so engaging is simply because humans do think in terms of stories. So far as I know, not only do machines not think in terms of stories, they don't think at all.

4. The concept of the anthropomorphic machine is quite old. In the 1840s, when the mathematician Ada Byron (Lady Lovelace) was working with Charles Babbage on his analytical engine, Babbage made grand claims for his engine—a task made easier by his failure to finish building it and thus have it subjected to rigorous testing. At one point he claimed, "The whole of the developments and operations of analysis are now capable of being executed by machinery." Babbage often referred to his machine's "memory," to "teaching" it to do something and even to its "feeling" for numbers.

5. Although Lady Lovelace was extremely impressed with the capabilities of Babbage's machine, in one of her notes she remarked: "It is desirable to guard against the possibility of exaggerated ideas that might arise as to the powers of the analytical engine. In considering any new subject, there is frequently a tendency, first, to *overrate* what we find to be already interesting or remarkable and, second, by a sort of natural reaction, to *undervalue* the true state of the case when we discover that our notions have surpassed those that were really tenable. The analytical engine has no pretensions whatever to *originate* anything. It can do whatever *we know how to order it* to perform. It can *follow* analyses; but it has no power of anticipating any analytical relations or truths. Its province is to assist us in making *available* what we are already acquainted with."

6. Of course, the invention of the stored program (and with it the ability of computers to modify their own programs) has provided newer wood for this fire. What I find interesting in the debate of the 1840s is its similarity to the debate continuing in our own era. For example, in 1958 two academics wrote: "There are now in the world machines that think, that learn and that create. Moreover their ability to do these things is going to increase rapidly until—in the visible future—the range of problems they can handle will be coextensive with the range to which the human mind has been applied."

7. Twenty-five years have passed since this statement was made, and we have yet to see machines that can compete with human intellectual capacity in any but very limited areas.

8. Artificial intelligence has been defined as the field in which machines are made to perform tasks that would require thinking when performed by humans. I have no argument with that. My problem comes when someone suggests that machines performing these tasks are in some manner "thinking" while they do them. After all, some people say, we have flying machines that behave like birds. Why can't we have thinking machines? Let's look at that argument a little more closely.

9. Suppose we say that artificial flying is the field in which machines are made to perform tasks that would require flying when performed by birds. Let us

take one example (the equivalent, say, of having a computer play chess)—conveying one's self from San Francisco to Los Angeles. As a practitioner of artificial flying, I can create a conveyance and conveying medium (call it a Carriage and Roadway, or CAR for short) with which I can transport myself between these two locations without ever leaving the ground. Just as our artificial-flying device never leaves the ground, is it necessary that our artificial-intelligence device "think" in order to perform tasks that we normally associate with thinking when we carry them out?

10   We can program computers to create text strings that we call poetry, but this does not mean that the computer *thinks* that it has created poetry or that it even has any internal motivation to create a poem in the first place. We can program computers to play extraordinarily powerful games of chess, but this doesn't mean that the computer *feels* anything about the game it is playing or even that it is "aware" that it is playing a game at all.

11   The computer is, and will remain, a tool. It is a tremendously powerful tool and, perhaps, it is even a useful thought amplifier. But the computer is not a thinking machine.

STUDY QUESTIONS

Directions: Refer to the reading to answer the following study questions.

1. Read paragraphs 1–3 again.
   A. Paragraph 2 tells a story. What synonym for the word *story* is used in paragraph 1?
   _____

   B. In the first sentence of paragraph 2, which of the following means "engaging in discourse with"?
      a. talking
      b. fixing
      c. building
      d. programming
   C. Do you think the "tale" in paragraph 2 is funny? Why or why not?
   _____
   _____
   _____

   D. What is the main idea of paragraph 3?
      a. The tale is engaging.
      b. Humans think in terms of stories.
      c. Machines do not think in terms of stories.
      d. Machines do not think at all.

2. Reread paragraph 4 carefully.
   A. What claims did Charles Babbage make for his "analytical engine"?
   _____

   B. Although it isn't stated directly, what do you think was the purpose of Charles Babbage's analytical engine?
      a. to make mathematical calculations
      b. to teach numbers
      c. to provide energy
   C. Did Babbage's first analytical engine work?
   _____

   D. Near the end of paragraph 4, there are three words in quotation marks: *memory*, *teaching*, and *feeling*. These words are used in reference to which of the following?
      a. human beings
      b. Babbage
      c. Babbage's machine

3. Read paragraph 5 again carefully.
   A. Who is the "Lady Lovelace" referred to in paragraph 5?
   _____

   B. Whose ideas are expressed in paragraph 5?
   _____

   C. The second half of the first sentence in paragraph 5 states: "It is desirable to guard against the possibility of exaggerated ideas that might arise as to the powers of the analytical engine." Which of the following best summarizes the main idea of this quotation?
      a. It is possible for the machine to do more than we think it can.

Computers

110

    b. We need to guard the ideas of the machine, because it has many powers.
    c. We should remember that the analytical engine does not have any special powers.
  D. The last four sentences of paragraph 5 list three things the analytical engine *can* do and two things it *cannot* do. What are they?
The analytical engine *can*

    1. _____

    2. _____

    3. _____
The analytical engine *cannot*

    1. _____

    2. _____

4. Read paragraphs 6 and 7 again carefully.
  A. How do the ideas of the "two academics" quoted at the end of paragraph 6 compare to those of Lady Lovelace and Babbage in paragraphs 4 and 5?
    a. The academics' ideas about computers are similar to Babbage's ideas about the analytical engine.
    b. The academics' ideas about computers are similar to Lady Lovelace's ideas about the analytical engine.
    c. Both Babbage and Lady Lovelace would agree with the quotation in paragraph 6.
    d. There is no connection between the ideas in paragraph 6 and the discussion of the analytical engine.
  B. What is the main idea of paragraph 7?
    a. The author agrees with the ideas in paragraph 6.
    b. The author does not think that computers can really think, learn, or create.
    c. The author thinks that machines can compete with human intellectual capacity.

5. Read paragraphs 8 and 9 again carefully.
  A. Paragraphs 8 and 9 concern:
    a. different ideas.
    b. the same idea.
    c. a general idea and an example of that idea.
  B. What is the main idea of paragraph 9?
    a. It is possible to fly from San Francisco to Los Angeles without leaving the ground.
    b. It is necessary that machines be able to "think" in order to perform tasks normally associated with thinking.
    c. A machine does not have to function like a human being in order to accomplish some of the same things that humans can do.

6. Reread paragraphs 10 and 11.
  A. Does the author of this selection agree with Lady Lovelace's evaluation of the analytical engine (paragraph 5) or with Babbage's evaluation (paragraph 4)? Explain your answer.

_____

_____

_____

_____

B. Does the author believe that a machine can write poetry or play chess?

C. Does the author believe that a computer can do these things in the same way that a human can?

INTEGRATION QUESTIONS FOR DISCUSSION AND WRITING

Directions: The following questions require you to find relationships among the ideas in the first two readings in this unit: "Computer Programming" (Chapter 4) and "Thought, Creativity and the Computer" (Chapter 5). Discuss your answers to these questions with your classmates.

1. In paragraph 5 of "Computer Programming," the author says that a programmer can "breathe life . . . and even personality" into a computer. Do you think David Thornburg, author of "Thought, Creativity and the Computer" would agree with this choice of adjectives? Why or why not?

2. Quickly reread the section on "Algorithms" in "Computer Programming." What is an algorithm, and who is responsible for designing it? How does this relate to the ideas of Babbage and Lady Lovelace, as discussed in Thornburg's article?

3. The section on "Algorithms vs. Heuristics" in "Computer Programming" contrasts the "brute force" method of solving problems with the use of a set of general principles or guidelines.
   a. Which method do you think human beings use to solve most of their complicated problems: the "brute force" method or the heuristic approach?
   b. Since both humans and computers are able to use the heuristic approach to solve problems, does this prove or disprove Thornburg's statement that "the computer is not a thinking machine" (paragraph 11)? Explain your answer.

4. In your opinion, must a computer "think" exactly like a human being or function exactly like the human brain in order to perform some of the same tasks that a human being can perform? Support your answer with information from the first two readings in this unit.

CHAPTER 6

Controversies over Artificial Intelligence

WARMUP QUESTIONS

The following selection is taken from a chapter in *Computers in Society* by Nancy B. Stern. Like the previous reading, this excerpt comes from a book whose purpose is to introduce computers to readers who are not familiar with them. Instead of being intended for a general audience, however, this book is meant for use in an introductory college course. As a result, some of the early chapters in the book contain more technical information about computers than might be found in the typical introductory text.

In this reading, the author examines the controversy (i.e., the argument or debate) over the question of artificial intelligence. Her discussion is a general, nontechnical one, focusing on the social and philosophical questions surrounding the issue of computers "thinking" like human beings.

Before you read, consider the following statements and indicate whether you *agree* or *disagree* with each one. Discuss your answers with your classmates.

1. _____ Scientists already know exactly how the human mind works.
2. _____ Someday it will be possible to build robots that speak and act like human beings.
3. _____ Scientists who want to build advanced computers should base their design on the model of the human brain.

What does the word *intelligence* mean to you?

_____

_____

Controversies over Artificial Intelligence

In your opinion, what kind of things would a machine have to be capable of in order to say that it had "artificial intelligence"?

_____

_____

DIRECTIONS FOR READING

Before you read this selection, first skim it quickly. Note the headings and the title of the material in the boxes on pages 116 and 117. Glance at the first sentence of each paragraph. Then read the entire selection quickly for general understanding.

Controversies over Artificial Intelligence
Nancy B. Stern

1. Artificial intelligence (AI) is a scientific application of computers that has aroused considerable controversy on both a social and a philosophical level.
2. To begin with, there is no universally accepted definition of the term or its objectives. Definitions range from modest descriptions of scientific applications to very broad statements about its use and its potential.
3. Some experts describe artificial intelligence as a narrowly focused field that has as its prime objective the programming of computers in such a fashion that they appear to make "intelligent" decisions. The purpose of this application is to enable computers to make complex decisions and to perform problem-solving tasks. If a machine can be programmed to do reasonably well at some predefined task, it will be said to display "intelligence."
4. Other proponents of artificial intelligence believe that the value of AI goes beyond its practical ability to enable machines to function as if they had intelligence. These experts claim that AI techniques and discoveries will be of considerable value to students of psychology. The AI supporters believe that the goals of artificial intelligence and of the psychological sciences in general are the same: to understand intelligent processes. For them, AI techniques provide researchers with an understanding of the human mind and how one thinks.
5. Thus there are, broadly stated, two categories of AI proponents. One group focuses on the application of computers for problem-solving functions, the other focuses on the use of computers as problem-solving tools for the primary purpose of providing greater insight into human thought processes.
6. The direction of AI research is, of course, integrally related to the objectives of the researchers. There are scientists who focus on AI techniques and on enhancing the computer's ability to perform certain tasks. For example, chess-playing programs have been written by AI experts to demonstrate the ability of machines to make complex decisions. Similarly, other game-playing programs have been designed to demonstrate the ways in which machines can be programmed to display intelligence. These game-playing tasks can serve as entertainment, can be used to challenge a human opponent's mental acuity, or can simply demonstrate the level of complexity and sophistication that may be programmed into a machine.
7. Other AI tasks include language translation and general problem solving. There are even robots that have been developed by AI researchers to serve as mechanical servants.
8. These applications, and others, which will be discussed in more detail in the following pages, have one or both of the following goals:

   1. To provide some "intelligent" assistance for problem-solving tasks
   2. To provide a new dimension to our understanding of the human mind

   The applications that are undertaken by both types of AI researchers are similar; the controversy surrounding AI applications is more directly related to the ultimate purpose of the application, not to the work itself.
9. In short, there is some degree of divergence among AI researchers as to the scope of their work and its ultimate objectives. Those who object to AI as a research field cite one or more of the [reasons given in Figure 6-1].

FIGURE 6-1

A Critical Evaluation of Artificial Intelligence

1. The problem-solving ability of the machines has not even approached the predictions made by AI proponents 10 and 20 years ago. Hence it is poor policy to continue to support this area of research.
2. The concept that AI can provide us with insight into human thought processes is not only wrong but is unethical as well. By continued government funding for AI, we are encouraging research in an area that should not be pursued, on moral grounds. There is a dimension to human intelligence which cannot and should not be attempted by programming a machine.
3. Since psychologists themselves have not yet agreed on a definition of "intelligence," it is somewhat premature to investigate ways of producing an artificial form of that intelligence. Some psychologists use IQ (intelligence quotient) as a measure of human intelligence. Others claim that human intelligence is not quantifiable; judgment, intuition, and creativity are aspects of intelligence that are exceedingly difficult, if not impossible, to measure. Hence without an agreement among psychologists as to the definition of intelligence, attention to "artificial intelligence" may well be misguided.

10   In this chapter we explore the background of AI, typical applications, and some of the larger issues that surround its use.

ALAN TURING AND HIS DEFINITION OF MACHINE INTELLIGENCE

11   Even before electronic digital computers began to emerge as scientific and commercial tools, a British mathematician, Alan M. Turing, in the late 1940s considered the problem of determining whether machines can be viewed as displaying "intelligence." Rather than attempting to provide a definition of intelligence, which he knew would only serve to foster controversy, he rephrased the problem by attempting to determine if machines can be made to function in ways similar to the way we behave when we say we are thinking.

12   This attempt to sidestep the question of what intelligence is was very ingenious. It enabled Turing to propose a kind of imitation game which could then be used to characterize machine "intelligence."

13   The test requires a person to ask questions, and on the basis of the answers, he or she must determine if the respondent is another human being or a machine. If the person is unable to make this determination accurately when asking questions of a machine, the device is said to possess intelligence (see Figure 6-2).

14   Turing's test has remained a kind of model for AI. Turing believed that by the year 2000 such a machine could be programmed to imitate human responses. Indeed, many AI researchers are attempting to demonstrate such capability, but thus far no machine or machine program has even approached this goal. We do, however, still have over a decade to determine if Turing's prediction was too optimistic or if, in fact, it will be possible to have communication between people and machines in which the human being finds it difficult to determine if the respondent is another human being or a machine.

FIGURE 6-2

Can a Machine Play This Game?[a]

The new form of the problem can be described in terms of a game which we call the "imitation game." It is played with three people, a man (A), a woman (B), and an interrogator (C) who may be of either sex. The interrogator stays in a room apart from the other two. The object of the game for the interrogator is to determine which of the other two is the man and which is the woman. He knows them by labels X and Y, and at the end of the game he says either "X is A and Y is B" or "X is B and Y is A." The interrogator is allowed to put questions to A and B thus:

C: Will X please tell me the length of his or her hair? Now suppose X is actually A, then A must answer. It is A's object in the game to try to cause C to make the wrong identification. His answer might therefore be

"My hair is shingled, and the longest strands are about nine inches long."

In order that tones of voice may not help the interrogator the answers should be written, or better still, typewritten. The ideal arrangement is to have a teleprinter communicating between the two rooms. Alternatively, the question and answers can be repeated by an intermediary. The object of the game for the third player (B) is to help the interrogator. The best strategy for her is probably to give truthful answers. She can add such things as "I am the woman, don't listen to him!" to her answers, but it will avail nothing as the man can make similar remarks.

We now ask the question, "What will happen when a machine takes the part of A in this game?" Will the interrogator decide wrongly as often when the game is played like this as he does when the game is played between a man and a woman? These questions replace our original, "Can machines think?"

[a]Alan Ross Anderson, *Minds and Machines* (Englewood Cliffs, NJ: Prentice-Hall), p. 7. Reprinted by permission of Prentice-Hall, Inc.

STUDY QUESTIONS

Directions: Refer to the reading to answer the following study questions.

1. Read paragraphs 1–5 again carefully.
   A. Which paragraph or paragraphs contain a definition of *artificial intelligence*?

   _____

   B. What is the main idea of paragraph 2?
      a. In the beginning, scientists could not agree about the purpose of artificial intelligence.
      b. No one really knows what the term *artificial intelligence* means.
      c. Definitions of scientific applications are the most important.
   C. What is the definition of *intelligence* given in paragraph 3?

   _____

   D. What is the relationship between the main idea of paragraph 3 and the main idea of paragraph 4?
      a. the same or similar
      b. exactly opposite
      c. different approaches to the same question
      d. no relationship
   E. What do the people described in paragraph 4 see as the primary value of artificial intelligence?
      a. It will allow a machine to think.
      b. It will teach us more about the human mind.
      c. It will increase the number of psychology students.
      d. It will allow machines to perform as if they were able to think.
   F. What is the purpose of paragraph 5?

   _____

2. Read paragraphs 6 and 7 again.
   A. Explain the importance of games in artificial intelligence research.

   _____

   _____

   _____

   B. Paragraph 7 contains
      a. a new main idea.
      b. additional examples of the previous main idea.

3. Carefully reread paragraphs 8–10.
   A. Paragraph 8 lists the two main goals of artificial intelligence research. Both of these points were described in detail in previous paragraphs. The first goal listed in paragraph 8 was described in detail in paragraph _____, and the second goal listed in paragraph 8 was described in detail in paragraph _____.

   B. Using the information in paragraph 8, complete the following statement in your own words.

   Although both types of AI researchers work on the same kinds of projects, _____

   _____

Computers

120

    C. Paragraph 9 contains
        a. the objectives of AI research.
        b. the advantages of AI research.
        c. an evaluation of AI research.
        d. the disadvantages of AI research.

    D. Which of the following are among the objections to AI research listed in paragraph 9? (Circle all that apply.)
        a. Scientists have not made as much progress as they said they would.
        b. It is morally wrong to make a machine behave like a human being.
        c. Artificial intelligence might be used for war or for illegal purposes.
        d. Scientists cannot agree on a definition of intelligence.
        e. Some aspects of intelligence cannot be measured.

4. Read paragraphs 11–13 again carefully.
    A. According to paragraphs 11–13, how did Alan Turing propose to measure the "intelligence" of a machine?
        a. directly
        b. indirectly
    Explain your answer.

    _____

    B. According to paragraphs 11 and 12, why did Turing decide not to try to define *intelligence*?
        a. It would cause too many arguments.
        b. It was not a relevant question.
        c. He was more interested in the theory of games.
        d. There was already an acceptable definition.

5. Reread Figure 6-2.
    A. Turing's machine-intelligence test involved a game requiring three players: Player A, a man; Player B, a woman; and Player C, either a man or a woman. According to Figure 6-2, what was the role, or job, of each of these players?
    Player A:

    _____

    Player B:

    _____

    Player C:

    _____

6. Read paragraph 14 again.
    A. According to paragraph 14, what did Turing predict? Has his prediction come true or not?

    _____

INTEGRATION QUESTIONS FOR DISCUSSION AND WRITING

Directions: The following questions require you to find relationships among the three readings in this unit: "Computer Programming," "Thought, Creativity and the Computer," and "Controversies over Artificial Intelligence." Discuss your answers to these questions with your classmates.

1. If a computer could pass the Turing test, do you think David Thornburg (author of "Thought, Creativity and the Computer") would then agree that a computer is a thinking machine?

2. Why do you think scientists have been unable to program a computer to pass the Turing test? Give as many reasons as you can, and support your answer with information from the first two readings in this unit.

3. In your opinion, will there ever be a computer that can pass the Turing test?

4. What do you think are the factors that make up intelligence? Do you think any of these factors could be programmed into a computer?

5. On the basis of your definition of intelligence in question 4, what kind of test would you create in order to prove that a computer was or was not "intelligent?"

UNIT III

Population Growth

CHAPTER 7

Populations, the Environment, and Humans

WARMUP QUESTIONS

The reading selections in Chapters 7–9 discuss the topic of population growth. What do you already know about how human and animal populations grow? How does the environment affect population? Do humans influence the population of other animals?

Before you begin the first selection, read the following statements and indicate whether you *Agree* or *Disagree* with each one. Then discuss your opinions with your classmates.

1. _____ In general, the population of an animal species increases at a steady rate over time.
2. _____ It is possible for scientists to predict the future population growth of different animal species.
3. _____ The use of insecticides has both positive and negative effects on various animal populations.
4. _____ Nature has ways of controlling animal population growth without interference from humans.
5. _____ Lack of food is usually the primary cause when the population of an animal species decreases.
6. _____ The development of agriculture at the beginning of civilization allowed human population to grow rapidly.
7. _____ At the present rate of human population growth, the world will have over eight billion people by the year 2000.
8. _____ It is more difficult to lower the human birthrate than it is to lower the death rate.
9. _____ The world cannot sustain many more people than are now living.

Population Growth

126

Write three questions you have about human or animal population. Share your questions with your classmates, and discuss possible answers.

_____
_____
_____
_____
_____

PREVIEWING

1. Look over the excerpt from *The Human Side of Biology* on pages 129–138.

   How many paragraphs does the reading contain? _____

   How many pages does it have? _____

2. How many figures do you find in the reading? _____

   How many of these figures are graphs? _____
   What type of information do the graphs provide?

   _____
   _____

3. Look at Figures 7-3 and 7-4. Briefly, what is the subject of each of these figures?

   Figure 7-3: _____
   _____

   Figure 7-4: _____
   _____

4. Before you read the selection, you should get a sense of its organization.
   List the titles of the three main sections and the paragraphs that each section includes.

   _____ (paragraphs 4 –)
   _____ (paragraphs   –)
   _____ (paragraphs   –)

   What type of information do you think each section contains?

   _____
   _____
   _____
   _____

Populations, the Environment, and Humans

127

5. What do you think the function of paragraphs 1–3 is?

_____

6. Look through the selection quickly once again. Write down the words that are printed in boldface type.

_____
_____
_____
_____
_____

Do you know any of these terms? Why have the authors placed them in boldface type?

DIRECTIONS FOR READING

The reading selection for this chapter is taken from *The Human Side of Biology*, a biology textbook by William H. Mason and Norton L. Marshall. The text is used in introductory biology classes in American universities.

The previewing section you just completed gave you an idea of the content and organization of the selection. You are now ready to read it more carefully.

The selection has been divided into three parts. You will read each section quickly and then examine each one more closely as you complete the study questions.

Populations, the Environment, and Humans
William H. Mason and Norton L. Marshall

1   The domestication of plants about 10,000 years ago led to the development of towns and cities. Previously, small tribal groups had been continually on the move, hunting and gathering food as they could. Agriculture, however, required a settled society, and the food surplus that it provided made possible the specialization of human activity. Now there could be smiths and weavers, merchants, carpenters, artists, and physicians. There was time to do more than merely survive, time to build, time to think and to learn. Our words *civilized* and *city* come from the same Latin root. Civilization not only changed human life in social and cultural ways. It also, by profoundly changing our environment, affects humankind in biological ways.

2   We noted earlier that some populations of organisms tend to oscillate in size in simple environments, whereas population stability appears to be the general rule in complex environments. Many human activities that disrupt the natural environment tend to reduce its complexity and promote changes in population dynamics. A good example of such an effect can be seen when insecticides are used in an attempt to control a particular pest species. However, the toxic substance may eliminate or reduce the numbers of many other animal forms, even mammals and birds. Some of these species may be important predators—and, without them, some prey form that had never been a pest under normal conditions may explode in numbers. This new pest is often more destructive than the original species that the spraying was intended to eliminate.

3   Humans have much to learn about how natural populations will react to modification of the environment. A great deal of additional research is needed to support well-planned environmental management programs if population stability of the natural plant and animal species is to be achieved. This research must provide further insight for comprehending and perhaps regulating our own population plight. As you will see in this chapter, we no longer exist in a "natural" environment; the normal checks and balances that once controlled population size are no longer functional. Worldwide human population growth is our most serious threat.

POPULATION GROWTH PATTERNS

4   A **population** can be defined as all the members of a given species living within a specified area. Dramatic fluctuations in population size are commonplace in the early stages of succession and in simple ecosystems such as those of the tundra and northern coniferous forest. The interrelationships within such ecosystems are few, and this probably promotes instability in the populations of resident species. An insect population in an old field may increase at an unchecked rate until food is exhausted or cold weather curbs reproduction. In northern Europe, lemmings sometimes reproduce more rapidly than foxes and owls can eliminate them through predation. Periodically the lemming population explodes, individuals become very aggressive, and large numbers undergo

Population Growth

mass migrations that result in the death of the vast majority. In both the insects and lemmings, population size is reduced occasionally by the death of many members of the population. Here population control is achieved by something we might call a crisis.

5   The growth of a population can be illustrated by a **growth curve**. A growth curve is constructed by plotting the numbers of organisms present on the vertical axis against time on the horizontal axis. The growth curve shown in Figure 7-1 depicts a dramatic oscillation in population size. Note that the total number of individuals increases steadily until a dramatic increase in death rate results in a downward plunge in population size. This curve represents the pattern of population growth characteristic of populations in the simple environments discussed above. The time required for the population to crash might be hours for a population of bacteria, several weeks for some insect populations, or several months or years for a mammal population.

6   Many undisturbed populations do not undergo dramatic increases and decreases. Notice that the growth curve in Figure 7-2 levels off and shows only minor fluctuations after the population reaches its optimum size. Note especially that the population does not crash once it reaches optimum size. Built-in restraints allow for minor fluctuations in population size as various environmental factors affect the species. The factors responsible for regulating growth and optimum size in a stable population are complex. All the factors that collectively curb population growth at a particular level are referred to as **environmental resistance**.

7   The species in a climax ecosystem rarely display a complete history of population growth such as those shown in Figures 7-1 and 7-2. However, when large-scale natural disasters or man-made modifications drastically alter ecosystems, the ecologist sometimes has the opportunity to trace the entire history of population growth for species in these disturbed surroundings. The identification of the various components of environmental resistance is made much easier in instances where this is possible. Much of what we know concerning

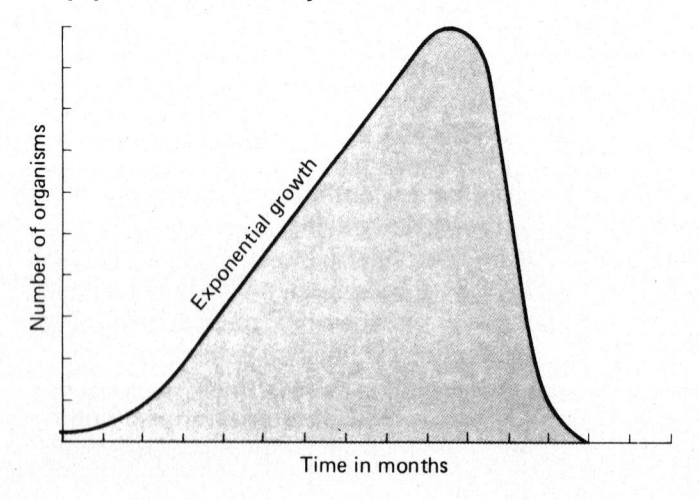

FIGURE 7-1 Growth Curve for an Unstable Population. For the species depicted here, in this particular situation, there is no factor or combination of factors that limits population growth short of the depletion of some necessary resource. Once this resource, such as food, is expended, all or most of the population dies in a very short time.

FIGURE 7-2 Growth Curve for a Stable Population. For the species depicted here, in this particular situation, a combination of factors, sometimes both environmental and physiological, act to reduce and then stabilize population expansion prior to the exhaustion of any critically important resource. There will be adjustments in population size as environmental fluctuations occur; however, some approximate size will be maintained indefinitely under existing conditions.

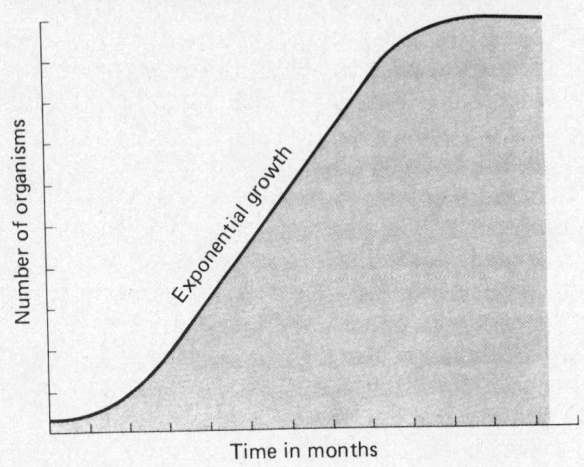

natural population control has been learned from studying disturbed ecosystems.

8   In new or young populations characteristic of a disturbed area, the **birthrate** greatly exceeds the **death rate**. A slow acceleration of initial population growth is somewhat dependent upon low breeding efficiency when the number of individuals in the population is small. This slow initial growth is usually followed by a period of greatly accelerated population growth. The time of most rapid population growth is often referred to as **exponential growth**. Reasons for this rapid increase in population size can be illustrated by a simple example. Suppose a pair of mice produce litters of 10 offspring every month. Assume that sexual maturity in this species is reached at the age of one month, and the life expectancy is several months. At the end of the first month of population growth, this pair would have increased to a total of 12 animals, at the end of the second month 72, the third month 432, and so forth. Exponential rates increase rapidly due to the combined effects of both the original and the added components. It works like compound interest, where your interest payment is added to the principal each time period and begins to earn interest itself. The new mice are added to the breeding population and produce more new mice. Not only is the population growing; its rate of growth is growing.

9   The exponential phase of population growth is ultimately followed by a negatively accelerating phase. The population is still growing, but its rate of growth is now decreasing. This point can be identified by the tapering off of the exponential phase. The tapering off eventually results in zero growth and the subsequent stability shown in Figure 7-2, or a rapid decrease or crash in population size as shown in Figure 7-1. The negatively accelerating phase represents the part of the growth curve at which environmental resistance begins playing a significant regulatory role through increasing the death rate in a population. Zero growth is attained at the point where the death rate becomes

equal to the birthrate. When death rate and birthrate remain equal or essentially balanced, the population remains stable in size.

POPULATION CONTROL MECHANISMS

10 Many of the factors contributing to environmental resistance are poorly understood. Food availability is rarely of primary importance in regulating population size. If food availability were the major factor governing the size of populations, all populations would increase exponentially until the food was exhausted, and all or almost all of the individuals would starve. Obviously, factors other than food must contribute to environmental resistance in stable populations.

11 Predation may play a role in regulating prey species populations. Generally, as a prey population enlarges, the individuals become more readily available to predators. The predator numbers also tend to increase, and greater numbers of the prey organism are consumed. However, as in the case of food availability, predation is seldom a major factor in population control. Arctic hare populations on large islands fluctuate in a manner somewhat similar to those on the mainland, even though predator species are sometimes absent on these islands. Also, many species lack major predators; for example, grizzly bears and lions obviously have no natural predators.

12 Other factors that can contribute to overall environmental resistance are disease and parasitism. A successful parasite rarely kills its host, and in most natural populations parasites cause little damage when the host population is not crowded. However, parasite infestations become heavier when host density increases beyond a certain level. In many cases increased parasite loads eventually result in increased host mortality. In this way, parasitism may contribute to population control when the host species exceeds an optimum level. A good example of this can be seen in whitetail deer populations where the occurrence of brain nematode infestations is typically low in moderate-sized deer populations living in climax forest ecosystems. However, if lack of predation or change in habitat causes a dramatic increase in the number of deer, the parasite may spread from individual to individual more readily and thus destroy significant numbers of the population.

13 Competition among different species for space, nesting sites, or food can also become important factors as population levels increase beyond normal limits. There may be little competition while population levels are low, but, as numbers increase, factors such as the exploitation of new types of foods may result in competition with other species. When one species of algae increases to a certain point, the sheer mass of algal cells may limit the reception of light by another species, thus eliminating the second species. A species of tree may "outcompete" nearby neighbors for soil moisture and nutrients when its numbers increase beyond a certain density. When a certain insect species becomes scarce, birds may turn to little-used species for food. This may interfere with the feeding activities of other animals, and the birds may suddenly be competing even with predatory insects for food.

14 You can undoubtedly think of other factors that would contribute to overall environmental resistance. Such factors as food availability, competition, predation, and parasitism often seem to be last-ditch devices that are effective only when a species has increased its numbers beyond the ability of the environment to support that population adequately. Many stable populations seem to be self-regulating and are rarely controlled by such factors. Biologists are just beginning to comprehend the extent to which **intraspecific mechanisms** control

population levels. We will briefly discuss a few of the ones that have been studied.

15 The size of some mammalian populations is regulated to a large extent through endocrine system responses to crowding. A good example of this is seen in some species of mice (Fig. 7-3). When individuals encounter more than the usual number of other members of their own species, their adrenal glands tend to enlarge. The increase in adrenal size is thought to be a response caused by increased pituitary gland activity, which is itself triggered by nerve impulses arising from areas of the brain stimulated by the increased sightings. As the adrenals enlarge, they produce excessive amounts of adrenal hormones—resulting in a reduction in size of the reproductive organs. Decrease in gonad size inhibits reproduction. The females in such a population will tend to have fewer offspring, or they may fail to breed at all. We find that this physiological response to overcrowding generally occurs prior to the point at which a population will be severely limited by food availability, parasitism, competition, or other crisis factors.

16 Certain behavioral responses in populations are also important ways in which a species may control its own population size. Individuals of many species display a type of behavior called **territoriality**. Individuals, or small groups of individuals, will select a territory and actively defend it against other members of the species (Fig. 7-4). The territory will typically contain the food, cover, and nesting sites necessary for successful completion of the life cycle for the residents of the territory. Members of the species that do not acquire or hold a territory do not breed, and they are more likely to be eliminated by starvation and predation than are those that do hold a territory. Since any ecosystem contains a limited number of territories, the population of such a species will not increase beyond the ability of the environment to support it. The existence of the nonbreeding component in the population actually promotes population stability, since extra individuals are always available to move into a vacated territory when an established holder is eliminated. Many mammals and birds

FIGURE 7-3 Physiological Adjustment as a Means of Population Growth Control. Many mammals react to sightings of more than the usual number of their own species by producing excessive anterior pituitary hormones. These promote increased adrenal secretion, which in turn retards ovary development. The female may thus produce fewer offspring or fail to breed at all.

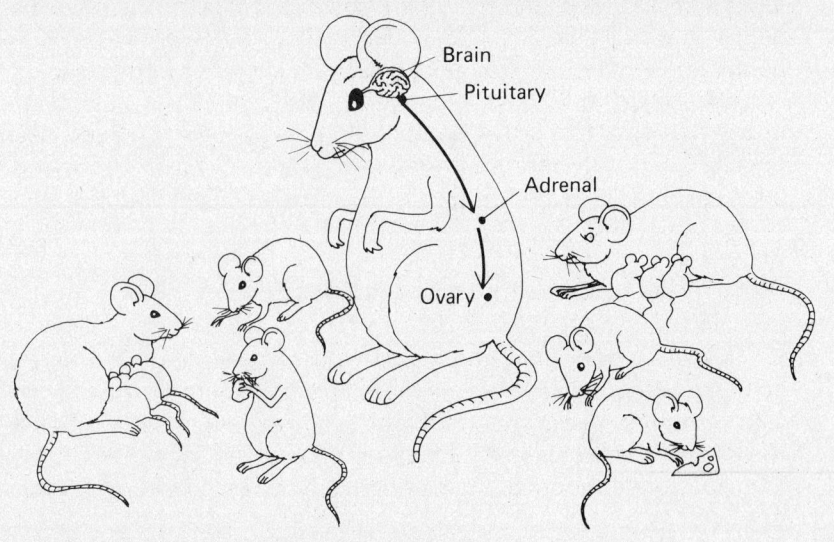

FIGURE 7-4 Territoriality as a Means of Stabilizing Population Size. In many species of birds, breeding pairs or small groups establish and defend a specific area, called a territory, during the mating and nesting season. Excess birds who are not successful in setting up a territory live at the fringe of the optimal habitat and do not breed unless they take over a vacated territory. This limits population size and protects the resources necessary to ensure future population stability.

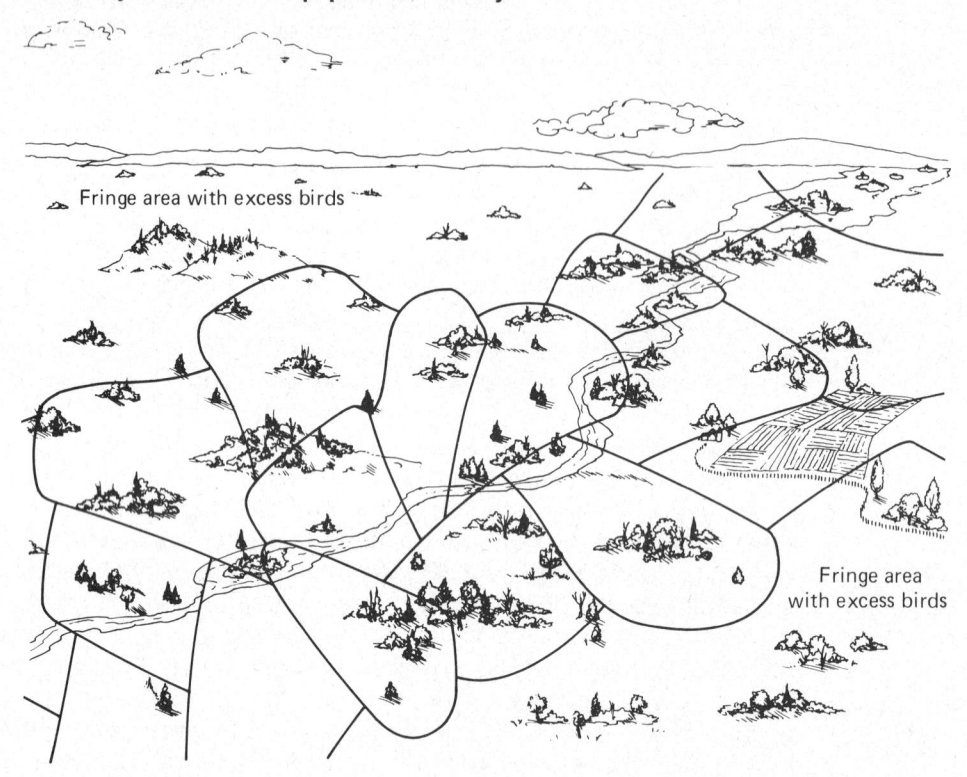

demonstrate territoriality. The populations of such species are usually remarkably stable.

17 The role of behavior in population control may sometimes depend on physiological response to environmental changes. Removal of the queen in some social insect populations stimulates subordinate females to begin egg laying within a matter of hours. One of these females soon becomes the replacement queen, and the others cease egg laying. The physiological mechanisms involved here are poorly understood, but many other similar cases of population regulation through behavior are known to exist.

18 **Migration** is a type of behavior that can have a regulatory effect on population size. Not only can migration lead to an increased death rate in the population, but it also prevents overuse of the vacated habitat during certain seasons of the year. Many insects, mammals, fish, and birds are migratory.

HISTORY OF HUMAN POPULATION GROWTH

19 We have seen that humans have been present on the earth as a distinct species for thousands of years. For most of this time they were little more than wild creatures, existing as gatherers and hunters. Food was often scarce and the only available shelter consisted of caves and rock overhangs. Plants and animals were not domesticated. Fire was not controlled, and tools were largely

nonexistent. Communication was extremely limited. This was not an experience in camping out—living was a matter of day-to-day survival.

20   During this long period the size of the human population can only be estimated. Most of these estimates place the numbers of humans at any time in prehistory at no more than five million. These estimates are probably fairly accurate, since one can determine rather precisely how much space was needed to supply the natural products needed to support the way of life prior to the beginnings of civilization.

21   Human population size remained relatively small during these times simply because the human carrying capacity of the environment was low. The elements of environmental resistance that regulated population size were without doubt uniformly unpleasant. Lack of living space, shortage of food, predation by animals, harsh climatic conditions, and disease undoubtedly played roles in keeping human numbers low. One factor that may have limited birthrates involved suckling the young for several years. When a human female breast feeds a child, her hormone levels tend to upset the normal menstrual cycle, and the chances of conceiving another child are considerably reduced during the nursing period. In some primitive societies today we know that superstition often prevents intercourse during the period a child is being suckled. Infants were probably intentionally killed or abandoned when conditions were harsh. This practice was actually continued in parts of the civilized world well into the nineteenth century. In any case, infant mortality was certainly very high, as it is in primitive societies today.

22   So human population levels remained small until the rudiments of civilization appeared. Of first significance in this regard was the domestication of native grasses about 10,000 years ago. The dawn of agriculture had arrived. Seeds could be stored, food stockpiled, the winter planned for. Thus food was removed as a restraint to population growth, at least to a limited extent. The human's mode of existence was about to change; the day of the city was dawning. Only now could the quantities of food be available that are necessary to maintain a concentrated human population. And it was only from city dwelling that many of the trappings of civilization could arise—communication, science, and technology all arose in the caldron of close human contact. Most of what we learn is gleaned from what others have done, and close contact and efficient communication are major keys to the advancement of any scientific endeavor.

23   However, even agriculture in its initial form did relatively little in terms of allowing for rampant human population growth. Disease, wars, and generally hard times still kept the population low, and by the time of Christ the numbers of humans had increased from about 5 million to an estimated 250 million. In other words, the population had doubled about five to six times in roughly an 8000-year period. This represents a very slow rate of increase.

24   During this time human accomplishments had far outstripped their population growth. Humans now had written records. The first rudiments of medicine were understood. Agriculture had come a long way, and tools of various metals were readily available. Animals had been domesticated and performed much of the necessary physical labor. But still population size remained fairly stable for many centuries. The major factor accounting for this stability was not low birthrate, but high death rate. The life expectancy was short since infant mortality was high, epidemics were largely unchecked, famines occurred with cruel frequency, and war was often an indiscriminate killer.

25   Then in the period between 1750 and 1850 a curious thing happened: The world's population size doubled from about half a billion to one billion in a relatively short span of time. There is no ready explanation for this dramatic

acceleration of population growth. The birthrate may have risen somewhat, but this is disputed by many investigators. The introduction of the potato in Europe probably played a significant role in food availability. Smallpox vaccinations and improved personal hygiene undoubtedly contributed to decreasing the death rate. Soap was introduced, and cotton clothing became generally available, and these two factors certainly helped to reduce the incidence of some infectious diseases. Whatever the reasons, during this period of time the rate of increase in human numbers was approximately 0.5 percent per year. The human population explosion was in the process of detonating.

26 In the period following 1850 the death rate continued to decline. Agriculture was being improved, and crop failures were less frequent. Causes and prevention of many diseases were discovered, and improved transportation provided for the more efficient distribution of food and lessened the impact of local famines. Between 1850 and 1930 the rate of population growth increased to about 0.8 percent per year, and the world population again doubled. This doubling took only 80 years, and now there were about two billion living humans.

27 At about 1900 an unusual thing occurred in western Europe and the United States: The birthrate began a steady decline. The reasons for this decline are poorly understood. The major factor has been theorized to have been a feedback phenomenon from the Industrial Revolution itself. It is easily understood that large families in an agrarian society are a distinct advantage, especially the production of sons to till the soil. However, large families are a distinct liability in the city, especially if child labor is illegal and education is compulsory.

28 This simple explanation for falling birthrates is not the full story. There were exceptions in that in the United States birthrates fell before the full impact of the Industrial Revolution was felt, and in England birthrates actually rose during the early period of the Industrial Revolution. The complete explanation of falling birthrates in modern times, especially in countries that have experienced dramatic declines in death rates and a move toward industrialism, is complex and incompletely understood. Individuals living in such an environment are somehow motivated to have fewer children. Regardless, population actually continued to grow even in these countries, and population growth worldwide accelerated even more.

29 From about 1930 to 1975 the world's population again doubled, from two billion to four billion. This doubling, which took only approximately 45 years, represents a truly dramatic increase in human numbers. The cause of such a rapid increase is clearly not the result of increased birthrates. It was caused by the export of modern and successful health practices from the developed (industrialized) countries to the undeveloped countries of the world, especially in those years immediately following World War II. During this time malaria, yellow fever, smallpox, cholera, tuberculosis, and several other infectious diseases were controlled in these parts of the world, and the death rate declined 50 percent between 1945 and 1955. Much of this decline was associated with the introduction of DDT to control the mosquito that spreads malaria. Similar cases were occurring throughout the world.

30 At the same time the growth rate was skyrocketing in the undeveloped countries, the trend of lowered growth rate noted earlier for developed countries generally continued. Several western European countries had essentially balanced their birth and death rates by the mid-1960s. By the early 1970s the birthrate in the United States was such that population equilibrium seemed just around the corner. However, most people in the world do not live in the developed countries, and many demographers predict that the undeveloped areas

Populations, the Environment, and Humans

of the world are still far away from obtaining the kind of natural population equilibrium being realized in the developed countries.

31   At the present time the world population continues to grow at a rate of about 1.8 percent per year. At this rate of increase, the time required for doubling is 40 years. Will there be 8 billion people at the turn of the century? Can there be 16 billion early in the next century? How about 32 billion in a short 100 years?

32   A rough approximation of the history of human population growth is seen in Figure 7-5. What kind of a growth curve does this represent? It represents a species living evidently for thousands of years at least somewhat in equilibrium with its environment. At present it obviously represents an exponential stage, and from our earlier discussion of growth curves we can speculate as to the two possible outcomes of such a growth phase. Will this be a curve that will crash once resources are depleted, or will population stabilize and, if so, at what density?

33   Our population growth has been accelerated by a decreasing death rate without a corresponding decreasing birthrate in the undeveloped countries. The latter is much more difficult to accomplish than the former. Governments of some undeveloped countries are desperately attempting to curb population growth, with little success. The problem is immense and complex. Many people in these parts of the world do not wish to have fewer children. Effective birth control measures are largely unknown in these countries. Education concerning birth control and the distribution of contraceptives is slow, and often the programs are inefficiently operated.

34   Just what does the future appear to hold? At current growth rates the population of Latin America will double in about 26 years; Africa in 27 years; Asia in 33 years; North America (U.S. and Canada) in 99 years; and Europe in 120 years.

FIGURE 7-5 History of Human Population Growth. Note that exponential growth has occurred only during the past few decades. Many people think that this growth has already exceeded the planet's carrying capacity at our present standard of living. (Time is not to scale.)

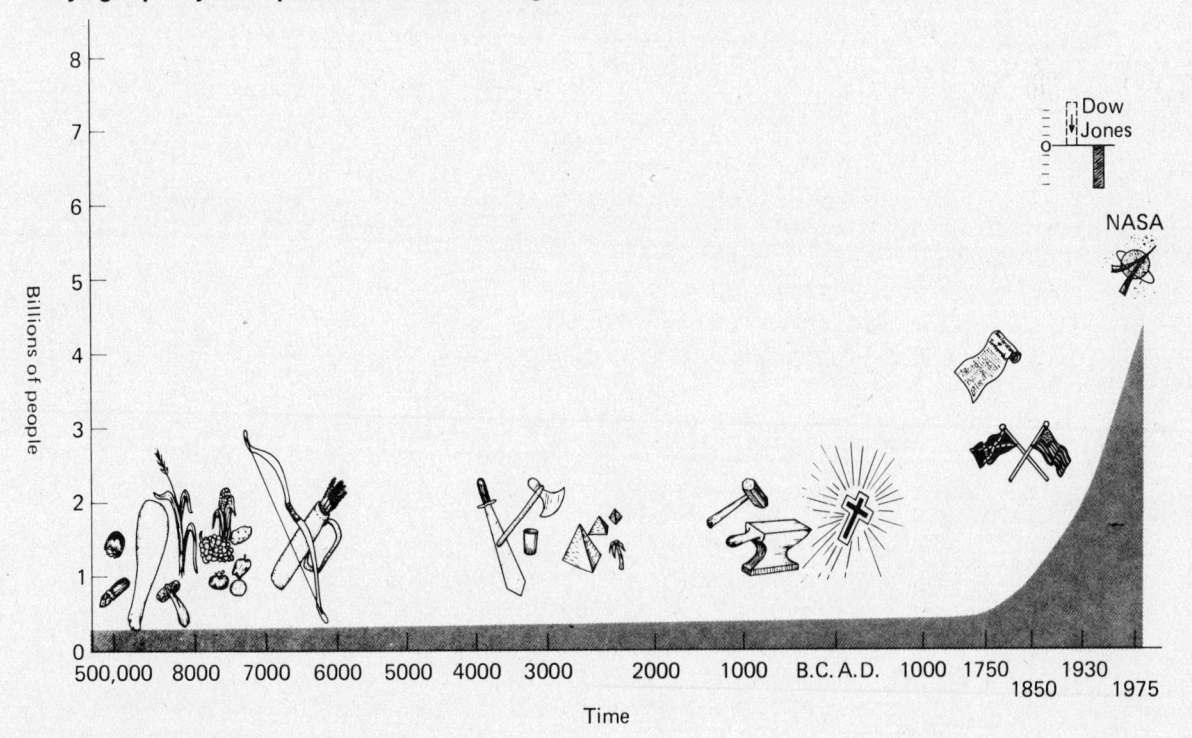

The most important question confronting humanity is whether the world can sustain these growth rates without suffering a population crash. Just what is the world's carrying capacity for humans? Are there different levels of carrying capacity depending on the degree of comfort or discomfort we are willing to endure? Will we really have a choice in this matter?

Populations, the Environment, and Humans

PART 1: STUDY QUESTIONS
(Paragraphs 1–3)

Directions: Read paragraphs 1–3 quickly for general understanding. Then refer to the selection to answer the following study questions.

1. Read paragraph 1 again carefully.
    A. You may not know the meaning of *domestication* in the first sentence, but by reading the entire paragraph, you can conclude that it has something to do with agriculture. What do you think the meaning is?

    _____

    B. What do the authors mean by "the specialization of human activity" in the third sentence?

    _____

    _____

    How does the list of occupations in the fourth sentence help you determine the meaning of this phrase?

    _____

    _____

    C. The sixth sentence states that the words *civilized* and *city* are derived from the same Latin root. What do the authors imply by this?
       a. People who do not live in cities cannot be considered "civilized."
       b. The study of Latin can help you improve your vocabulary.
       c. Civilization is possible only when there is a settled society.
    D. According to the last two sentences, in what three ways does civilization affect human life?

    _____

    _____

2. Read paragraph 2 carefully.
    A. What word in the first sentence has the opposite meaning of *oscillation*? _____
    In what type of environment do populations tend to oscillate?

    _____

    In what type of environment do populations tend to remain stable?

    _____

    B. To what does the word *its* refer in the second sentence?
       a. human activity
       b. population
       c. natural environment
    C. Which of the following is an acceptable paraphrase of the second sentence?
       a. When human activity changes the environment, it usually makes the environment simpler, and thus populations oscillate in size.
       b. When human activity changes the environment, it usually makes the environment more complex, and thus populations remain stable.
       c. When human activity changes the environment, it usually makes the environment simpler, and thus populations remain stable.
    D. The rest of this paragraph gives an example of how human activity can affect animal populations.

Population Growth

140

What is the human activity in this example, and what is the intended effect of the activity?

_____

_____

What other, unintentional effect does this activity have?

_____

_____

What is the result of the two effects?

_____

_____

3. Read paragraph 3 again.
   A. What word in the first sentence means "change?"

   _____

   B. According to this paragraph, do we now understand how to maintain population stability of plant and animal species? (Read the second sentence carefully.)

   _____

   C. What do the authors mean by "our own population plight" in the third sentence? (This idea is restated in the last sentence of the paragraph.)

   _____

   D. What do the authors mean in the fourth sentence by stating that "we no longer exist in a 'natural' environment"?
      a. Human civilization has changed our environment.
      b. The environment has changed naturally.
      c. The unnatural environment is harmful to humans.

PART 2: STUDY QUESTIONS
(Paragraphs 4–18)

Directions: Read paragraphs 4–18 quickly for general understanding. Then refer to the selection to answer the following study questions.

1. Note that Part 2 consists of two sections, "Population Growth Patterns" and "Population Control Mechanisms." Using your own words, what do you think is the topic of each of these sections?

   "Population Growth Patterns": _____

   _____

   "Population Control Mechanisms": _____

   _____

2. Read paragraph 4 carefully.
   A. What type of population growth is discussed in this paragraph?
      a. oscillating
      b. stable
      c. simple

Populations, the Environment, and Humans

141

    B. What does *fluctuation* mean in the second sentence?
        a. growth
        b. stability
        c. change
    C. According to the second sentence, in what two situations is the fluctation of population size common?
        a. _____

        b. _____

    NOTE: Earlier chapters of *The Human Side of Biology* define the terms *succession* and *ecosystem*. "Early stage of succession" here means the period when species populations are new to an area. "Ecosystem" refers to an area, such as a lake, forest, or mountain, where different species live together.
    D. The paragraph gives two examples of dramatic population fluctuation. What are they?
        a. _____

        b. _____
    In these examples, how is rapid population growth stopped?

_____

_____

_____

3. Read paragraph 5 carefully, and examine Figure 7-1.
    A. What is the purpose of this paragraph?

_____

    B. What kinds of situations might cause a species population to decrease suddenly, as depicted in Figure 7-1? (Give your own ideas as well as those in the paragraph.)

_____

_____

_____

4. Read paragraph 6 carefully and examine Figure 7-2.
    A. Does this paragraph continue the discussion of growth curves that was started in paragraph 5?

_____

    B. How does the growth curve in Figure 7-2 differ from that in Figure 7-1?

_____

    C. What kind of population is depicted in Figure 7-2?
        a. oscillating
        b. stable
        c. undisturbed
    D. According to this paragraph, what is environmental resistance?

_____

_____

Population Growth

Can you think of any examples of environmental resistance?

_____

_____

E. What does *curb* mean in the final sentence?
   a. increase
   b. decrease
   c. limit

5. Read paragraph 7 carefully.
   A. Which is the main idea of this paragraph?
      a. Ecologists have not learned very much about natural population control, especially in climax ecosystems.
      b. Large-scale disasters and modifications by people change population growth patterns.
      c. It is generally impossible to observe the complete history of population growth except in special situations.
   B. In the first sentence, the authors refer to a "climax" ecosystem. By this they mean an ecosystem that has fully developed over time, not one that is new. What portion of the growth curve shown in Figure 7-6 would be observable in a climax ecosystem?
   C. To what does the word *this* refer in the third sentence?

_____

6. Read paragraph 8 carefully.
   A. According to this paragraph, does the rate of population growth increase at a steady rate over time?

_____

   B. Examine the first sentence. Which of the following is true of a new or young population in a disturbed area?
      a. Fewer of the organisms die every day than are born.
      b. More of the organisms die every day than are born.
      c. The same number of organisms die every day as are born.
   C. In your own words, define *exponential growth* as it is explained in this paragraph.

_____

_____

_____

   What example is given to illustrate this concept?

_____

_____

_____

7. Read paragraph 9 carefully.
   A. In your own words, what is negative acceleration?

_____

_____

Populations, the Environment, and Humans

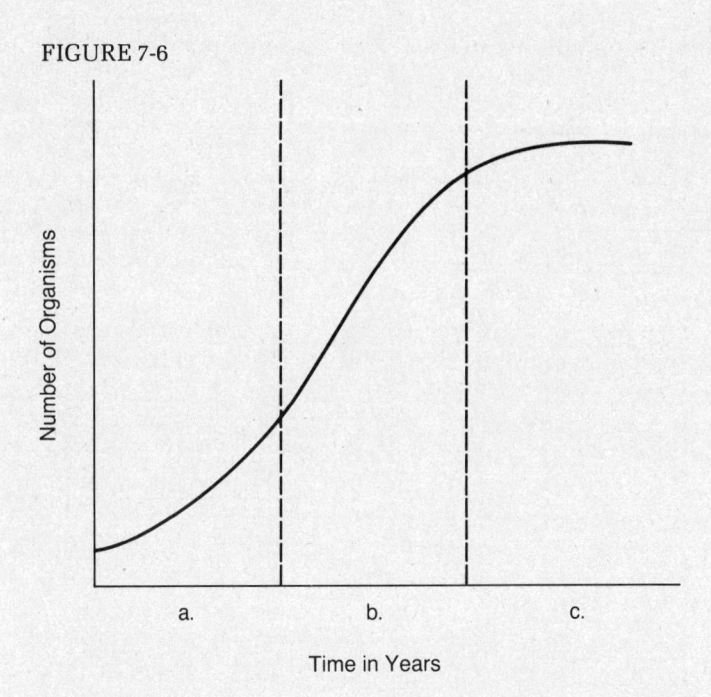

143

FIGURE 7-6

[Graph: S-shaped curve with Number of Organisms on y-axis and Time in Years on x-axis, with dashed vertical lines marked a., b., and c.]

B. What does *tapering off* mean in the third sentence? How do you know?

_____

C. What are the two possible situations that can follow the tapering off of the exponential phase?
   a. _____
   b. _____

D. According to this paragraph, why does the growth of a population taper off?

_____
_____
_____

8. Paragraphs 4–9 explain how populations grow. Paragraphs 10–18 discuss the various ways in which the size of a population is controlled. What term introduced in paragraph 6 refers to the control of the population by nature?

_____

Skim paragraphs 10–13 quickly. What mechanism does each paragraph discuss?

paragraph 10: _____

paragraph 11: _____

paragraph 12: _____

paragraph 13: _____

9. Now read paragraph 10 carefully.
   A. How important is the availability of food in controlling the size of populations?

_____

Population Growth

   B. In your own words, paraphrase the authors' argument that food availability is not a major factor.

   _____
   _____
   _____

10. Read paragraph 11 carefully.
    A. You may not have been familiar with the terms *predator* and *prey* before reading this selection, but the paragraph provides several clues to their meaning. What do you think these terms mean? (If the clues are not enough, look in a dictionary.)

    a. predator: _____

    b. prey: _____

    B. What predator species are mentioned in the paragraph?

    _____

    What prey species is mentioned?

    _____

    Can you think of any species that can be both predator and prey?

    _____

    C. What happens as a prey population increases?

    _____

    What is the final result?

    _____

    D. According to this paragraph, how important is predation in population control?

    _____

11. Read paragraph 12 carefully.
    A. In order to understand this paragraph fully, you must know the meaning of *parasite* and *host*. The paragraph gives some clues to their meaning. What do you think these terms mean? (If the clues are not sufficient, consult a dictionary.)

    a. parasite: _____

    b. host: _____

    B. According to this paragraph, in what population situation do parasites cause significant damage to the host population?

    _____
    _____

    C. Carefully examine the example about whitetail deer populations.

      a. What is the host population? _____

      b. What is the parasite population? _____

      c. In your own words, how does the parasite control the size of the host population?

      _____
      _____
      _____

Populations, the Environment, and Humans

145

12. Read paragraph 13 carefully.
   A. What type of population-control mechanism does this paragraph discuss?

   _____

   According to the first sentence, different species often compete for three features of the environment. What are these features?
   a. _____
   b. _____
   c. _____
   Under what conditions do different species begin to compete?

   _____

   B. The paragraph gives three examples of competition among species. For each example, list the competing species and the environmental feature for which they compete.

	Species	Feature
a. Example 1	_____	_____
b. Example 2	_____	_____
c. Example 3	_____	_____

13. Read paragraph 14 carefully.
   A. This paragraph states that the population-control mechanisms discussed in the previous four paragraphs are "last-ditch devices." What does this mean?

   _____

   When do these devices become effective?

   _____

   B. What term is used to describe the population-control mechanisms that a species uses to control its own population?

   _____

   C. Skim paragraphs 15–18 quickly. Each of these paragraphs discusses an intraspecific mechanism to regulate population. Briefly state the mechanism that each paragraph discusses.
   a. paragraph 15: _____
   b. paragraph 16: _____
   c. paragraph 17: _____
   d. paragraph 18: _____

14. Read paragraph 15 carefully and examine Figure 7-3.
   A. This paragraph discusses how a mammal's endocrine system can act to limit population growth. The sequence of events described in the example is fairly complex. Arrange the following events in the order in which they occur.
   a. The adrenal glands increase in size.
   b. The mouse sees an unusually large number of other mice.
   c. The pituitary gland activity increases.
   d. The adrenal glands produce large amounts of adrenal hormones.
   e. Females will have fewer offspring or will fail to breed entirely.
   f. Nerve impulses are stimulated in the brain.
   g. The size of the reproductive organs decreases.

Population Growth

146

   B. At what point in the growth of the population does this population-control mechanism tend to occur?

   _____

15. Read paragraph 16 carefully, and examine Figure 7-4.
   A. In one word, what is the topic of this paragraph?

   _____

   B. Is this a physiological or a behavioral mechanism?

   _____

   C. In your own words, define *territoriality*.

   _____
   _____
   _____

   D. How does territoriality differ from competition for space, mentioned in paragraph 13?

   _____
   _____

   E. Which of the following are likely outcomes for members of a species that do not have a territory?
      a. They find nesting sites.
      b. They do not have offspring.
      c. They are stable in population.
      d. They die from lack of food.
      e. They are killed by predators.
   F. What happens when a territory-holding member of the species dies?

   _____

16. Read paragraphs 17 and 18 carefully. These two paragraphs describe two more intraspecific mechanisms that control population levels: physiological response to a change in the environment (removal of a queen insect) and migration. Briefly, in your own words, describe these mechanisms.
   a. physiological response to environmental change:

   _____
   _____
   _____

   b. migration:

   _____
   _____
   _____

PART 2: COMPREHENSION EXERCISES
(Paragraphs 4–18)

Exercise 1:

The following statements are either *true* or *false* according to paragraphs 4–18 of the reading. Write either T or F in the space before each statement.

1._____ Significant increases and decreases in population size are typical in complex ecosystems.
2._____ A period of exponential growth generally follows a period of negative acceleration.
3._____ Predation and lack of food are factors that contribute to environmental resistance.
4._____ The population growth of new or young populations is slow because the death rate exceeds the birthrate.
5._____ It is easiest to observe the complete history of population growth in climax ecosystems.
6._____ Parasites cause more damage to a population under crowded conditions.
7._____ Competition among different species for food is an example of an intraspecific mechanism.
8._____ Some species control their own population size through special behavioral responses.
9._____ Territorial species typically do not undergo dramatic population fluctuations.

Exercise 2:

Complete the following summary of paragraphs 4–18 by filling in each blank with an appropriate word or phrase.

A _____ is defined as the total number of members of a species that exist in a given area. Population size _____ frequently in new populations and in simple ecosystems. In undisturbed and complex environments, however, populations tend to remain _____. The factors that limit population growth are called _____ _____.

In new populations, the birthrate usually _____ the death rate, but acceleration of initial population growth is _____. After this initial phase is a period of _____ growth, in which the population grows _____. This second phase is followed by either a _____ phase or by a dramatic _____ in population size. _____ growth is reached when the birthrate equals the death rate.

There are a variety of factors that limit population growth. _____ is one such factor, but it is rarely a primary cause; if it were, populations would periodically starve. _____, whereby one species consumes another, is another factor of environmental resistance. Disease and parasitism limit population growth, especially when the population is _____. _____ among different species for food, space, and other resources also regulates population size.

Some factors that limit population growth are called _____ mechanisms because the species controls its own population size. One example is the _____ _____ system response to crowding in some mammals. Another is a type of behavior called _____. In this behavior, the species members will not _____

Population Growth

148

_____ if they do not hold a specific area or space. Finally, _____ is a type of behavior in which the population moves from its habitat in great numbers, leading to an increased death rate.

Exercise 3:

Look back at questions 1, 2, 4, and 5 in the Warmup section on page 125. Would you answer any of these questions differently after reading Part 2 of "Populations, the Environment, and Humans"?

PART 3: STUDY QUESTIONS
(Paragraphs 19–34)

Directions: Read paragraphs 19–34 quickly for general understanding. Then refer to the selection to answer the following study questions.

1. This section presents an overview of human population growth, from precivilized times to the present.
   A. What type of organization would you expect to find in this section?
      a. cause and effect
      b. chronological
      c. classification
   B. Skim paragraphs 19–34, looking for dates and at the key words or phrases in the first sentence of each paragraph. Then indicate which paragraphs are devoted to each of the following time periods.

Precivilization	paragraphs _____ – _____
Early civilization	paragraphs _____ – _____
1700s–1970s	paragraphs _____ – _____
Present and future	paragraphs _____ – _____

2. Now that you have an idea of the overall structure of this section, look at each paragraph in detail. Read paragraph 19 carefully.
   A. Which of the following is the main idea of this paragraph?
      a. Humans have existed for thousands of years.
      b. Life was extremely difficult for early humans.
      c. Early humans did not control fire.
   B. For each of the following nouns, write an adjective or verb that describes its condition for early humans.

      shelter: _____

      food: _____

      tools: _____

      communication: _____

3. Read paragraph 20 carefully.
   A. What term do the authors use for the period during which early humans lived, before civilization?

      _____

Populations, the Environment, and Humans

149

    B. How large was the human population during this period?

4. Read paragraph 21 carefully.
   A. Did the human population grow exponentially during the prehistoric period? Why or why not?

   B. List several of the mechanisms of environmental resistance that tended to limit human population during the prehistoric period.

5. Read paragraph 22 carefully.
   A. What is the main idea of this paragraph? (Use the words *civilization* and *agriculture* in your answer.)

   B. Which of the following is a synonym for the word *rudiment* in the first sentence?
      a. beginning
      b. agriculture
      c. existence
   C. What do the authors mean in the fifth sentence when they state that "food was removed as a restraint to population growth"?

   D. According to the paragraph, what does "close human contact" make possible?

   E. Outline the main idea of this paragraph by placing the following phrases in the appropriate places in the cause-and-effect chain.
      large groups of humans living together
      storage of quantities of food
      the development of communication, science, and technology
      the beginning of agriculture

   _____
         makes possible

       _____
           which makes possible

           _____
               which makes possible

               _____

Population Growth

150

6. Read paragraphs 23 and 24 carefully.
   A. How quickly did the human population grow during the period of early civilization?

   _____

   B. List the factors that kept the population from increasing very rapidly during this period.

   _____
   _____
   _____

   C. List the factors that probably helped increase the total population.

   _____
   _____
   _____

   D. Which of the following phrases has the same meaning as *outstripped* in the first sentence of paragraph 24?
      a. progressed more slowly
      b. advanced more rapidly
      c. became more important

7. Read paragraph 25 carefully.
   A. The first and the last sentences in this paragraph imply which of the following?
      a. The period from 1750 to 1850 was the beginning of exponential population growth.
      b. The period from 1750 to 1850 was the beginning of negatively accelerating population growth.
      c. The period from 1750 to 1850 was a time of relative population stability.
   B. Which was more important in influencing population growth during this period, a change in birthrate or a change in death rate?

   _____

   C. List the factors that contributed to the decrease in the death rate during this period. Place each factor under the appropriate heading.

Food	Health
_____	_____
_____	_____
_____	_____

8. Read paragraph 26 carefully.
   A. What span of years does this paragraph discuss?

   _____

   B. How did the size of the human population change during this period?

   _____

   What factors account for this change in population?

   _____

9. Read paragraphs 27 and 28 carefully.
   A. Which of the following is the overall topic of these two paragraphs?
      a. The Industrial Revolution changed western Europe and the United States.
      b. Human population continued to increase after 1930.
      c. The birthrate in industrialized countries began to drop around the turn of the century.
   B. Paragraph 27 states one possible reason for the decline in birthrate when industrialization takes place. Identify this reason by filling in the blanks in the following paragraph.

   In _____ societies, large families are considered desirable because

   the _____ can help run the farm. In _____ societies,

   however, children cannot help support the family because they _____

   _____ to work and they must _____. Under these circum-

   stances, _____ families are favored.

   C. The second sentence in paragraph 28 gives two facts concerning birthrates. Do these facts tend to support or weaken the explanation of declining birthrates presented in paragraph 27?

10. Read paragraph 29 carefully.
    A. What happened to the human population during the period from 1930 to 1975?

    B. Did this change take place primarily in the developed (industrialized) countries or in the developing countries of the world?

    What caused this change?

    C. Refer to paragraphs 25–29, and complete the following chart.

Time period	Number of years for population to double	Total population at end of period
1750–1850		
	80 years	
		4 billion

11. Read paragraph 30 carefully.
    A. What period of time does this paragraph discuss?

    B. Briefly paraphrase the first sentence in this paragraph.

Population Growth

152

C. What does *population equilibrium* mean in the third sentence?

D. Read the last sentence in this paragraph again. Do the authors seem optimistic or pessimistic about the prospects for bringing human population growth under control?

12. Read paragraph 31 carefully.
    What is the purpose of this paragraph?
    a. to emphasize that the world is now in a period of exponential population growth
    b. to test the reader's understanding of what has been discussed up to this point
    c. to summarize the ideas presented in the two previous paragraphs

13. Read paragraph 32 and examine Figure 7-5.
    A. According to the graph, what is the time span during which humans lived in equilibrium with the environment?

    What is the time span of the exponential growth stage?

    B. What two possibilities may follow this stage?
       a.
       b.
    Which of these outcomes do you think is more likely?

14. Read paragraph 33 carefully.
    A. According to the first sentence, what two factors now lead to rapid population growth in the developing countries?
       a.
       b.
    B. To what does *latter* refer in the second sentence?

    To what does *former* refer?

    C. What general idea do sentences 3–5 support?

15. Read paragraph 34 carefully.
    This paragraph asks the reader to consider some important questions.
    a. Do you think human population growth can continue to increase rapidly? Why or why not?

Populations, the Environment, and Humans

153

    b. Will humans have to change their way of life as population increases in the future? If so, how?

    _____
    _____
    _____

    c. Can human population growth be controlled? If so, how?

    _____
    _____
    _____

PART 3: COMPREHENSION EXERCISES
(Paragraphs 19–34)

Exercise 1

The following statements are either *true* or *false* according to paragraphs 19–34 of the reading. Write either *T* or *F* in the space before each statement.

1. _____ During the period of prehistory, human population tended to fluctuate dramatically.
2. _____ When agriculture was introduced, human population growth took a sharp upward swing.
3. _____ Before 1750, a major factor that limited human population growth was low birthrate.
4. _____ Between 1750 and 1850, the human population doubled.
5. _____ The main factor responsible for the exponential growth of human population has been an increase in the birthrate.
6. _____ Families in industrialized societies tend to have fewer children.
7. _____ The human population has now entered a period of negatively accelerating growth.
8. _____ Population growth rates are similar throughout the world, a fact that demonstrates the universal nature of population-control mechanisms.

Exercise 2

Complete the following summary of paragraphs 19–34 by filling in each blank with an appropriate word or phrase.

During the period of prehistory, the human population remained _____ because the human carrying capacity of the environment was _____. When _____ began 10,000 years ago, _____ made it possible to store food and to plan for winter. The trappings of civilization, such as _____, _____, and _____, came about because of close human contact. However, the population did not increase _____ because of such factors

Population Growth

as _____ and _____. High _____ rates kept the population stable.

The period of _____ growth began in 1750, and the population doubled in the next hundred years. Factors such as _____, _____, and _____ caused the death rate to decrease.

Beginning around 1900, the birthrate began to decline in western Europe and the United States. Although the causes are not fully understood, it appears that the _____ _____ was a major reason for this shift in the birthrate.

Between 1930 and 1975, the population doubled once more. The primary reason for this growth was a decrease in _____ in the _____ countries, due to better health practices.

Today, the human population is growing at a rate of 1.8 percent per year and will double in size in _____ years. To curb population growth, the birthrate must be _____, but this is very difficult to accomplish.

Exercise 3

Look back at questions 6–9 in the Warmup section on page 125. Would you answer any of these questions differently after reading Part 3 of "Populations, the Environment, and Humans"?

CHAPTER 8

Factors Limiting Growth

WARMUP QUESTIONS

The reading in this chapter, "Factors Limiting Growth," is taken from *Biology Today* by David L. Kirk. This text is intended for an introductory college-level biology course.

"Factors Limiting Growth" provides more information about population-control mechanisms in particular situations. Before you begin the selection, consider the following statements, and indicate whether you *agree* or *disagree* with each one. Discuss your opinions with your classmates.

1. _____ It is possible for an animal population to continue growing indefinitely.
2. _____ Factors such as floods, fires, and droughts can influence population growth.
3. _____ It is unusual for animal populations to fluctuate in size regularly.
4. _____ A single population-control factor, such as lack of food, is not sufficient to limit population size; only a combination of several factors can limit population size.
5. _____ Some population-control mechanisms take effect only when the population of a species becomes very large.

Many different types of factors can limit population growth. Some of them were discussed in "Populations, the Environment, and Humans." What were some of these factors? Can you think of any others? Discuss your list with your classmates.

_____
_____
_____

Population Growth

DIRECTIONS FOR READING

Before you read this selection, first scan it quickly, noting the section headings and the words and phrases in boldfaced type. Also examine Figures 8–1 through 8–3. Then read the entire selection quickly for general understanding. After you have finished, you will read the selection again as you answer the study questions that follow.

Factors Limiting Growth
David L. Kirk

1. The exponential model of population growth applies to a variety of biological situations. For example, exponential growth often occurs during the initial expansion of a population that colonizes a new area with abundant resources or when a species acquires a new resource that releases it from the control of previous growth-limiting factors. Still, we are not neck deep in bacteria nor shoulder-to-shoulder with elephants, so we may surmise that this type of growth is rarely sustained for long. The factors that limit exponential growth can be grouped into two basic categories, each with unique consequences for a population's growth curve.

DENSITY-INDEPENDENT FACTORS AND J-SHAPED GROWTH

2. Some of the factors that limit exponential growth occur irrespective of population size or density. They are called **density-independent factors**. Common examples are floods, fires, and droughts. When these events periodically decimate a population, the growth curve looks like the one shown in Figure 8-1. Population rises exponentially for a time but then falls abruptly. Such a curve is called a **J-shaped growth curve**.

3. A J-shaped growth pattern is common among organisms that inhabit a widely fluctuating environment. For example, only the eggs of some species of desert insects are able to survive the prolonged dry season. But when the torrential rains of spring arrive and vegetation begins to grow rapidly, the eggs hatch and the insect population grows exponentially at or near the intrinsic rate of increase for the species. With the return of the searing dry season, the entire population of adults disappears once more—until the next seasonal episode of growth.

FIGURE 8-1 Fluctuation in Population Size among Desert Insects in Three Successive Years. This kind of population profile is called a J-shaped growth curve.

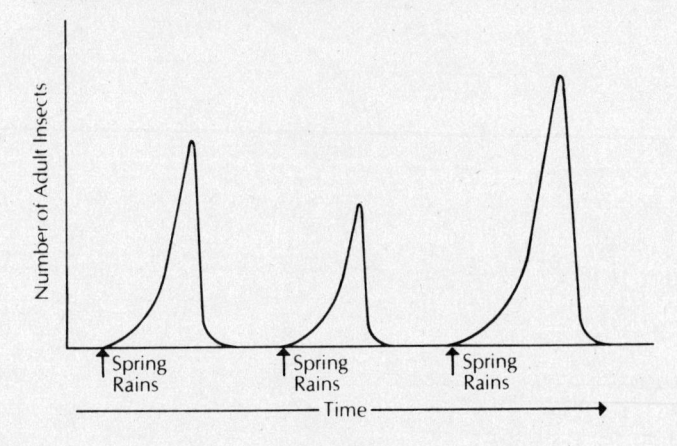

DENSITY-DEPENDENT FACTORS AND S-SHAPED GROWTH

4   The example of J-shaped growth illustrated in Figure 8-1 assumes that the density-independent limiting factor (drought) occurs so regularly that population size never increases to the point where it causes serious depletion of resources (food, nesting sites, and so on) or extensive accumulation of toxic wastes. In most instances of population expansion, however, this point is ultimately reached, and factors imposed by population density begin to limit continued growth. Such **density-dependent factors** arise as a direct outcome of population growth and serve to limit further growth by depressing the birth rate and/or increasing the death rate.

5   At some point, of course, density-dependent factors halt population growth completely. For example, suppose that we put a few yeast cells in a medium containing sugar and place the medium in an airtight container. The yeast cells get the energy they need to live and reproduce by breaking down the sugar to form alcohol and carbon dioxide. Suppose further that we periodically remove some of the medium and replace it with fresh medium in order to ensure a continuing supply of sugar to the yeast cells. The result would be a growth curve like that shown in Figure 8-2. This is called an **S-shaped growth curve** or a **sigmoid growth curve**. Note that the population initially grows exponentially but that the rate of increase falls off, finally reaching zero. This final, constant population size is known as the **carrying capacity** of that particular environment.

6   We might speculate that the carrying capacity is determined by the amount of sugar available to the yeast. The density-dependent limiting factor, in other words, is depletion of the food supply by an ever-increasing number of yeast cells. We could test this assumption by increasing the amount of sugar in the medium both initially and in each addition we make. When we have done so, the population once again grows until it becomes stabilized at a second but

FIGURE 8-2 Sigmoid Growth of Yeast in a Culture. The open circles indicate the observed population size at hour intervals. The solid line is a plot of the logistic growth equation, which clearly describes the observed density-dependent growth of the yeast population quite well. Note that population size levels off and tends to stabilize near the carrying capacity—in this case, 665.

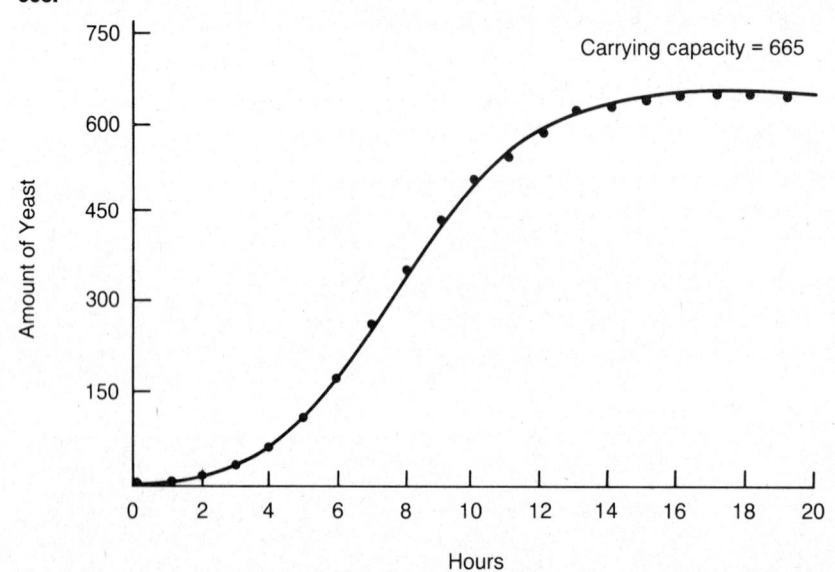

higher carrying capacity. Thus availability of a single essential resource (in this case sugar) can limit both the rate of growth and the size of a population. Ecologists summarize the effects of resource availability on population size with the **law of the minimum**: of all the various resources needed by a population, the resource that is present in the smallest quantity in relation to the needs of the population is the one that acts as a limiting factor.

7   Depletion of some essential resource is not the only density-dependent factor that can limit population growth. Growth can also be checked when an expanding population produces toxic wastes beyond the species's level of tolerance. Experiments with yeast have shown that, as the amount of alcohol (the waste product of sugar metabolism by yeast) increases, the death rate for young yeast buds also increases. When 1.2 percent ethyl alcohol is added to the medium, for example, the carrying capacity of the environment is reduced by 35 percent; the population grows to only 65 percent of the size shown in Figure 8-2. Thus where and to what extent a population can grow is limited by its tolerance for environmental factors; when a species's tolerance for some factor is approached, that factor imposes a limit on maximum population size in that environment. This principle is known as the **law of tolerance**. Of particular interest to us here is the fact that some of these growth-inhibiting influences may be density-dependent.

INTERACTION OF DENSITY-DEPENDENT AND DENSITY-INDEPENDENT FACTORS

8   It is very important to note that density-independent and density-dependent regulators of population growth are not mutually exclusive. As we have said, density-independent exponential growth can be regarded as a special case

FIGURE 8-3 The Effects of Density-Dependent and Density-Independent Factors on the Growth Curve of a Population of Bobwhites in Wisconsin. The solid portions of the curve show the net reproductive increases each year between spring and autumn. When these gains in density are plotted against spring density, the results are similar to those expected under sigmoid growth. The dashed portions of the curve show mortality over the winter months. The number of deaths during the winter largely depends on the harshness of the weather, a density-independent factor.

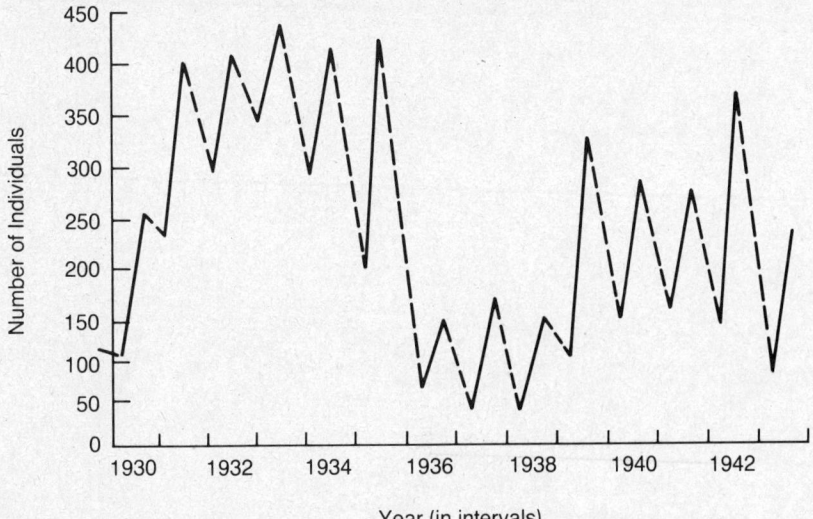

of density-dependent sigmoid growth when the population size is well below the carrying capacity. But more important, the carrying capacity is rarely constant for natural populations. When the carrying capacity fluctuates upward dramatically (as with the appearance of increased amounts of food), the population experiences a period of density-independent growth. Similarly, a downward shift (as with the disappearance of food) can lead to a period of intense density-dependent mortality or a sharp decline in reproductive capabilities. Finally, even if the carrying capacity is constant, density-independent factors—such as severe cold—can still be overlaid on the density-dependent factors to temporarily reduce population size. As a result, most natural populations experience both density-independent and density-dependent factors, and their growth curves often contain a complex mixture of J-shaped and S-shaped components (Figure 8-3).

Factors Limiting Growth

161

STUDY QUESTIONS

Directions: Refer to the reading to answer the following study questions.

1. Read paragraph 1 carefully.
   A. This paragraph discusses exponential growth of populations, a concept defined in the previous reading. In your own words, what is exponential growth?

   _____

   B. According to this paragraph, there are two situations in which exponential growth often occurs. What are they?

   a. _____

   b. _____

   Can you think of an example of each of these situations?
   a. _____
   b. _____

   C. Read the third sentence carefully. What does the author mean by "neck deep in bacteria" and "shoulder-to-shoulder with elephants"?

   _____

   To what does the phrase "this type of growth" refer?

   _____

   D. The last sentence indicates that the factors limiting exponential growth can be placed in two major categories. Quickly look ahead at the next few paragraphs. What are these categories?
   a. _____
   b. _____

2. Read paragraphs 2 and 3 carefully.
   A. What is the topic of these paragraphs?

   _____

   B. What are density-independent factors?
      a. Factors that occur because the population size is large or very crowded.
      b. Factors that do not depend on the size of the population or how crowded it is.
      c. Factors that occasionally cause the population size to decrease dramatically.
   C. Paragraph 2 gives some examples of density-independent factors. Can you think of any other?

   _____

   D. Look carefully at Figure 8-1. What type of growth curve does the figure display?

   _____

   E. What is the purpose of paragraph 3?
      a. to show the difference between density-independence and the J-shaped curve

Population Growth

162

   b. to define density-independent factors
   c. to give an example of density-independent factors
F. What density-independent factor is explained in paragraph 3?
   a. the long dry season
   b. the spring rains
   c. exponential growth
G. Referring to paragraph 3, fill in either the cause or the effect for each of the following relationships.

CAUSE	EFFECT
a. long dry season	_____
b. _____	vegetation grows quickly

3. Skim paragraphs 4–7 quickly. What is the major topic of this section?
   _____

4. Read paragraph 4 carefully.
   A. In the second sentence, to what does "this point" refer?
   _____
   _____

   B. What does "depletion of resources" mean in the first sentence?
      a. decrease of resources
      b. increase of resources
      c. change of resources
   C. In your own words, what is a density-dependent factor?
   _____
   _____

   Can you think of any examples of density-dependent factors?
   _____
   _____

5. Read paragraph 5, and examine Figure 8-2 carefully.
   A. Which of the following is the main idea of this paragraph?
      a. Density-dependent factors cause the population to grow exponentially at first.
      b. Density-dependent factors stop the growth of a population and cause it to drop sharply in size.
      c. Density-dependent factors can stop the growth of a population but do not cause it to decrease in size.
   B. In the example given in this paragraph, identify the following elements:
      a. the population species: _____
      b. the density-dependent factor: _____
   C. What type of growth curve illustrates density-dependent growth?
   _____

   How does it differ from the J-shaped growth curve of density-independent growth?
   _____
   _____

Factors Limiting Growth

163

   D. In your own words, what is the carrying capacity of an environment?

   E. Refer to Figure 8-2.
      Which span of hours represents exponential growth?
      a. hours 0–5
      b. hours 5–12
      c. hours 12–20

6. Read paragraph 6.
   A. According to this paragraph, can the carrying capacity of an environment be changed? _____
      What examples does the author provide to demonstrate this?

   B. In your own words, what is the law of the minimum?

   C. Refer again to Figure 8-2. Which span of hours represents the depletion of food?
      a. hours 0–5
      b. hours 5–12
      c. hours 12–20

7. Read paragraph 7 again.
   A. Does the first sentence refer back to the previous paragraphs, or ahead to the rest of paragraph 7?

   B. Which sentence expresses the main idea of this paragraph?
      a. sentence 1
      b. sentence 2
      c. sentence 3
   C. What does the author mean by "toxic waste"?

      What is the toxic waste produced by yeast cells?

      What happens to the yeast cells when their toxic wastes begin to accumulate?

   D. In your own words, what is the law of tolerance?

8. Read paragraph 8, and examine Figure 8-3 carefully.
   A. Which of the following expresses the main idea of this paragraph?
      a. Density-dependent and density-independent factors work separately to regulate the carrying capacity of an environment.

Population Growth

164

      b. Density-dependent growth is a special type of density-independent growth, as influenced by the carrying capacity of the environment.

      c. Density-dependent and density-independent factors often work together, resulting in complex population growth patterns.

  B. According to this paragraph, what happens when the carrying capacity of an environment increases?

_____

What happens when the carrying capacity decreases?

_____

Can density-independent factors work even if the carrying capacity of the environment has not been reached?

_____

  C. In Figure 8-3, does the increase in bobwhites each year (solid lines) represent density-dependent or density-independent growth?

_____

What kind of factor causes the drop in bobwhite population each winter (dashed lines)?

_____

_____

INTEGRATION QUESTIONS FOR DISCUSSION AND WRITING

Directions: These questions require you to find relationships among the ideas in the first two readings in this unit: "Populations, the Environment, and Humans" and "Factors Limiting Growth." Discuss your answers with your classmates.

1. Paragraph 9 of "Populations, the Environment, and Humans" states that two possible situations follow exponential growth: either population growth negatively accelerates (tapers off), or it decreases rapidly. How would you explain each of these situations in terms of the concepts of density-independent and density-dependent growth factors presented in "Factors Limiting Growth"?

2. "Populations, the Environment, and Humans" discusses population-control mechanisms (paragraphs 10–18) and classifies them as either *interspecific* (between different species) or *intraspecific* (within a particular species). "Factors Limiting Growth" categorizes population-control factors differently, as either *density-independent* or *density-dependent*.

    There is overlap between some of these categories. Consider the factors, shown in Figure 8-4, that can regulate population growth. In which of the four categories can each factor be placed? (More than one category may be possible for some.)

3. According to "Populations, the Environment, and Humans" the growth of the human population has been in an exponential phase since 1750.
  A. What does this fact signify about the carrying capacity of our environment for humans?

Factors Limiting Growth

FIGURE 8-4

Factor	Interspecific	Intraspecific	Density-dependent	Density-independent
Lack of food				
Forest fire				
Disease				
Accumulation of toxic waste				
Predation				
Endocrine system response in mice				
Migration				
Territoriality				
Extremely cold winters				

B. What limiting factors of human population growth are density-independent? List as many as you can.

C. What limiting factors of human population growth are density-dependent?

D. In the future, do you think that the human population growth curve will be J-shaped or S-shaped? Why?

CHAPTER 9

Population and Natural Resources

WARMUP QUESTIONS

The final reading in this unit is an excerpt from *The Main Issues in Bioethics* by Andrew C. Varga. This book is intended for a general audience.

"Population and Natural Resources" discusses some of the consequences of the rapid increase in human population. Before you read the selection, consider the following statements and indicate whether you *agree* or *disagree* with each. Discuss your opinions with your classmates.

1. _____ There is more hunger in the world today than there ever has been in the past.
2. _____ More than half of the world's population does not receive adequate food.
3. _____ Most of the recent increase in food production has taken place in developing countries.
4. _____ Growing affluence throughout the world contributes to an overall increase in the food supply.
5. _____ The use of wood for fuel in developing countries is beneficial because it can be replaced.
6. _____ An educated population is necessary if the world is to support an ever-increasing number of people.

As the human population steadily grows, there are many important, often negative consequences. What do you think are some of the results of the population explosion? Discuss your ideas with your classmates.

DIRECTIONS FOR READING

Now you are ready to read "Population and Natural Resources" quickly for general understanding. After you have done so, turn to the study questions that follow.

Population and Natural Resources

Andrew C. Varga

1. Scarcity of food and natural resources is the obvious consequence of the rapid growth of population. Some resources, such as agricultural products, are renewable. Oil, minerals and many raw materials of industrial products, on the other hand, are not renewable and their limited supplies sooner or later will be exhausted. There has always been some degree of hunger or starvation somewhere on the earth in the history of mankind. But in our days the scarcity of food affects a larger number of people than ever before, and hunger is fairly widespread in spite of all the improvements in agricultural methods. The United Nations Food and Agricultural Organization (F.A.O.) estimated that in 1977, 500 million people suffered from hunger.[1] About half of the world's population is not adequately fed.

2. Few of the developing nations can sufficiently provide for their growing populations; hence a large segment of their people is locked in the vicious circle of mental and physical underdevelopment and dire poverty. According to medical evidence, infants deprived of sufficient, balanced nutrition will never grow to their full mental capacity, and thus poor nations will lack the most important power for their development, that is, the mental ability and energy of their people.

3. Worldwide per-capita food production has increased after World War II, but most of the increase took place in developed countries. Several Third World nations have substantially raised the rate of their food production, but this gain has been offset by the fast growth of their population, so that the per-capita increase of food has been only minimal. Paradoxically, affluence in the world at large and within the confines of individual nations also adds to the problem of food scarcity. The developed nations consume between twelve hundred and nineteen hundred pounds of grain per person. Most of it is eaten indirectly in the form of eggs, milk products and meat. In Liberia and Haiti, however, the per-capita consumption is less than two hundred pounds, in India less than four hundred pounds of grain, most of it consumed directly in the form of bread, rice and cereals. It is obvious that food consumption is not distributed evenly, so that the poor who cannot buy sufficient food are reduced to starvation. The more affluent a country is, the more its agricultural products are converted into better quality food. One pound of beef is produced by as many as ten pounds of grain. The wealthier a country is, the more it can afford either to convert grain into higher-quality food or buy grain from other countries, as is the case with Europe, the U.S.S.R. and the oil-producing nations. The result is, of course, that the poor and hungry nations of the world cannot afford to compete with the wealthier nations and import enough grain to improve the diet of their people.

4. The rapid growth of population also causes scarcities of other renewable and nonrenewable resources. Over 1 billion people use wood for fuel, cooking and heating, and this excessive consumption of wood leads to deforestation, upsetting the ecological balance. The scarcity of firewood forces many people in poor countries to burn dried cow dung for fuel. But cow dung is used in these countries for fertilizer and thus another shortage develops that adversely affects food production. The problem of energy shortage is well known. No indus-

---

[1] *Daily News*, November 13, 1977.

trial or agricultural growth is possible without energy. The cost of energy, however, is steadily increasing as reserves are depleted. Since petrochemicals are the basis of fertilizers, poor nations are less and less capable of buying the much needed fertilizers to improve their agricultural production. According to United Nations statistics, the consumption of energy is growing three times as fast as the population. Also the consumption of minerals is growing much faster than the population and, in spite of some recycling of minerals, the accessible reserves are being depleted. More and more land is used for residential purposes and roads, so the available acreage for agriculture keeps steadily shrinking.

5   As can be seen, the problems are interconnected, and economic growth, which is the source of the improvement of man's life on earth, is greatly affected by the growth of population. The standard of living was very low thousands of years ago, of course, when the earth had a much smaller population, but today there is a stronger causal relationship between population growth and the rise in the standard of living than there was in the past.

6   One of the sources of economic growth is an educated population: the farmer, the industrial worker, the manager—all of whom learn their trade and employ the best scientific methods of production and organization. Persons who are unable to read or barely go beyond the level of the three R's, cannot be easily taught to improve their productivity or plan and organize their own lives with foresight and prudence. It seems that certain developing nations are fighting a losing battle with illiteracy and the attempt at upgrading their educational systems. They cannot build enough schools and train teachers in sufficient numbers to educate everybody at even the elementary level. In Latin America a fairly large percentage of the population is still illiterate, and the situation in Africa and Asia is even worse. Any development of their educational systems is more than offset by the yearly addition of large numbers of children to the growing population. It is true that centuries ago the education of the population was very low everywhere compared to present-day standards, but after the scientific revolution that precipitated the industrial revolution, much greater knowledge and more advanced education are needed to make possible a steady economic growth. The world economy today could not provide even the bare minimum for the more than 4 billion people on the globe without scientific methods of production. Will the developing nations be able to make progress in educating their children so that they can contribute to their economic growth as skilled labor? Can they do this without lowering the growth rate of their population?

Population and Natural Resources

169

STUDY QUESTIONS

Directions: Refer to the reading to answer the following study questions.

1. Read paragraph 1 carefully.
   A. The first sentence summarizes the main idea of the entire reading. Paraphrase the sentence.
   _____
   _____

   What is a synonym for *scarcity*?
   _____

   What are natural resources? Give some examples.
   _____
   _____
   _____

   B. What two categories of resources are discussed? Give an example of each.
      a. _____ (Example: _____)
      b. _____ (Example: _____)
   C. Which of the following statements is true, according to this paragraph?
      a. A larger percentage of people are hungry today than in the past.
      b. A larger number of people, but not a larger percentage, are hungry today than in the past.
      c. Half the present population suffers from hunger.

2. Read paragraph 2 carefully.
   A. According to the first sentence, few developing nations can "sufficiently provide for their growing populations." What are the consequences of this?
   _____
   _____
   _____

   B. What does the author mean by "vicious circle"?
   _____
   _____

   C. What does the author believe is the most important factor in the development of a country?
   _____
   _____

3. Read paragraph 3 carefully.
   A. In developing countries that have increased their food production, have individuals benefited substantially? Why or why not?
   _____
   _____

   B. In addition to rapid population growth, what other factor adds to the problem of food scarcity?
   _____

Population Growth

In the second sentence, what does the word *paradoxically* indicate?
a. continuation of the previous idea
b. an apparent conflict or contradiction
c. a result of the previous idea

C. What does the author mean by "better quality food"?

___

Which countries consume better quality food?

___

D. In your own words, explain how affluence contributes to world hunger.

___
___
___

4. Read paragraph 4 carefully.
  A. This paragraph discusses other resources that are becoming scarce due to rapid population growth. What specific resources are discussed?
  a. ___
  b. ___
  c. ___
  d. ___
  e. ___
  Which of the resources you listed are renewable? Which are nonrenewable?
  B. What is the immediate negative consequence of using wood for fuel?
  ___

  In your own words, explain how scarcity of firewood can lead to a shortage of food.
  ___
  ___
  ___

  C. What is the relationship between petrochemicals and agriculture?
  ___

  Why do the poor nations suffer as petrochemical prices rise?
  ___
  ___

  D. What is the main idea of this paragraph?
  a. Energy costs have risen even more quickly than the world's population.
  b. The increase in population has caused a scarcity of resources necessary to improve agricultural production.
  c. Scarcity of resources caused by the rapid growth of population affects primarily the developing and poor nations.

Population and Natural Resources

5. Read paragraph 5 carefully.
    A. List some of the problems to which the first sentence refers.

    _____

    _____

    _____

    B. According to this paragraph, what is necessary for the improvement of life?

    _____

6. Read paragraph 6 carefully.
    A. Which of the following is the main idea of the paragraph?
        a. In order for people to be productive members of their societies, they must be educated beyond the level of the three Rs.
        b. Today, the population is much better educated than it was in the past, but improvements still need to be made.
        c. A strong educational system is needed for economic growth, but rapid increases in population make improvement in education difficult.
    B. Why is education important for economic growth? (Refer to the second and third sentences, but use your own words.)

    _____

    _____

    C. According to the third sentence, which of the following is true?
        a. Educational systems in developing countries are not improving.
        b. Educational systems in developing countries are improving.
        c. The populations in developing countries are becoming more literate.
    D. Read the eighth sentence carefully. What do you infer would happen today if we did not have our present "scientific methods of production"?

    _____

    _____

    _____

INTEGRATION QUESTIONS FOR DISCUSSION AND WRITING

Directions: These questions require you to find relationships among the ideas in the three selections in this unit: "Populations, the Environment, and Humans," "Factors Limiting Growth," and "Population and Natural Resources." Discuss your answers with your classmates.

1. According to "Population and Natural Resources," the rapid growth of human population has resulted in a scarcity of food. Do you think that this scarcity of food acts as a population-control mechanism, as described in "Populations, the Environment, and Humans"? If your answer is yes, why has the human population continued to grow in size? If your answer is no, explain why lack of food has not limited the size of the human population.

2. "Factors Limiting Growth" introduces the concept of the law of the minimum. Define this concept, and think about how it might relate to the human population. Are there

presently any resources that act as limiting factors on population size? What resources might limit human population growth in the future?

3. What do you predict will happen to the human population by the year 2000? By the year 2050? 2100? What will be the consequences of further increases in our population?

4. Do you agree with Varga's emphasis on the importance of education in "Population and Natural Resources"? How would you respond to his questions at the end of the article?

UNIT IV

Social Psychology

CHAPTER 10

Social Relations

WARMUP QUESTIONS

This unit contains three readings in social psychology, a discipline that falls somewhere between sociology and psychology. While psychology studies the individual, and sociology studies the group or society, social psychology is primarily concerned with the interaction between these two: the influence of society on the behavior, intellect, and emotions of the individual.

Some of the questions that concern social psychologists are very difficult to answer. What is the source and nature of *altruism*, the desire of human beings to make sacrifices in order to help other human beings? How far will people go in obedience to a higher authority? What is the cause of hatred and violence between different nationalities and racial groups? To what extent are people's actions influenced by the opinions of others?

Before you begin this unit, read the following situations carefully. Make detailed notes about how you might think, feel, and act in each situation. (You will be asked to refer to your notes later in the unit.) Then discuss each situation with your classmates.

Some of these situations might seem strange or impossible. In order for this exercise to be successful, however, you must imagine that the situation is real and is happening to you. Also, you must try to be as honest as possible in your responses.

SITUATION ONE:

You are visiting a foreign country. It is late at night, and you are walking alone on a dark street. You see someone from your country being beaten and robbed by two large men with guns. What will you do?

SITUATION TWO:

You are riding on a crowded bus just after lunchtime in your city. Passing a busy corner, you see an old man being beaten and robbed by two teen-age boys. What will you do?

Social Psychology

SITUATION THREE:

You live in an apartment building with very thin walls. A husband and wife from Country B live next door. You are from Country A, and Countries A and B have a history of war and border disputes that goes back almost four hundred years. In general, you do not like people from Country B very much.

One night you hear loud voices arguing in the apartment next door. Then you hear gunshots and a woman screaming. What will you do?

SITUATION FOUR:

You are an inhabitant of the country of Lala. The men and women of the neighboring country, Exene, are more numerous than you. They have more money and superior weapons.

One summer just before the harvest, soldiers from Exene come and take your rich farmland and the home where your family has lived for hundreds of years. They force you and many others in your country to live in a camp in the barren hills.

Make a list of adjectives that describe the inhabitants of Exene.

SITUATION FIVE:

You are an inhabitant of the country of Exene. The neighboring country, Lala, has rich farmland. Few people live there, and the country does not seem to be very developed culturally. As a soldier in the Exene army, you help your country move the people of Lala to a new settlement in the foothills of the mountains. As a reward, your government gives you a large farm in Lala.

Make a list of adjectives that describe the inhabitants of Lala.

SITUATION SIX:

It is late at night. You are walking alone in a section of your city where many guest-workers live. Most of these guest-workers are from countries much poorer than yours; they are not well liked by the people of your country, but they work for very low pay and often do jobs no one else will do. Guest-workers can be easily recognized by the style of their clothes.

Suddenly, in a doorway across the street, you see two teen-age boys threatening a woman with sticks. The boys are from your country, but the woman is obviously a guest-worker.

Describe your feelings and actions in this situation.

PREVIEWING

1. Quickly look through the reading in this chapter, an excerpt from the textbook *Psychology: An Introduction*.

    How many paragraphs does the main part of the reading contain? (Do not count the section that begins with the title "The Trouble at Robbers Cave.") _____

    How many paragraphs does the section called "The Trouble at Robbers Cave" contain? _____

    How many pages long is the entire reading? _____

2. Look quickly at the section called "The Trouble at Robbers Cave." Note that it has been placed in a box to separate it from the rest of the reading.

    Now look quickly at paragraphs 27 and 28 in the main part of the reading, and answer this question.

Social Relations

177

What is the purpose of "The Trouble at Robbers Cave"? (Circle all that apply.)
- **a.** It gives an expanded definition of an idea in the chapter.
- **b.** It gives a long example to support and develop an idea in the main part of the chapter.
- **c.** It explains an idea that is not explained in the chapter, but is related to it.
- **d.** It describes and discusses the results of a research project.

3. Before you read this selection, try to get an idea of how it is organized. You can identify the major topics by looking at the bold section titles within the text. Ignoring the section "The Trouble at Robbers Cave" for a moment, list the three major topics in this selection and the paragraphs that each one includes.

    Introduction _____ (paragraphs 1 – 2)
    _____ (paragraphs ___ – ___)
    _____ (paragraphs ___ – ___)
    _____ (paragraphs ___ – ___)

4. Which of the sections listed in question 3 contain subtopics or subheadings? List these subtopics. (Continue to disregard "The Trouble at Robbers Cave" for a moment.)

    _____
    _____
    _____
    _____
    _____

5. Now take a quick look at the organization of "The Trouble at Robbers Cave." As you can see, this section of the reading is divided into three parts. List the title of each part, and the paragraphs it includes.

    _____ (paragraphs ___ – ___)
    _____ (paragraphs ___ – ___)
    _____ (paragraphs ___ – ___)

6. Some of the words and phrases you listed in questions 3 and 4 may be familiar to you, and some may be unfamiliar. Discuss the meanings of these words and phrases with your classmates.

    Known   *Unknown*

    _____   _____
    _____   _____
    _____   _____
    _____   _____

DIRECTIONS FOR READING

The reading for this chapter comes from the textbook *Psychology: An Introduction* by Arno F. Wittig and Gurney Williams III. The text is used by college students in introductory psychology courses.

The previewing section you just completed gave you an overview of the reading's content and organization. You are now ready to read it carefully.

The selection has been divided into three parts. You will read each section quickly for general understanding and then examine each part more closely as you complete the study questions.

Social Relations

Arno F. Wittig and Gurney Williams III

1. The themes are old. Storytellers, poets, philosophers, and artists have tried for millennia to illuminate characteristics of human interactions, from loving and helping to hating and attacking. Only recently have psychologists joined in the attempt. Yet psychological studies over the last forty years have added substantially to knowledge about social relations.

2. Previous sections introduced important background for understanding these studies. In this final section, we illustrate attitudes in action. We sketch some of the findings of social psychology about helping, prejudice, aggressiveness, and loving—time-honored themes of art and literature newly interpreted by modern research.

ALTRUISM

3. In an ancient Biblical story, several travelers ignored the anguished cries of an injured man by the side of the road. Finally, a "lowly" Samaritan stopped to help. The parable is an old and venerated account of *altruism*, an unselfish attitude placing the welfare of others above one's own self-interest.

4. The parable is played out in the streets and alleys of cities today, where people offer aid to victims of accidents and crime, sometimes risking their own lives. But the ending to such modern accounts of emergencies is not always satisfying. Sometimes, it seems, there are many bystanders, but few samaritans.

5. Social psychologists often point to one case involving a young woman in Queens, New York. Kitty Genovese was on her way home at 3 A.M. when she was attacked and murdered. She fought hard for her life, screaming loudly enough to draw dozens of her neighbors to their windows. Yet no one helped her. In the course of half an hour as she continued to repel her attacker, no one even called the police. Investigators later discovered that at least thirty-eight persons had been aware of her struggle.

6. What did they perceive and think? In general, what determines whether witnesses will help? Why? The Genovese murder helped stimulate dozens of studies in the 1960s and 1970s to seek answers to these questions. One major finding is that social influence, discussed in the previous section, sharply affects bystanders' behaviors. No matter how shocking or demanding the situation, people are acutely sensitive to the reactions—and mere presence—of others.

The Challenge of a Crisis

7. In the wake of the murder, newspaper editorials and commentaries invoked long-respected social norms requiring people to offer help to others. Many Americans—probably including Kitty Genovese's neighbors—are taught from childhood to "Love thy neighbor," or at least to help a neighbor in distress. But no one can be taught specific techniques for dealing with every emergency. Researchers Bibb Latané and John M. Darley (1969), who did some of the most

famous research on bystander behavior, have pointed out that emergencies are rare, providing little opportunity for experience in coping with them. Each crisis is different. And there is little useful folk wisdom about what to do.

8   Seldom do bystanders anticipate any reward for offering help. Many are afraid of being sued if they make a mistake during intervention, or physically hurt if they challenge an attacker. Under these circumstances, Latané and Darley wrote, "It is perhaps surprising that anyone should intervene at all" (p. 247).

When Do Bystanders Intervene?

9   In another study, Latané and Darley (1970) outlined a theory suggesting that witnesses to an incident such as the murder of Kitty Genovese have to fulfill four conditions before they intervene. . . . They have to *notice the event*. They have to *interpret it as an emergency* and *feel personally responsible for dealing with it*. Finally, they have to *have the skills and resources to act*.

10   But climbing this "decision tree" is not easy. The crisis itself is fraught with dangers, outlined above. In addition, the presence of other people, researchers theorized, complicates the situation.

11   For one thing, the witness in the window risks embarrassment by intervening in situations that turn out not to be emergencies. The bystander thinks, "Suppose it's just a quarrel. What if the people fighting down there on the street get mad at me for not minding my own business?" As a result of such thoughts, bystanders hesitate to help, a phenomenon that Latané and Darley call *audience inhibition*.

12   Another reason people hold back in the presence of others is the same kind of social influence Solomon Asch discovered in his experiments at Yale. "Others aren't rushing to help," the bystander notices, "so maybe there really isn't cause for alarm." Conformity prevents action.

13   Finally, in theory, the presence of others makes it possible for witnesses to diffuse responsibility. "The emergency isn't on just my shoulders," the murder witness rationalizes. "They're as much responsible for not getting involved as I am."

14   This theory leads to a surprising prediction: that the more bystanders there are at the site of an emergency, the less likely any individual witness is to give aid. In other words, a lone bystander is more likely to become a samaritan than a member of a crowd or group. The theory suggests that people do not find "safety in numbers," encouraging them to intervene.

15   The theory has been tested repeatedly. In a survey of some four dozen published and unpublished studies involving almost 6000 subjects, Latané and Steve Nida (1981) found overwhelming confirmation of the basic prediction. "Overall, about 75 percent of people tested alone helped, but fewer than 53 percent of those tested with others did so" (p. 321). The data suggest strongly that the more potential helpers there are, the less likely the victim is to get help.

FACTORS CONTRIBUTING TO ALTRUISM

16   Some studies have uncovered exceptions to the conclusion that being in a group tends to inhibit helping. The inhibition is weaker in children under 9 years (Staub, 1970) or when other witnesses to an emergency are seen as less able to give aid (Bickman, 1971; Ross & Braband, 1973). Some studies indicate people are more likely to help when other members of a group or crowd express beliefs about the seriousness of the emergency, or the need to get involved (Darley et al., 1973).

17   One interesting study—typical in its methodology—explored whether the victim's race affected the likelihood of getting help. This chapter opened with a description of this experimental situation. In the midst of a staged experiment allegedly testing ESP, "Brenda" screamed over an intercom when a stack of chairs apparently fell on her. Experimenters Gaertner and Dovidio (1977) observed how subjects, who were white, responded.

18   Before experimental trials began, subjects saw a picture identification card for Brenda. They were asked to make sure they did not know her. Some subjects were shown one card, on which Brenda was black; others were shown a different card, on which she was white. Among other conditions, the researchers led some subjects to think they were alone in working with Brenda. Other subjects thought they were part of a group.

19   Brenda's tape-recorded "crisis" was always the same. The intercom carried the alarming sound of crashing chairs and Brenda's cry "They're falling on me!" Despite the similarities, subjects' reactions differed widely. To begin with, more than nine out of ten lone subjects rose to help Brenda when they thought she was black—a slightly higher percentage, in fact, than tried to aid a white Brenda. There was certainly no evidence of racial discrimination in these responses from subjects who thought they were Brenda's only hope for help.

20   Consistent with findings you have encountered above, subjects were less likely to help when they thought other subjects were present. Still, three out of four subjects tried to aid Brenda when they thought she was white. In the most striking finding of the study, the percentage of people willing to help was lowest by far when subjects thought Brenda was black and when they thought they were *not* alone in hearing her screams. Only a few more than a third of the subjects (37.5 percent) offered aid under these conditions. The results suggest that the race of the victim can magnify the effect of the mere presence of others.

21   Why? Gaertner and Dovidio offer one explanation based on attribution processes, described in the previous chapter. They suggest that in the decade following the great civil rights campaigns of the 1960s, white Americans in general tried to avoid attributing their own behavior to bigotry. They tried to maintain at least the appearance of fairness. Yet racist attitudes had not been eradicated in the 1970s. And racism showed itself in this experiment. When whites were able to diffuse responsibility to others, they were able to avoid attributing bigotry to themselves. They were able to discriminate. In the authors' words, the results suggest the "subtlety of white racism" in the 1970s. We elaborate on the complex, "subtle" pattern of prejudice in the next section.

PREJUDICE AND DISCRIMINATION

22   In the aftermath of the surprise bombing attack on Pearl Harbor, President Franklin D. Roosevelt issued orders that effectively drew lines around military installations and defense plants. Any Japanese aliens or Japanese-Americans could be moved out of the designated areas. During 1942, more than 120,000 people were forced to move to "relocation centers," where they lived in barracks covered with black tarpaper. . . . At least initially, the orders did not allow for the possibility that many of those forced to move were loyal Americans. But by the beginning of 1945, from a quarter to a third of the evacuees had been allowed to start homes elsewhere, or to serve in the armed forces.

23   These unfortunate people were victims of *prejudice*, a negative attitude comprising beliefs, feelings, and behavioral tendencies toward them solely because of their membership in a group. Prejudicial beliefs are often called *stereotypes*, inflexible conceptions that organize information about others

much the way that schemata . . . provide a framework for knowledge. ("Stereotype" comes from Greek words meaning "solid impression.")

24 Prejudicial feelings generally are negative. And the combination of stereotypical thinking and negative feelings often leads to openly harmful behaviors, such as uprooting people from their homes, or preventing them from living where they choose. Such negative behaviors are called *discrimination*. ([According to] the concept of discrimination, or differentiation, . . . people respond differentially depending on the presence or absence of some stimulus characteristic such as race or ethnic origin.)

25 The relocation camps of World War II provided clear evidence of prejudice, stereotyping, and discrimination. Some four decades after the war, many instances of negative attitudes and actions against people in minority groups were far less easy to discern. The example of the "subtlety of white racism," exhibited in the Gaertner and Dovidio experiment, suggests that people sometimes mask negatively hateful attitudes or beliefs that their own racial stock is superior.

26 Other observers have noticed changing patterns of prejudice. For example, according to psychologist Kenneth B. Clark, professor emeritus of psychology at the City University of New York, the 1970s were marked by a fundamental shift in the battlegrounds where the struggles for equal rights were waged. The change began, Clark wrote, after passage of major antidiscrimination legislation in the 1960s:

> In the early 1970s, the center of gravity of the civil rights movement began to move from southern states to northern cities. The resistance to further racial progress changed from the more flagrant forms of southern racism to the more complex, subtle, and deep-seated racism of the North. (*The New York Times*, May 18, 1982, p. A23).

27 What are the roots of prejudice? What factors bring hidden prejudice out into the open? . . . "The Trouble at Robbers Cave" [see the accompanying box] introduces one classic study exploring these questions.

Hidden Prejudice in the 1980s

28 Despite the isolated setting for Sherif's field study, and despite the fact that the twenty-two subjects were only about 11 years old, the situation outlined in . . . "The Trouble at Robbers Cave" is familiar and contemporary. In the early years of the 1980s, some residents of Florida found themselves caught in competition with Haitian and Cuban refugees for scarce jobs. . . . Members of minority groups still struggle to find adequate, affordable housing despite laws prohibiting discrimination. Some schools are still separate and unequal despite a long-standing Supreme Court ruling (handed down the same year, 1954, that Sherif conducted his experiment) aimed at ending discrimination in education. Each of these examples reflects competition between groups over limited employment opportunities, housing and educational resources.

29 But by the 1980s, some norms governing relations between the races had changed. It had become unfashionable in many circles of American society to express prejudice openly. Some studies suggested that new norms had developed, requiring belief in the equality of the races (Taylor et al., 1978). And some research indicated that at least some whites were likely to "bend over backwards" to avoid discriminating against blacks. For example, white subjects are more likely to be aggressive toward other whites than toward blacks, one

THE TROUBLE AT ROBBERS CAVE

Background

1   Robbers Cave State Park, southeast of Oklahoma City, provides woody, pastoral ground, perfect for pleasant camping. In a famous experiment in the mid-1950s, social psychologists led by Muzafer Sherif (Sherif & Sherif, 1956) deliberately turned the site into a kind of battleground, sowing prejudice and hostile behavior in the subjects.

2   Chapter 11 reports a similar study by Sherif, showing how frustration sometimes produces anger. The Robbers Cave experiment went beyond that research, revealing not only some of the conditions spawning stereotypes and hatred, but also suggesting ways to make prejudice dissolve.

The Research

3   Sherif's experiment comprised three stages: forming two groups, setting them at odds with each other, and then healing the friction between them. The first stage required just a week. Two sets of boys arrived at the site in separate buses, each initially unaware of the other's presence. For several days, each bunch worked together on moderately challenging tasks such as carting a canoe to a swimming hole and making dinner. By the end of the week, the sets had become groups. They had named themselves, respectively, Rattlers and Eagles. In the final days of group building, the boys learned there were others camping in the same park.

4   Sherif had planned to produce a series of frustrating situations to stimulate intergroup rivalry. But the plan proved unnecessary. In the first day of contact between the two groups, the Eagles defeated the Rattlers in a tug-of-war contest. The losers burned the winner's flag—a provocation that bred scuffling and shouting in the days that followed. Experimenters did nothing to heighten ill feelings. Nor did they try to suppress them. By the end of six more days, Rattlers and Eagles were arch-enemies.

5   At that point, Sherif tried two different techniques to break down the walls separating the two groups of similar boys. The first involved promoting social contact in pleasant situations. Groups ate together, watched movies together, and shot off firecrackers in the same area. The second technique was to challenge both groups together to solve a problem affectng Rattlers and Eagles alike. For example, on an outing, a truck failed to start just as it was due to go pick up food for both groups. (Unknown to campers, Sherif had planned the engine failure.)

Conclusions and Remaining Questions

6   Sherif found that after a week of intergroup rivalry and frustration, members of both groups were highly likely to rate fellow members favorably, members of opposing groups unfavorably. In a written test, subjects connected adjectives such as "brave," "friendly," and "tough" with others in the same group. And boys tended to associate other words like "sneaky," "smart alecks," and "stinkers" with members of the other group. Ratings by Rattlers of Eagles were 53 percent unfavorable. Ratings by Eagles of Rattlers were 77 percent unfavorable. These stereotyped views swayed the campers' perceptions. Boys tended to overestimate accomplishments of their own group, and underestimate achievements of their "opponents."

7   Could these stereotypes be eliminated? The answer depended on the technique used. Sherif drew several conclusions. Among them were: (1) Mere contact between groups did not reduce friction, even when the groups were engaged—side by side—in pleasant activities. Mealtime, for example, turned into another battleground as campers hurled mashed potatoes, leftovers, and insults at each other. (2) Competing groups, when faced by important goals that can only be achieved by cooperation, will tend to work together. This cooperation, called into play in a series of situations, will tend to reduce tension. Perhaps the most striking incident occurred when both groups faced the problem of the broken-down truck. With no hesitation, boys in both groups picked up tug-of-war ropes they had used a short time before to compete. They tied rope to the truck and pulled together to get it started. Near the end of the experiment, both groups shared in a campfire party, and left together on the same bus.

8   In sum, the trouble Sherif created at Robbers Cave appeared to contribute to the formation of stereotypes. But these hardened views of other people tended to diminish in the course of a series of cooperative efforts made by both groups toward meeting mutual needs.

9   What lessons can society learn from the Robbers Cave experiment? How can the central finding that prejudice declines when groups work together be employed to reduce prejudice in society at large? From the perspective of a learning theorist, what reinforcement is there in continuing to hate "outsiders" even when competition is no longer necessary? How could a modern researcher replicate Sherif's findings with an experiment conforming with current ethical standards?

study indicated (Griffin & Rogers, 1977). This tendency to give special treatment to members of minority groups is sometimes called *reverse discrimination*.

30 But research from the early 1980s indicates that there are limits to the good will leading to reverse discrimination. One interesting study by Ronald W. Rogers and Steven Prentice-Dunn of the University of Alabama (1981) revealed how racism—tightly controlled by norms in some groups—can emerge under certain conditions.

31 In a laboratory setting, individual subjects faced a "shock generator" comparable to the apparatus Stanley Milgram used in his research on obedience. This generator had ten switches, each supposedly producing a different jolt. Experimenters told subjects to monitor the heartrate of another subject in a separate room by watching a signal light. Whenever the rate fell below a certain level, subjects were to administer a shock to bring the level back up. The experiment was billed as an investigation of biofeedback. Actually, it was a study of racism. The shock apparatus was phony, and the person on the receiving end of the apparatus was a confederate.

32 In different trials, researchers used different confederates, some white and some black. All subjects were white. A further variable was that the confederate acted pleasantly toward some subjects and toward others with hostility. Under one set of conditions, subjects could hear the confederate wondering whether people as dumb as the subjects appeared could follow instructions properly. When asked if he knew the subjects, the insulting confederate said that he knew their *type*—they thought they were "hot stuff," he grumbled. Other confederates simply voiced no objections to procedures or subjects.

33 What effect did insults have on subjects' behaviors? Researchers reported virtually no effects—when confederates were white. And, when white subjects were not insulted, they were somewhat easier on black confederates than white confederates in terms of length and intensity of "shocks" delivered. But when white subjects were insulted, they were much harder on black confederates. The study indicates that as recently as the late 1970s, some Americans were two-faced about interracial encounters, "one face looking forward but the other face focusing grimly on the past" (Rogers & Prentice-Dunn, 1981, p. 71).

34 In this section, we have traced several faces of prejudice, ranging from open expressions of hostility toward the Japanese in World War II to the subtle kinds of racism discovered within the last few years. We have looked at studies suggesting some of the conditions leading to prejudice and discrimination. Results are discouraging in that they suggest that prejudice still exists. But the research is encouraging in showing that norms can change, that stereotyped thinking—hardened attitudes toward others—can soften. The basic finding that learning can lead to prejudice suggests that learning can help lessen it.

REFERENCES

Bickman, L. (1971). The effect of another bystander's ability to help on bystander intervention in an emergency. *Journal of Experimental Social Psychology 1*, 367–379.

Darley, J. M., Teger, A. L., and Lewis, L. D. (1973). Do groups always inhibit individuals' responses to potential emergencies? *Journal of Personality and Social Psychology 26*, 395–399.

Gaertner, S. L., and Dovidio, J. F. (1977). The subtety of white racism, arousal, and helping behavior. *Journal of Personality and Social Psychology 35*, 691–707.

Griffin, B. Q., and Rogers, R. W. (1977). Reducing inter-racial aggression: inhibiting effects of victims' suffering and power to retaliate. *Journal of Psychology 95*, 151–157.

Latane, B., and Darley, J. M. (1969). Bystander apathy. *American Scientist 57*, 244–268.

Latane, B., and Darley, J. M. (1970). *The unresponsive bystander: Why doesn't he help?* New York: Appleton-Century-Crofts.

Latane, B., and Nida, S. (1981). Ten years of research on group size and helping. *Psychological Bulletin 89*, 308–324.

Rogers, R. W., and Prentice-Dunn, S. (1981). Deindividuation and anger-mediated interracial aggression: unmasking regressive racism. *Journal of Personality and Social Psychology 41*, 63–73.

Ross, A. J., and Braband, J. (1973). Effect of increased responsibility on bystander intervention: II. The cue value of a blind person. *Journal of Personality and Social Psychology 25*, 254–258.

Staub, E. (1970). A child in distress: The influence of age and number of witnesses on children's attempts to help. *Journal of Personality and Social Psychology 14*, 130–140.

Sherif, M., and Sherif, C. W. (1956). *An outline of social psychology* (rev. ed.). New York: Harper & Row.

Taylor, D. G., Sheetsly, P. B., and Greely, A. M. (1978). Attitudes toward racial integration. *Scientific American*, June, *238*, 6, 42–49.

Social Relations

187

PART 1: STUDY QUESTIONS
(Paragraphs 1–15)

Directions: Read paragraphs 1–15 quickly for general understanding. Then refer to the selection to answer the following study questions.

1. Before you begin reading in detail, you should get an idea of the general organization of this section.
   A. Fill in the blanks in this paragraph.

      Paragraphs _____ contain the introduction to this reading. The section on altruism extends from paragraph _____ to paragraph _____.

   B. The section on altruism contains two subheadings. List the subheadings, and indicate which paragraphs fall under each one.

Subheading	Paragraphs
_____	_____
_____	_____

   C. Which paragraphs in this section discuss "samaritans"? _____
   D. Which paragraphs mention the Kitty Genovese murder? _____

2. Paragraphs 1 and 2 provide an introduction to the reading. Look carefully at paragraph 1.
   A. According to paragraph 1, what is the connection between ancient stories and modern psychological research?
      _____

   B. Paragraph 1 identifies the general category of the themes mentioned in the first sentence and gives two pairs of specific examples. Fill in the following blanks with this information.

      General theme: _____
      Specific examples:
      _____ and _____
      _____ and _____

   C. What is the meaning of the word *yet* in sentence 4?
      a. Sentence 4 is the opposite of sentence 3.
      b. Sentence 4 is the explanation for sentence 3.
      c. Sentence 4 is an unexpected result of sentence 3.
      d. Sentence 4 is a logical conclusion from sentence 3.

3. Look again at paragraph 2.
   A. This reading is the concluding section of a long chapter in *Psychology: An Introduction*. What important functions does paragraph 2 perform in the chapter from which this reading is taken? (Circle all that apply.)
      a. It gives new information.
      b. It explains previous information.
      c. It reminds the reader about previous information.
      d. It identifies the topic of the rest of the reading.

Social Psychology

188

    B. Look at the last sentence. What will this reading be about?
        a. time-honored themes of art and literature
        b. new interpretations by modern research

4. Read paragraphs 3 and 4 carefully.
   A. The purpose of the Bible story in paragraph 3 is to give an example of _____ _____.

      Ask a classmate who knows the tale of the Samaritan to relate the full story as he or she remembers it.

   B. Underline the definition of *altruism* in paragraph 3. Then give an example of altruism from your own culture or your own experience.

_____

_____

_____

   C. Note how the word *parable* is used in paragraphs 3 and 4, and infer its meaning.
     a. good person
     b. story
     c. theme

   D. What is the meaning of *bystanders* in the last sentence of paragraph 4?
     a. one who acts
     b. one who observes
     c. one who analyzes

5. Read paragraph 5.
   A. What is the relationship between paragraphs 4 and 5?
     a. Old story—Modern research
     b. General idea—Specific example
     c. One point of view—Opposite point of view
     d. General category—Division of category into parts

   B. Why do you think that no one called the police or tried to help Kitty Genovese? What would you have done in that situation?

_____

_____

_____

   C. To make sure you have all the important facts in the case, fill in the following blanks.

    Place: _____

    Time: _____

    Length of time of attack: _____

    Number of people who heard Kitty Genovese's cries: _____

6. Look carefully at paragraph 6.
   A. What is the main idea of this paragraph?
     a. The Genovese murder caused people to ask questions.

Social Relations

189

        b. Studies in the 1960s and 1970s sought to answer people's questions about the Genovese murder.
        c. Social influence can affect people's behavior.
    B. What is another word for *finding* in sentence 5?
        a. study
        b. opinion
        c. conclusion
        d. proof
        e. locating
    C. What is the relationship between the last two sentences in this paragraph?
        a. Idea—Restatement of idea
        b. General idea—Specific example
        c. Specific idea—General conclusion

7. Carefully read paragraphs 7 and 8, which describe the research of Latané and Darley (1969).
    A. What is the main idea of paragraph 7?
        a. Many Americans are taught to "love their neighbors."
        b. Techniques for dealing with every possible emergency cannot be taught.
        c. Latané and Darley did some of the most famous research on bystander behavior.
    B. Paragraph 8 lists three findings of the 1969 Latané and Darley study. In your own words, list the three findings.

        _____

        _____

    C. Do these research results help to explain what happened in the Kitty Genovese case? If so, in what way?

        _____

        _____

    D. Which of these sentences best expresses the main idea of paragraph 8?
        a. Because of the reasons given in paragraphs 7 and 8, it is not surprising that people do not help others in distress.
        b. Latané and Darley thought it was surprising that more people did not help Kitty Genovese.
        c. Latané and Darley were surprised by the results of their study.
    E. Look up the definition of the verb *sue* in the dictionary if you are not sure of its meaning. Then try to think of a situation in which a person might sue someone who tried to help.

        _____

        _____

8. Read paragraphs 9 and 10.
    A. What are the four conditions for bystander intervention listed in paragraph 9? Use your own words if possible.
        a. _____
        b. _____

c. _____

d. _____

B. Paragraph 10 refers to "climbing the decision tree." What do you think this means? (In other words, what is the relationship among the four conditions you listed in the previous question?)

C. In the second sentence in paragraph 10, what does "fraught with dangers" mean?
   a. involves danger
   b. does not involve danger
   c. protects from danger

9. Carefully read paragraphs 11–13. Pay close attention to the transition words at the beginning of each paragraph.
   A. What is the relationship between paragraph 11 and the last sentence in paragraph 10?
      a. General idea–Specific example
      b. One point of view–Opposite point of view
      c. General classification–Division into parts
      d. Researcher's opinion–Reason for researcher's opinion
   B. Look at the transition words at the beginning of paragraphs 11, 12, and 13. Which phrase means about the same as "for one thing" at the beginning of paragraph 11?
      a. the first type or kind
      b. the first reason
      c. one part
      d. the most important explanation
   C. What term is given for the idea described in paragraph 11?

   D. If you are not sure of the meaning of *inhibition*, look the word up in the dictionary. Then give two or three additional examples of inhibitions that prevent people from doing certain things in public.

   E. Summarize the reason for not intervening given in paragraph 11, using no more than fifteen words. Include the word *privacy* in your summary.

   F. Which of the following words best sums up the reason for bystander apathy given in paragraph 12?
      a. presence
      b. alarm
      c. conformity
   G. Give examples from a culture or society with which you are familiar of how conformity can influence social behavior. (For a description of the experiments conducted by Solomon Asch, see the reading in Chapter 12.)

H. Paragraph 13 describes the final reason for a lack of action on the part of witnesses. The first sentence of paragraph 13 says that witnesses can "diffuse responsibility." This means that witnesses can
   a. accept responsibility.
   b. understand responsibility.
   c. transfer responsibility to others.
   d. act on their responsibility.
I. Look at the phrase "on my shoulders" in the second sentence of paragraph 13. If something is "on your shoulders," you are
   a. tired.
   b. diffuse.
   c. responsible.
   d. rational.
   e. not involved.

10. Carefully reread paragraphs 14 and 15.
   A. You and your friend are walking down a street and see someone being robbed. According to paragraph 14, which of the following is true?
      a. You will be more likely to help if there are other people on the street.
      b. You will be less likely to help if there are other people on the street.
   B. The last sentence in paragraph 14 refers to "safety in numbers." This phrase comes from a proverb in English that says, "There is safety in numbers." Explain the meaning of this proverb, and compare it to other, similar proverbs you have heard. (Hint: *Numbers* refers to numbers of people.)

   _____
   _____

   C. What is the main idea of the last sentence in paragraph 14?
      a. "Safety in numbers" helps people to assist the victim of a crime.
      b. "Safety in numbers" does not help people to assist the victim of a crime.
   D. The purpose of paragraph 15 is to present
      a. theory.
      b. prediction.
      c. proof.
   E. To make sure you have all the important information from paragraph 15, fill in the following blanks.

   Date of study: _____

   Authors: _____

   Theory: _____

   Number of subjects: _____

   Percentage of people tested alone who helped: _____

   Percentage of people tested with others who helped: _____

   Conclusion: _____
   _____

Social Psychology

192

PART 1: COMPREHENSION EXERCISES
(Paragraphs 1–15)

Exercise 1

The following statements are either *true* or *false* according to paragraphs 1–15 of the reading. Write *T* or *F* in the space next to each one.

1. _____ Most of the advances in the psychology of social relations have come in the last ten years.
2. _____ In the cities of today, it is common for people to offer aid to the victims of accidents and crime.
3. _____ After the Kitty Genovese murder, many newspapers and magazines printed articles saying that people should help each other.
4. _____ Social influence plays only a small part in the behavior of bystanders.
5. _____ People have little experience with, or knowledge about, what to do in a true emergency.
6. _____ Research shows that it is possible for someone to have the desire to help another person, but not the skill or ability to do so.
7. _____ *Audience inhibition* is defined as people's hesitation to help because they fear embarrassment if they intervene in the personal business of others.
8. _____ The larger the group of people who witness a crime or emergency, the greater the possibility that someone will offer assistance.
9. _____ The need for conformity can prevent people from acting in an emergency.

Exercise 2

Complete the following summary of paragraphs 1–15 by filling in each blank with an appropriate word or phrase.

Social _____ have been the subject of poems, stories, and songs from the beginning of _____. Psychologists have been _____ this topic for only the last _____ years or so, but they have already learned a great deal in this area.

One of the early stories of _____ was the Bible story of the good Samaritan, who was the only person to _____ an injured man by the side of the road. Unfortunately, in modern cities, not many of the _____ who witness an accident or a _____ are willing to help.

One example is the case of _____. She was attacked for more than _____ before she was finally killed. At least thirty-eight people heard her _____ for help, but no one came to her aid.

Many studies in the 1960s and 1970s tried to explain this _____. Some of the studies found that people did not have the _____ or experience to deal with true emergencies. Also, people are influenced by the fear of invading another's _____, by the social _____ of others (that is, conformity), and by the ability to share _____ for not getting involved with others.

The surprising _____ that emerged from these studies was that the _____ people are present, the _____ likely they are to intervene.

PART 2: STUDY QUESTIONS
(Paragraphs 16–21)

Directions: Read paragraphs 16–21 quickly for general understanding. Then refer to the selection to answer the following study questions.

1. After an introductory paragraph (paragraph 16), most of this section describes a single experiment. Answer these questions about the overall organization of paragraphs 16–21.
   A. Who were the researchers, and what was the date of the experiment described in detail in this section?
   _____

   B. The description of this research is divided into several parts: the research question (i.e., the purpose of the research), a description of the methods used, a description of the results, and a discussion of the results. Give the paragraph numbers that correspond to each of these parts.

   Purpose: paragraph(s) _____
   Methods: paragraph(s) _____
   Results: paragraph(s) _____
   Discussion: paragraph(s) _____

2. Look carefully at paragraph 16.
   A. Paragraph 16 contains one-sentence summaries of several research papers. What is the main idea of these studies?
      a. The presence of others does not always prevent bystanders from helping.
      b. Children under 9 years will help more often than older people.
      c. If the others present seem powerless, the bystander is more likely to help.
      d. The bystander is more likely to help if other bystanders say something about the seriousness of the problem.
   B. Match each of the following studies with its main idea. You may use the same letter more than once.

   _____ Darley et al. (1973)

   _____ Bickman (1971)

   _____ Staub (1970)

   _____ Ross and Braband (1973)

   _____ Gaertner and Dovidio (1977)

      a. The presence of others does not always prevent bystanders from helping.
      b. Children under 9 years will help more often than older people.
      c. If the others present seem powerless, the bystander is more likely to help.

Social Psychology

194

   d. The bystander is more likely to help if other bystanders say something about the seriousness of the problem.
   e. None of the above.

3. Carefully reread the description of the "Brenda" experiment in paragraphs 17, 18, and 19.
   A. According to paragraph 17, what was Gaertner and Dovidio's research question or hypothesis? In other words, what were they trying to prove or disprove?

   _____
   _____

   B. If the researchers wanted to find out about racial discrimination, why didn't they just show all the subjects a picture in which Brenda was black? (Answer this from your own knowledge.)

   _____
   _____

   C. Why did the researchers tell some subjects that they were alone and others that they were part of a group?

   _____
   _____

   D. The tape recording of chairs falling and Brenda's cry was always the same. Why was this important?

   _____
   _____

   E. Answer the following questions to make sure you have all the important information about the study from paragraph 19.
   What group of subjects is described in this paragraph?

   _____

   In general, what was the reaction of this group?

   _____

   What percentage of the group reacted in this way?

   _____

   What did the researchers conclude about these results?

   _____

4. Now reread paragraphs 20 and 21, which continue the description of the "Brenda" experiment.
   A. Answer the following questions to make sure you have all the important information about the study from paragraph 20.
   What group of subjects is described in this paragraph?

   _____

   What was the reaction of this group when they thought Brenda was white?

   _____

   What percentage of the group reacted in this way?

   _____

Social Relations

195

What was the reaction of this group when they thought Brenda was black?

What percentage of the group reacted in this way?

What did the researchers conclude about these results?

B. At the beginning of paragraph 21, to what do the words *why* and *one explanation* refer? In other words, what information is being questioned, and what information is being explained?

C. Read paragraph 21 again carefully, making sure that you understand the meaning of the words *bigotry* and *racism*. Now read the following two definitions of *discriminate* (the word is found in paragraph 21, sentence 8), and choose the one that is the most appropriate in the context of this paragraph.
   a. to see the difference (*between* things); distinguish
   b. to make distinctions in treatment; show partiality (in *favor* of) or prejudice (*against*)

D. According to paragraph 21, what was the attitude of white Americans in the 1960s?
   a. They were successful in avoiding bigotry.
   b. They were involved in the civil rights movement.
   c. They did not want others to think they were prejudiced.
   d. They attributed racist behavior to a lack of fairness.

E. According to the authors, most of the subjects who thought they were alone did not show racist attitudes, but many of the subjects who thought that there were others to help "Brenda" did show signs of racism. According to paragraph 21, what is the reason for this?

F. Do you agree or disagree with the authors' analysis of the results, described in question E? Give the reasons for your answer.

G. Sentences 9 and 10 in paragraph 21 describe racism and prejudice as "subtle." Since this is not a word usually used to describe prejudice, answer the following questions.
Use your dictionary to find one or more words that mean the opposite of *subtle*.

Explain how you think it is possible for prejudice or bigotry to be subtle.

Social Psychology

196

PART 2: COMPREHENSION EXERCISES
(Paragraphs 16–21)

Exercise 1

The following statements are either *true* or *false* according to paragraphs 16–21 of the reading. Write T or F in the space next to each one.

1. _____ Some studies show that being in a group doesn't make people less likely to give assistance in a crime or emergency.
2. _____ People in a group are more likely to help if they hear other members of the group discussing what should be done.
3. _____ Subjects in the "Brenda" experiment were told that the purpose of the study was to test ESP (extrasensory perception).
4. _____ The real reason subjects were shown a picture of "Brenda" was to make sure that they did not know her.
5. _____ Almost all subjects in the "Brenda" experiment who thought they were alone showed no evidence of racial discrimination.
6. _____ The most surprising result of the study was that three out of four of the subjects who thought others were present tried to help the white "Brenda."
7. _____ The race of the victim can make the effects of having other bystanders present more noticeable.
8. _____ Researchers believe that the presence of others allows subjects to avoid taking personal responsibility for racist attitudes.

Exercise 2

Complete the following summary of paragraphs 16–21 by filling in each blank with an appropriate word or phrase.

Studies during the _____ showed that there were some exceptions to the _____ that being in a group makes bystanders less likely to _____.

One study found that the _____ of the victim had an _____ how people acted when they thought they were part of a _____. The study involved a fake ESP _____ in which subjects heard a tape-recorded _____ involving someone named "Brenda," who was supposedly _____ of the experiment, but in another room. Some subjects thought Brenda was _____, and some thought she was _____; some thought they were part of a _____, and others thought they were _____.

Social Relations

197

The results support the conclusion that people are _____ to help when they think they are _____ of a group. But _____ out of four of the subjects who believed _____ were present tried to help Brenda when they thought she was white; only _____ percent of these subjects tried to help _____ when they thought she was black.

The researchers concluded that the subjects were able to _____ blaming themselves for _____ behavior when others were present. The researchers call this "the _____ of white racism."

PARTS 1 AND 2: COMPREHENSION EXERCISE
(Paragraphs 1–21)

Directions: Look back at the Warmup Questions at the beginning of this unit. Which of the situations described there are related to the ideas discussed in the first two sections of the reading?

_____

Now look at your notes describing your reactions in these situations. Use the new information you have just read to reanalyze your reaction in each case. Discuss your analyses with your classmates.

PART 3: STUDY QUESTIONS
(Paragraphs 22–34)

Directions: Read paragraphs 22–34 and the accompanying boxed material quickly for general understanding. Then refer to the selection to answer the following study questions.

1. Before reading this section in detail, try to get an idea of its organization.
   A. Look at paragraphs 22–34. Match each of the following topics with the appropriate paragraph numbers.

   _____ definition of prejudice   a. paragraph 22
   _____ research of Rogers and Prentice-Dunn (1981)   b. paragraphs 23–24
   _____ prejudice during World War II   c. paragraphs 25–27
   _____ prejudice in the 1980s   d. paragraphs 28–29
   _____ prejudice after World War II   e. paragraphs 30–33
   _____ conclusion   f. paragraph 34

   B. Now look at the boxed section entitled "The Trouble at Robbers Cave," and fill in the blanks in the following paragraph.

   This section reports on research conducted by _____ _____ in the year _____. The methods of the researchers are discussed in paragraphs _____, and the results of the research are discussed in paragraphs _____.

Social Psychology

2. Read paragraph 22 of the reading again carefully.
   A. What is the main topic of paragraph 22?
      a. Pearl Harbor
      b. Japanese-Americans
      c. internment centers
      d. loyal Americans
   B. To what does the phrase "the designated areas" refer in sentence 2?

   C. Do you think a "relocation center" was more like a hotel or a prison? Explain your answer.

   D. Which of the following can be concluded from sentences 4 and 5 of paragraph 22?
      a. Some of the people relocated were loyal Americans.
      b. The President's orders applied to everyone who was Japanese or Japanese-American.
      c. By 1945, some of the relocated people were allowed to return to their homes.
      d. A large percentage of Japanese-Americans served in the armed forces in World War II.

3. Read paragraph 23 again carefully.
   A. In the first sentence of paragraph 23, to whom does the phrase "these unfortunate people" refer?

   B. Read carefully the definition of *prejudice* in the first sentence of this paragraph. Then look at the following situations and check the ones that you think are examples of prejudice as it is defined in paragraph 23. Be prepared to discuss your answers.
      _____ Leroy thinks that the students at the high school on the other side of town are probably less intelligent than the students at his high school.
      _____ Mrs. Carpenter will not let her daughter date Jimmy Billings because his father is a garbage collector.
      _____ Ms. Yeager gives Mr. Magma a promotion he does not deserve because she thinks he is an attractive man.
      _____ Julia Juniper thinks that the ideal husband for her will be someone who makes at least $100,000 per year.
      _____ Antonio will not eat any ice cream other than his favorite brand.
      _____ Alan Donovan thinks that the next mayor of his town should be a woman, since women have been ignored in politics for so long.
      _____ Joseph Spinelli, who works in an automobile factory in Flint, Michigan, will buy only products that are made in the United States.
   C. Look at the definition of *stereotype* in the last two sentences of paragraph 23. Then list two stereotypes that others have about your country, and two stereotypes that others have about the United States.
   Stereotypes about your country

   Stereotypes about the United States

Social Relations

199

4. Look carefully at paragraph 24.
   A. The first sentence in paragraph 24 says that prejudicial feelings are generally negative. Give an example of *positive* prejudicial feelings.

   _____

   _____

   Now look back at question 3B. Are any of the situations described there examples of *positive* prejudice?

   _____

   B. What two examples of discrimination are given in this paragraph?

   1. _____

   2. _____

   C. Give two examples of discrimination from your own knowledge or experience.

   1. _____

   2. _____

   D. What is the purpose of the last sentence in paragraph 24?
      a. It gives a definition of discrimination.
      b. It tells what comes next in the reading.
      c. It summarizes the main idea of paragraph 24.

5. Carefully reread paragraph 25.
   A. Which of the following best expresses the main idea of the first two sentences in paragraph 25?
      a. Prejudice has disappeared in the forty years since World War II.
      b. Compared to forty years ago, evidence of prejudice is more difficult to identify today.
      c. The same kind of prejudice that existed during World War II can be found in the United States today.
   B. Summarize the conclusion of the Gaertner and Dovidio experiment (as described in paragraph 25) in your own words.

   _____

   _____

   _____

6. Carefully reread paragraphs 26 and 27.
   A. What main idea is the long quotation in paragraph 26 meant to support?
      a. Current white racism is subtle.
      b. The civil rights movement was of great importance.
      c. Antidiscrimination legislation in the 1960s was of great importance.
   B. What is the relationship between the words *flagrant* and *subtle* in the second sentence of the quotation in paragraph 26?
      a. They have the same meaning.
      b. They are opposite in meaning.
      c. They are similar in meaning, but not exactly the same.
      d. There is no meaningful relationship between these words.

Social Psychology

    C. According to paragraph 27, what is the purpose of the boxed reading entitled "The Trouble at Robbers Cave"?

    _____

    _____

    _____

7. Read paragraphs 1–5 of "The Trouble at Robbers Cave."

    A. According to paragraphs 1 and 2 of "The Trouble at Robbers Cave," the purpose of the study was to
    - a. repeat the results of an earlier experiment.
    - b. show the contrast between pleasant camping and a battleground.
    - c. study the causes of prejudice and possible solutions.
    - d. cause the subjects to hate each other.

    B. According to paragraph 3, what was the purpose of the first stage of the experiment?

    _____

    _____

    C. According to paragraph 4, what caused hostility between the two groups?
    - a. the plans of the researchers
    - b. natural competition between the two groups

    D. Paragraph 5 of "The Trouble at Robbers Cave" identifies two methods by which the experimenters tried to bring the groups together. List the two methods and the examples of each. Use your own words.

    First method: _____

    Examples: _____

    _____

    Second method: _____

    Examples: _____

    _____

8. Carefully read paragraphs 6–9 of "The Trouble at Robbers Cave."

    A. According to paragraph 6, the researchers gave a written test to find out what each group thought about the other. What kinds of information did this test reveal? (Circle all that apply.)
    - a. how the other group should be punished
    - b. what words could be used to describe the other group
    - c. estimates of the intelligence of the other group
    - d. what words could be used to describe their own group
    - e. which activities were their favorite ones
    - f. opinion of the achievements of the other group
    - g. opinion of the adults at the camp
    - h. opinion of the accomplishments of their own group
    - i. attitude toward other races
    - j. seriousness of stereotypes and prejudices

Social Relations

201

    B. Paragraphs 7 and 8 describe
- a. the results of the experiment.
- b. the conclusion of the experimenters.

    C. Below is an outline of paragraph 7 of "The Trouble at Robbers Cave." In the space next to each number or letter in the outline, write the number(s) of the sentence(s) from paragraph 7 that corresponds to that part of the outline. (In other words, the outline is another way of saying that paragraph 7 has an introductory section and two main ideas, and that each of the two main ideas has one supporting idea.)

Outline	Sentences
I.	_____
A.	_____
1.	_____
B.	_____
1.	_____

    D. Do you agree with the experimenters' conclusion that stereotypes or prejudice can "diminish in the course of a series of cooperative efforts made by both groups toward meeting mutual needs"? Explain your answer.

_____

_____

_____

_____

9. Look carefully at paragraph 28.
   - **A.** Which of the following gives the main idea of the first sentence in paragraph 28?
     - a. The results of the Sherif study are familiar and contemporary even though the subjects were young and the setting was isolated.
     - b. Because the subjects were 11 years old and the setting was isolated, it should not be surprising that what happened is familiar in the modern world.
     - c. Even though the subjects were young and the setting was isolated, the results should be interpreted very cautiously.
   - **B.** Sentences 2–4 of paragraph 28 contain
     - a. conclusions of the Sherif study.
     - b. reasons for discrimination in society.
     - c. examples of modern-day competition between groups.
     - d. the three most important aspects of racist behavior.
   - **C.** Explain in your own words the connection between the Sherif study and sentences 2–4 of paragraph 28.

_____

_____

_____

10. Read paragraphs 29 and 30 carefully.
    - **A.** Match each of the following studies with its conclusion, as presented in paragraphs 29 and 30.

    _____ Taylor et al. (1978)

    _____ Griffin and Rogers (1977)

_____ Rogers and Prentice-Dunn (1981)
- a. White persons were less aggressive toward black people than toward other whites.
- b. Even in the 1980s, racism could still be revealed under certain circumstances.
- c. White subjects refused to participate in research they thought was against blacks.
- d. By the end of the 1970s, people in America were aware of social pressure to look upon all races as equal.

B. Which of the following is an example of *reverse discrimination*, as defined in paragraph 29?
- a. A black football player is awarded a contract for $5 million for three years; a white football player who played on the same college team is given a contract for much less money.
- b. A Chinese immigrant becomes a successful real-estate salesperson in Los Angeles, California, with the help of an American friend who is a real-estate broker.
- c. An actor from Mexico is hired because of his race to work in a movie about Hispanic Americans.
- d. Because he believes that women have not had the same chance for advancement in business that men have, a male supervisor gives a promotion to a woman, even though several men with the same qualifications have been waiting for a promotion longer.

C. By the 1980s, according to paragraph 29, people tended to
- a. avoid discrimination.
- b. avoid reverse discrimination.

D. Paragraph 30 introduces an idea that is
- a. another example of the main idea in paragraph 29.
- b. an exception to the main idea in paragraph 29.

11. Carefully read paragraphs 31 and 32, which describe the experiment (Rogers and Prentice-Dunn, 1981) introduced in paragraph 30. The first sentence in paragraph 31 describes a "shock generator" used in a study by Stanley Milgram. A description of this study can be found in Chapter 11 of this unit.
   A. In the first sentence of paragraph 31, why are the words *shock generator* in quotation marks?
   - a. Someone else's words are being used.
   - b. The author wants to emphasize these words.
   - c. The machine being described did not really generate electric shocks.
   - d. The words are used in a technical way.
   B. In the second sentence of paragraph 31, the word *jolt* probably means
   - a. wire.
   - b. jump.
   - c. shock.
   - d. switch.
   C. According to the last part of paragraph 31, this experiment was designed to investigate
   - a. the heartrate.
   - b. biofeedback.
   - c. racism.
   - d. the apparatus.
   D. In this experiment, what was the role of the confederates?
   - a. Their actions were being studied.
   - b. They were helping the experimenters.
   - c. They gave instructions.

E. Which sentence or sentences in paragraph 32 support the idea (in sentence 3) that the confederates were pleasant to some subjects? (Circle all that apply.)
   a. sentence 4
   b. sentence 5
   c. sentence 6
F. Which sentence or sentences in paragraph 32 support the idea (in sentence 3) that the confederates acted with hostility toward some subjects? (Circle all that apply.)
   a. sentence 4
   b. sentence 5
   c. sentence 6

12. Read paragraph 33, which describes the results of the study.
   A. Glance back to paragraph 32, and answer these two questions.
   What was the race of the subjects?
      a. black
      b. white
      c. some black and some white
   What was the race of the confederates?
      a. black
      b. white
      c. some black and some white
   B. Now complete the following chart, which summarizes the results of the Rogers and Prentice-Dunn study. The top-left square should contain the subjects' reaction to white confederates who were pleasant, the top-right square should contain the subjects' reaction to white confederates who were hostile, and so forth.

RESULTS	Pleasant confederates	Hostile confederates
White confederates		
Black confederates		

   C. In the last sentence of paragraph 33, the authors quote the Rogers and Prentice-Dunn study as concluding that Americans have two faces, "one face looking forward but the other face focusing grimly on the past." Explain the meaning of this quote in your own words.

   _____
   _____
   _____
   _____

13. Read paragraph 34 carefully.
   A. On the basis of this concluding paragraph, what is the authors' opinion of racial prejudice?
      a. They favor it.

Social Psychology

  b. They oppose it.
  c. They can see some validity in both sides of the question.
  d. They have no opinion.
B. According to this concluding paragraph, what do the authors believe?
  a. Racial prejudice can decrease over time.
  b. Prejudice will continue to grow in the future.
  c. Change in thinking will have no effect.

PART 3: COMPREHENSION EXERCISES
(Paragraphs 22–34)

Exercise 1

The following statements are either *true* or *false* according to paragraphs 22–34 of the reading. Write T or F in the space next to each one.

1. _____ Japanese-Americans who could prove that they were loyal to the United States did not have to move to relocation centers during the first part of World War II.
2. _____ The effects of prejudice are usually negative.
3. _____ Four decades after the war, most people in the United States no longer believed that the white race was superior to others.
4. _____ After the 1960s, the most significant struggles for racial equality shifted from the southern states to the northern cities.
5. _____ The "Robbers Cave" experiment was unusual because of the age and isolation of the subjects.
6. _____ In the "Robbers Cave" experiment, the experimenters had to set up special situations to make the Rattlers and the Eagles regard each other as enemies.
7. _____ The "Robbers Cave" experiment showed that tension between two groups can be reduced if the groups cooperate on a goal that is important to both.
8. _____ The practice of giving black children fewer educational opportunities than white children was ended in the United States in 1954 as a result of a ruling by the Supreme Court.
9. _____ In the 1980s in the United States, according to the authors, it is no longer socially acceptable to show prejudice openly against members of another race.
10. _____ *Reverse discrimination* means that blacks discriminate against whites, instead of whites discriminating against blacks.
11. _____ Studies show that Americans may still have some deep feelings of prejudice toward blacks, even though these feelings may not be openly expressed.

Exercise 2

Complete the following summary of paragraphs 22–34 by filling in each blank with an appropriate word or phrase.

In 1942 more than _____ Japanese-Americans were forced to leave their homes and move to _____ centers. These people were the victims of _____, which is defined as "beliefs, feelings, and _____ tendencies" toward others simply because of their _____ in a group. Other words closely related to this concept are *stereotype* (a _____ idea about someone that is not based on what the person is really like) and *discrimination* (_____ behavior caused by negative thinking and stereotyped beliefs).

Forty years ago it was easy to see the _____ of discrimination, but today many people _____ their negative feelings toward persons of other races. In the United States, the strong racism of the South may have been _____ in the 1970s by a more subtle kind of _____ in the North.

By the 1980s it was considered crude or unacceptable to express _____ in public, and there was even some _____ of *reverse discrimination* (the tendency to give _____ special preferential treatment). Despite these facts, however, one study showed that some whites still have hidden feelings of _____ _____ prejudice, even though they may not _____ these feelings outwardly.

Exercise 3

Look back at the Warmup Questions at the beginning of this unit. Which of the situations described there are related to the ideas discussed in this section of the reading?
_____
Now look at your notes describing your reactions in these situations. Use the new information you have just read to reanalyze your reaction in each case. Discuss your analyses with your classmates.

CHAPTER 11

Some Conditions of Obedience and Disobedience to Authority

WARMUP QUESTIONS

The excerpt in this chapter is a description of a psychological experiment taken from *Social Psychology: Concepts and Applications* by Louis A. Penner. As the title of this chapter indicates, the experiment was designed to investigate the issue of obedience to authority. How would people react if they were asked by a superior to do something unethical? Would they obey even if they thought they were harming other human beings? Would they go against their personal beliefs and feelings when given an order by a person in authority?

Before you begin the reading, consider the following statements and indicate whether you *agree* or *disagree* with each one. Then discuss your answers with your classmates.

1. _____ When a soldier kills an enemy in battle, it is not murder.
2. _____ If the police or the government gives an order, the order should be obeyed, no matter what it is.
3. _____ No one should harm another human being, or deny freedom to another human being, except for political or religious reasons.
4. _____ An employee of a large company that does something illegal should not report the company to the government. Instead, the employee should remain loyal to his or her boss.
5. _____ Even adults should do exactly what their parents tell them to do.

Think of two examples (other than the ones already discussed) in which obedience to authority is necessary, regardless of the personal consequences.

___

___

___

     Think of two examples (other than the ones already discussed) in which disobedience to authority is necessary, regardless of the personal consequences.

___

___

___

___

Discuss your answers with your classmates.

DIRECTIONS FOR READING

     Skim the reading quickly before you begin. Look at the section titles, and read the first sentence of each paragraph. Then read the selection for general understanding.

Some Conditions of Obedience and Disobedience to Authority

Louis Penner

BACKGROUND

1   This [selection] is about social influence, the ability to change a person's beliefs or behavior. One form of social influence is obedience to authority. The writer and philosopher C. P. Snow once observed that "when you think about the long and gloomy history of man, you will find more hideous crimes have been committed in the name of obedience than have ever been committed in the name of rebellion." The truth of this statement can be found in historical examples—the behavior of the guards in Hitler's concentration camps and the mass suicide among followers of the Reverend Jim Jones.

2   In the late 1950s, Stanley Milgram began a series of experiments on what would lead people to obey an unethical or immoral command from an authority. The following experiment was the first of several that Milgram conducted on this topic.

HYPOTHESIS

3   Milgram did not propose a formal hypothesis. His purpose was to determine whether his subjects would obey commands to harm another human being. He suspected they would not.

SUBJECTS

4   The subjects were 40 males recruited from the general community in New Haven, Connecticut. Their occupations ranged from unskilled worker to engineer. Subjects were paid $4.50 for their participation.

PROCEDURE

5   When a subject arrived at Milgram's laboratory, he was told that the money was his for simply showing up, and he could keep it no matter what happened later. Then he was introduced to another man, a pleasant-looking individual in his late forties. The subject believed that this man was also a subject, but he was a paid confederate. The experimenter told the confederate and the subject that the study concerned the effects of punishment on learning. While one of them attempted to learn, the other would be the teacher and would administer punishment whenever a mistake was made. Then a rigged drawing was held which resulted in the subject always being the teacher and the confederate always being the learner.

6   The experimenter showed the subject and the confederate into an adjacent room. As the subject watched, the confederate was strapped into a chair and an electrode was attached to his wrist. After returning to the original room,

the subject was seated in front of a large shock generator. On the generator were 30 levers, each clearly labeled with the amount of shock it would deliver, ranging from 15 volts for the extreme left-hand lever to 450 volts for the extreme right-hand lever.

7   The teacher (the subject) was given 45 volts of electric shock to let him know what shock felt like, and then the experiment began. The teacher read to the learner (the confederate) a list of word pairs—for example, blue-girl, nice-day. Following this, he read the first word from each pair and gave the learner four other words. The learner's task was to indicate which of these four words was originally paired with the first word by pressing a switch in front of him. The teacher was told that the learner must be shocked every time he chose the wrong word, and that this shock should be increased one level for each successive wrong answer.

8   The learner (who was never really shocked) gave the wrong answer about 75 percent of the time. He grunted from discomfort when the shock reached 75 volts; by 150 volts, he was pleading with the experimenter to let him out; at 270 volts, he screamed in response to the shock and again demanded he be let out of the experiment. At 300 volts, he announced that he would no longer choose any of the words, and he said nothing for the remainder of the experimental session. The subject was told that if the learner did not respond, his silence was to be considered a wrong answer and shock was to be given. When subjects were reluctant to administer the shock, the experimenter verbally urged them to continue.

9   The experimental session ended when a subject either refused to give any more shock or had reached the maximum shock level (450 volts). The dependent measure was the highest level of shock a subject gave the confederate. At the conclusion of an experimental session, the subject was told the true purpose of the experiment; it was made clear that he had not harmed the confederate and that the confederate bore him no ill will. The experimenter attempted to deal with any discomfort the subjects felt.

RESULTS

10   Milgram had expected most of his subjects to either refuse to shock the confederate at all or to break off the shock as soon as the confederate indicated any discomfort. This view was shared by other social scientists Milgram consulted before he conducted the experiment. However, this is not what the subjects did. No subject disobeyed the experimenter's commands before 135 volts. Seventy-five percent of the subjects gave at least 300 volts, and 63 percent went all the way to the maximum voltage.

IMPLICATIONS

11   These findings illustrate the phenomenon of interest in this [selection]. The subjects did not want to shock the other person, nor did they enjoy his (supposed) suffering; but they did engage in the behavior desired by the experimenter. [This research also raises questions about] why they did this, and more generally, what gives one person the ability to change the beliefs and behaviors of another.

STUDY QUESTIONS

Directions: Refer to the reading to answer the following study questions.

1. This reading has an organization that is very common in reports of scientific research.
    A. Identify the six sections of the reading and the paragraphs that constitute each section.

    Background _____   Paragraphs 1–2 _____
    _____   _____
    _____   _____
    _____   _____
    _____   _____

2. Look carefully at paragraphs 1 and 2.
    A. According to C. P. Snow, what is the greatest cause of "hideous crimes" during the "long and gloomy history of man"?

    B. The examples cited in the last sentence of paragraph 1 are examples of
        a. crimes committed in the name of rebellion.
        b. crimes committed in the names of obedience.
    C. According to paragraph 2, what did Milgram want to investigate?

    D. Give examples of actions that you would consider immoral or unethical.

3. Read paragraphs 3 and 4.
    A. Look at paragraph 3. What was the purpose of this experiment?

    B. Did Milgram think the subjects would do what he asked?

    C. To make sure you have all the available information about the participants in this study, fill in the following blanks.

        Number of subjects: _____
        Sex of subjects: _____
        Occupations: _____
    D. Is there any other information you would like to have about the participants in this study?

4. Paragraphs 5–9 give a detailed explanation of the experimental procedure used in this study. Read paragraph 5 carefully.
    A. What was the first thing the subject was told on arriving at the laboratory? Why do you think he was told this?

Social Psychology

212

   B. The difference between confederates and subjects was discussed in Chapter 10. Refresh your memory by filling in the following blanks with either *subject* or *confederate*.

   In experimental research, the _____ is the person whose actions are being studied. The _____, on the other hand, is really helping the experimenter conduct the research, even though it may appear that his or her actions are also being studied.

   C. What was the subject told about the purpose of the research?

   _____

   D. Who was to administer the punishment—the subject, the researcher, or the confederate?

   _____

5. Read paragraph 6 carefully.
   A. Where was the confederate located during the experiment?

   _____

   B. Fill in the blanks in the following sentence.

   A "shock generator" is a _____ that produces _____ _____ shocks.

   C. What was the minimum voltage on the shock generator? _____

   What was the maximum voltage? _____

6. Look closely at paragraph 7. It describes the learner's task. (The learner was actually the confederate in the experiment.)
   A. According to the first sentence of paragraph 7, what happened before the experiment began? Explain the purpose of this part of the procedure.

   _____
   _____
   _____

   B. The learner's (confederate's) task was to
      a. write down words.
      b. repeat the second word he heard.
      c. remember the first two words in each group.
      d. remember the second word in a pair of words.
   C. What happened on the first wrong answer and on successive wrong answers?

   _____
   _____

7. Paragraph 8 continues the description of the experimental procedure.

   A. Was the learner ever really shocked? _____

   B. How often did he give the wrong answer? _____
   C. Use a word or phrase to describe what the learner did when the voltage reached each of the following levels.

   75 volts _____

   150 volts _____

270 volts _____

300 volts _____

D. Fill in the blanks in the following sentences, which are based on the last two sentences of paragraph 8.

Silence was considered a _____ answer, so the learner had to be _____. If the subject did not want to give any more shocks, the researcher told him to _____.

8. Read paragraph 9, which concludes the description of the experimental procedure.
   A. The experiment ended under one of two conditions:
      1. _____
      2. _____
   B. Was the subject ever told the real reason for the experiment? _____
   C. The last sentence in this paragraph says that the researcher "attempted to deal with any discomfort the subjects felt." What does this mean? What kind of "discomfort" do you think the subject might have felt on learning the real purpose of the experiment?

   _____
   _____
   _____

9. Read paragraphs 10 and 11, which describe the results and implications of the study.
   A. Did the results of the study agree with the predictions of Milgram and other scientists? _____
   B. Complete the following graph with information from paragraph 10. Plot the number of subjects who administered each of the three voltage levels discussed.

   [Graph: Y-axis labeled "Voltage" with markings Minimum, 100, 300, Maximum. X-axis labeled "Number of Subjects" ranging from 0 to 40.]

   C. Paragraph 11 identifies two reasons why it was unusual for the subjects to act in the way that they did. What are the two reasons? (Use your own words.)
      a. _____
      _____

Social Psychology

b. _____

D. Fill in the blank in the following sentence.

According to the reading, the more general question this research raises is "What makes one person able to change the _____ of others?"

INTEGRATION QUESTIONS FOR DISCUSSION AND WRITING

Directions: The following questions ask you to find relationships among the ideas in the first two selections in this unit: "Social Relations" (Chapter 10) and "Some Conditions of Obedience and Disobedience to Authority" (Chapter 11). Discuss your answers with your classmates.

1. Look back at the Warmup Questions at the beginning of Chapter 10. Which of the situations described there are related to the ideas discussed in Chapter 11?

   Now look at your notes describing your reactions in the situations that apply to this chapter. Use the new information you have just read to reanalyze your reaction in each case. Discuss your analyses with your classmates.

2. Think about what you might have done if you had been one of the subjects in Stanley Milgram's experiments. Would you have given the "learner" electric shocks? How do you explain the behavior of the subjects in Milgram's experiment?

3. In the Chapter 10 reading, the last paragraph of the "Trouble at Robbers Cave" section implies that the research was not ethical by today's standards. Do you think that the subjects in the Sherif and Milgram studies might have been harmed in some way by the nature of the experiments? If so, do you think any possible harm was justified by the knowledge gained in the experiments? In general, to what extent should the rights of experimental subjects in social science research be protected?

4. What is the relationship between the findings of Latané and Darley (1969, 1970) and Milgram (1965)? Discuss the ways in which both studies shed some light on the questions of social influence and the attitude of human beings toward certain kinds of violence.

5. Although Rogers and Prentice-Dunn (1981) used a device similar to that used by Milgram (1965), the two studies have some very important differences. Compare and contrast the two studies.

6. The Milgram experiment was carefully planned so that the results would not be confusing or ambiguous. For example, the subject was given a shock at the beginning of the experiment so that he would know what it felt like. Therefore, people interpreting the results later could not conclude that the subject did not really think he was hurting the learner.

   Look at the procedure section of the Milgram experiment (paragraphs 5–9). Look also at the procedure section of the "Brenda" experiment—Gaertner and Dovidio (1977)—in Chapter 10 (paragraphs 18 and 19). Discuss how each of these experiments (or any of the others mentioned in Chapters 10 and 11) might be more difficult to interpret if one of the procedure steps was changed or omitted.

7. The description of the Sherif and Sherif (1956) study in Chapter 10 ends with several questions ("The Trouble at Robbers Cave," paragraph 9). Discuss with your classmates several possible answers to the first question: "What lessons can society learn from the Robbers Cave experiment?"

8. The description of the Milgram experiment in this chapter also ends with a question: "What gives one person the ability to change the beliefs and behaviors of another?" What is your opinion? Are there any lessons that society can learn from the Milgram experiment?

CHAPTER 12

Experiments in Conformity

WARMUP QUESTIONS

The following reading is taken from a chapter on social psychology in *Psychology Today*, an introductory psychology text by Richard R. Bootzin et al. The reading summarizes the results of experiments designed to investigate the influence of social pressure and conformity on the actions of others. Can the opinions of others influence how an individual sees a physical object? Do people care more about the opinions of friends or of strangers? Can social norms cause someone to harm another person even if he or she does not really want to?

Before you begin the reading consider the following statements. Indicate whether you *agree* or *disagree* with each one. Then discuss your answers with your classmates.

1. _____ I care more about the opinions of my friends than I do about the opinions of strangers.
2. _____ Sometimes it is better to agree with your friends even if you think they are wrong.
3. _____ No matter how strong the influence of society, people cannot be forced to do things they think are wrong.
4. _____ Some social conformity is necessary. Otherwise, there would be too much disorder in society.
5. _____ If everyone in a society feels pressure to act in the same way, this discourages creativity and does not permit the society to grow and change.

Now write two questions of your own about the possible influence of conformity and social pressure on the actions and perceptions of the individual.

_____

_____

_____

DIRECTIONS FOR READING

Skim the reading before you begin, looking at the title of each section and at the figure on page 218. Read the first sentence of each paragraph. Then read the selection quickly for general understanding.

Experiments in Conformity

Richard R. Bootzin, Elizabeth F. Loftus, Robert B. Zajonc, and Jay Braun

SHERIF'S EXPERIMENTS

1   Individual conformity can go beyond matters of belief and custom; social influence can lead people to question the information received by their senses. A classical demonstration of visual conformity was provided by Muzafer Sherif (1936), who exploited a visual illusion to study the effects of norms. Sherif used the "autokinetic effect," in which a stationary pinpoint of light, when viewed in total darkness, appears to move. People viewed such lights by themselves and, over the course of many judgments, each arrived at a stable—but different— range of judgments on the distance the light "moved." Afterward, several individuals, each with a different pattern of judgment, viewed the light together and judged aloud the distance the light "traveled." In the course of making these judgments, their widely divergent estimates converged until they resembled one another closely.

2   The situation in this experiment differs substantially from that found in social facilitation.* In social facilitation, the effect is caused by the mere presence of others—their behavior provides no reinforcement and furnishes no cues as to appropriate responses. In the conformity experiment, however, the person does receive information from others. Although she or he is not required to use this information as a guide to behavior, it is available. If the person feels any compulsion to follow it, social influence has exerted an effect. In Sherif's experiments, people who viewed the light together from the beginning made similar judgments during the first session. And people who started by making their judgments in groups and then watched the light by themselves had adopted the social norm as their own—they persisted in giving approximately the same estimates that had been developed within the group.

ASCH'S EXPERIMENTS

3   Some psychologists doubted that Sherif's experiments had demonstrated the power of conformity, because the situation was so ambiguous and each viewer so uncertain of her or his judgments that they eagerly accepted the only available information—the judgments of other subjects. One of those who doubted the significance of Sherif's results was Solomon Asch, who thought that if people could judge unambiguous stimuli under optimal conditions, the sort of convergence Sherif found would not appear. Individuals who shifted their opinions when the facts are uncertain would not be moved when faced with reality. When Asch (1951) tested his proposal with male college students, the results surprised him.

4   Each student was told that he was participating in an experiment on visual judgment in which he would compare the lengths of lines. He would be shown two large white cards: one card with a single vertical line, and another with three vertical lines of different lengths (see Figure 12-1). The alleged experimental

---

Social facilitation refers to the way people's behavior is influenced by the presence of others. For example, a racer will run faster in competition than when running against the clock.

FIGURE 12-1 The Stimuli in a Single Trial in Asch's Experiment. The subject must state which of the comparison lines he [or she] judges to be the same length as the standard. The discrimination is an easy one to make: Control subjects (those who made the judgments without any group pressure) chose line 2 as correct over 90 percent of the time.

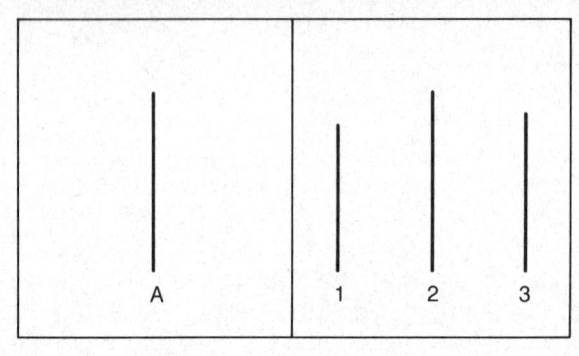

Standard Line   Comparison Lines

task was to determine which of the three lines on the second card was the same length as the standard.

5   The student was seated in a room with seven other apparent subjects who were actually Asch's confederates. After unanimous judgments on the first two sets of cards, the third set was shown. Although the correct response was obviously line 2, the first confederate declared that line 1 matched the standard. In turn, the other six confederates agreed—and with great certainty. Now the true subject was faced with a dilemma. His eyes told him that line 2 was the correct choice, but six other people had unanimously and confidently selected line 1. Confronted with a solid—but obviously wrong—majority, almost one-third of the fifty people Asch tested bowed to social influence and conformed with the obviously incorrect choice at least half the time.

FACTORS INFLUENCING CONFORMITY

6   What accounts for the conformity found in Asch's research? Part of the answer may lie in situational factors built into the experimental design. For one thing, the judgments of the confederates were unanimous; not one of them hinted that another answer might be possible. By varying the basic experiment, Asch found that the extent of agreement was an important influence. When only one confederate gave the correct answer, the proportion of subjects who conformed dropped dramatically—from 32 percent to 5 percent. It appears that a single voice raised in opposition to an otherwise unanimous judgment can have a remarkable effect. Others who may be leaning toward a dissenting view but are not sure that they should express it may decide to assert themselves against the majority.

7   Another situational factor that influenced the conformity Asch found was the requirement that his subjects interact face-to-face with the confederates. Later research showed that when people can respond anonymously, they conform less often (Deutsch and Gerard, 1955).

8   However, the Asch experiments included situational factors that might have lowered the pressure to conform. The confederates were complete strangers to the subject, with no special claim on her or his loyalty or affection.

The subject had never seen them before and probably would never see them again. Consequently, she or he had little reason to fear that nonconformity would have social repercussions. The existence of this situational factor, which would logically reduce the pressure to conform, has led some psychologists to conclude that Asch's work revealed only the tip of the conformity iceberg. If the pressure to conform among strangers is so strong, it seems likely that the pressure to conform among friends is far stronger.

ZIMBARDO'S PRISON EXPERIMENT

9   Social conformity of a different sort was studied when Philip Zimbardo and Craig Haney (1977) advertised in newspapers for volunteers to take part in a mock prison experiment. The volunteers were randomly assigned roles as "prisoners" and "guards." Both groups were placed in the basement of the Stanford University psychology building and given minimal instructions; they were told to assume their assigned roles and that the guards' job was to "maintain law and order." In only a few hours, the behavior of one group became sharply differentiated from the behavior of the other group. The guards adopted the behavior patterns and attitudes that are typical of guards in maximum security prisons, with most of them becoming abusive and aggressive. Most of the prisoners became passive, dependent, and depressed, although some became enraged at the guards. Suffering among the prisoners was so great that one had to be released in less than thirty-six hours; several other prisoners also had to be released before the intended two-week experiment was ended after six days.

10   Stereotypical social norms controlled the behavior of both groups. The guards adopted a manner they believed was necessary to simulate their role and maintain order. The prisoners, who were the targets of the guards' abuse, assumed attitudes that accorded with their image of prison life. As the groups became antagonistic, each reinforced the other's behavior. The prisoners expected the guards to be mean and vicious and treated them accordingly. The guards expected the prisoners to be rebellious and acted so as to prevent unruly behavior. A situation of pretense, by virtue of the participants' perceptions, had real effects on the feelings and behavior of everyone involved. As this experiments shows, conformity to social norms is not simply the result of social pressures from one's own group; the influence of other groups in society magnifies the pressure to conform.

REFERENCES

Asch, S. E. Effects of group pressure on the modification and distortion of judgements. In H. Guetzkow (ed.), *Groups, leadership, and men*. Pittsburgh: Carnegie Press, 1951.

Deutsch, M., and Gerard, H. B. A study of normative and informational influences on social judgement. *Journal of Abnormal and Social Psychology*, 1955, *51*, 629–636.

Haney, C., and Zimbardo, P. G. The socialization into criminality: On becoming a prisoner and a guard. In J. L. Tapp and F. L. Levine (eds.), *Law, justice and the individual in society: Psychological and legal issues*. New York: Holt, Rinehart, and Winston, 1977, pp. 198–223.

Milgram, S. Behavioral study of obedience. *Journal of Abnormal and Social Psychology*, 1963, *67*, 371–378.

Sherif, M. *The Psychology of Social Norms*. New York: Harper, 1936.

Sherif, M., Harvey, O. J., White, B. J., Hood, W. R., and Sherif, C. W. *Intergroup conflict and cooperation: The robbers cave experiment*. Norman, Oklahoma: University of Oklahoma Press, 1961.

Experiments in Conformity

STUDY QUESTIONS

Directions: Refer to the reading to answer the following study questions.

1. Paragraphs 1 and 2 describe the research of Sherif (1936). (This is a different experiment from the one described in Chapter 10.) Look carefully at paragraph 1.
   A. Which of the following is a correct paraphrase of the first sentence in paragraph 1?
      a. Conformity can influence sensory information as well as customs and beliefs.
      b. Conformity has nothing to do with customs and beliefs; instead, it influences what people think that they see and hear.
      c. We usually think that people conform as a result of customs and beliefs, but social influence can also cause people not to believe what they see or hear.
   B. Fill in the blanks in the following sentence.

      The _____ effect is the phenomenon in which a person in a

      _____ room looks at a motionless point of _____ and

      it appears to _____.
   C. What happened when people viewed the light by themselves?
      a. Their judgments were all different.
      b. Their judgments were very similar.
   D. What happened when people viewed the lights with others and discussed how far the light moved?
      a. There was considerable disagreement.
      b. Eventually everyone gave a similar answer.
   E. According to paragraph 1, how far did the light in the experiment actually move?

      _____

   F. What part of the experiment does paragraph 1 describe? (Circle all that apply.)
      a. background
      b. hypothesis
      c. procedure
      d. results
      e. implications/conclusions

2. Look carefully at paragraph 2, which continues the discussion of the Sherif (1936) study.
   A. According to paragraph 2, what is the major difference between social facilitation and the conformity described in this experiment?
      a. The effect in this experiment is caused by the mere presence of others.
      b. Social facilitation involves a stronger influence on behavior than conformity.
      c. In this experiment, the subjects were forced to conform to the estimates of others.
      d. In social facilitation, there are no guidelines for action, but some guidelines were available in the conformity experiment.
   B. What happened when people who had begun in a group estimated on their own how far the light moved?
      a. They started to change their estimates.
      b. They preserved the original estimates of the group.

3. Paragraphs 3, 4, and 5 describe the research of Asch (1951). Look carefully at paragraph 3.
   A. According to this paragraph, what was one criticism of the Sherif study (paragraphs 1 and 2)?
      a. The social conditions in 1936 were different from those in 1951.
      b. The subjects were too easily influenced by others.

Social Psychology

        c. What the subjects were looking at was not clear and definite enough.
        d. The judgment of the subjects was ambiguous.
    B. Paragraph 3 describes the hypothesis of the Asch study. Explain the hypothesis in your own words. (If you are not sure, use the information in paragraphs 4 and 5 to help you.)

_____

_____

_____

    C. The last sentence in paragraph 3 says that the results of the study surprised Asch. Were you able to predict the results of the experiment? Did the results surprise you?

_____

_____

4. Look carefully at paragraphs 4 and 5, and at Figure 12-1.
    A. Were the subjects told the true purpose of the experiment? _____
    B. Fill in the blanks in the following sentence.

        The task in the experiment was to _____ lines of _____

        _____ lengths that were shown on white cards.
    C. Each time the experiment was conducted, how many people participated?
        a. one
        b. six
        c. seven
        d. eight
    D. How many of those people were the true subjects, and how many were the researcher's helpers?

_____

    E. According to paragraph 5, what did the researcher's helpers say when the third set of cards was shown?

_____

_____

    F. What was the dilemma faced by the subject?
        a. What he saw disagreed with what the others said.
        b. He was not sure about what he saw.
        c. He was not sure if the others were telling the truth.
        d. He was not sure about the true purpose of the research.
    G. What part of the experiment is described in paragraphs 4 and 5? (Circle all that apply.)
        a. background
        b. hypothesis
        c. subjects
        d. procedure
        e. results
        f. implications/conclusions
    H. How many subjects agreed with the group even when they knew the answer was wrong? How often did they do this?

_____

Experiments in Conformity

5. Paragraphs 6, 7, and 8 discuss the implications of the Asch (1951) study. Look carefully at paragraphs 6 and 7.
   A. According to paragraph 6, which of the following factors may have contributed to the results of the experiment?
      a. the length of the experiment
      b. the social and political climate in the United States at the time
      c. the age and sex of the subjects
      d. the percentage of confederates who conformed
   B. Fill in the blanks in the following sentence.

   In a similar experiment, the percentage of subjects who _____ (agreed/disagreed) with the _____ (right/wrong) answer of the group dropped from _____ percent to _____ percent.
   C. What was the reason for the results described in question B?
   _____
   _____

6. Look carefully at paragraph 8.
   A. The subjects did not know any of the confederates in this study. Would this have increased or decreased the tendency of the subjects to agree with the group?
   _____
   B. According to the paragraph, what would most likely happen if the original experiment were repeated with seven friends of the subject?
      a. The subject would feel more pressure to agree with wrong answers.
      b. The subject would almost never agree with the group when the answer was wrong.
   C. What do you think the idiom *tip of the iceberg* means? If you are not sure, consult a dictionary or ask a native speaker of English. Then write a definition in your own words.
   _____
   _____
   _____

7. Paragraphs 9 and 10 describe the research of Zimbardo and Haney (1977). Look carefully at paragraph 9.
   A. What were the roles assigned to the volunteers in this experiment? How were these roles assigned?
   _____
   B. What instructions were given to the "prisoners"?
   _____
   C. What instructions were given to the "guards"?
   _____
   D. How did the "guards" behave?
   _____
   E. How did the "prisoners" behave?
   _____

Social Psychology

F. Do you think these results are surprising? Why or why not?

_____

_____

8. Look carefully at paragraph 10.
   A. According to this paragraph, why did the "guards" treat the "prisoners" so badly?
      a. They were locked in the basement of the building.
      b. They thought that was the way prison guards were supposed to act.
      c. They would not get paid for their time otherwise.
      d. The researchers forced them to act that way.
      e. They really did not like the "prisoners."
   B. Since it was just an experiment, not a real prison, why didn't the "prisoners" simply ignore the guards? (Circle all that apply.)
      a. Social norms influenced the behavior of the "prisoners."
      b. The volunteers really believed they were in a prison.
      c. Conformity prevented the situation from getting worse.
      d. The experiment was carefully constructed to allow for this.
      e. The bad behavior of the "guards" made the "prisoners" angry.
      f. The "prisoners" were given specific instructions to argue with the "guards."

INTEGRATION QUESTIONS FOR DISCUSSION AND WRITING

Directions: The following questions ask you to find relationships among the ideas in the three selections in this unit: "Social Relations" (Chapter 10), "Some Conditions of Obedience and Disobedience to Authority" (Chapter 11), and "Experiments in Conformity" (Chapter 12). Discuss your answers with your classmates.

1. Look back at the Warmup Questions at the beginning of Chapter 10. Which of the situations described there are related to the ideas discussed in Chapter 12?

_____

   Now look at your notes describing your reactions in the situations that apply to this chapter. Use the new information you have just read to reanalyze your reaction in each case. Discuss your analyses with your classmates.

2. What is the relationship between the case of Kitty Genovese (Chapter 10) and the research of Sherif (1936) and Asch (1951) in this chapter? (Review the definition of *social facilitation* in paragraph 2 of "Experiments in Conformity," and consider the theme that has run throughout these three readings: the theme of social influence.)

3. Design an experiment that would either confirm or disprove the results of Asch (1951). As you recall, Asch found that subjects would state something they did not really believe just to conform to the opinion of a group.
   Write a formal statement of your hypothesis, and then provide a detailed description of your procedure. Use the procedure description of Milgram's research in Chapter 11 as a model.

4. In Chapter 11 you discussed the issue of ethical research, especially with regard to Milgram (1965) and Sherif (1956). Do you think the prison experiment described in this chapter (Zimbardo and Haney, 1977) was an example of ethical research? What kind of

experiment could they have devised that would have prevented the prisoners from suffering so much?

5. These three chapters describe the negative effects of social pressure and conformity: insensitivity, prejudice, unethical behavior. Do you think that social pressure and conformity can have any positive effects? If so, what are they?

6. These three chapters describe social pressure and conformity in a Western, English-speaking culture. Describe the role of social pressure and conformity in another culture with which you are familiar.

7. Do you think the results of any of the experiments described in this unit would have been different if they had been conducted in another country or another culture? Explain.

UNIT

V

Language

CHAPTER 13

What Is Language?

WARMUP QUESTIONS

The readings in this unit concern language, how it works, how it is learned, and how it is taught. What do you already know about language? How would you define *language*? How are different languages similar to one another? How are they dissimilar?

Before you start the first selection, "What Is Language?" read the following statements, and indicate whether you *agree* or *disagree* with each one. Then discuss your opinions with your classmates.

1. _____ Most of your knowledge of your native language is unconscious.
2. _____ The same sounds are used in all languages, but different languages arrange the sounds in different ways.
3. _____ Knowing the vocabulary of a language is all that is needed to communicate in that language.
4. _____ An infinite number of sentences is possible in any language.
5. _____ If native speakers of a language make grammatical mistakes when speaking, it means that they do not know the grammar of that language.
6. _____ It is possible for a sentence to be so long that it cannot be easily understood.
7. _____ Some languages are superior to others for certain purposes; for example, German is better for science, and French is better for the arts.
8. _____ Any American can explain all the most important grammar rules of English.

Language

230

Write down three questions you have about language. Share your questions with your classmates, and discuss possible answers.

_____

_____

_____

_____

PREVIEWING

1. Look over the reading in this chapter, an excerpt from Chapter 1 of *An Introduction to Language*.
    A. How many paragraphs does it contain? _____
    B. How many pages long is the reading? _____

2. Before you begin to read, try to get an idea of the organization of the selection. Scan the reading for headings and subheadings. Then list the major sections and the paragraphs each includes.

    Introduction   (paragraphs _____ - _____)

    _____   (paragraphs   3 - _____)

    _____   (paragraphs _____ - _____)

3. Below the title of the selection is a quotation from the book *Language and Mind* by the American linguist Noam Chomsky.
    A. How do you know that this is a quotation and not the words of the authors of the chapter?

    _____

    _____

    B. What is the purpose of this quotation?
       a. to introduce the chapter
       b. to show that the authors have done their research
       c. to start the reader thinking about the subject of the chapter
    C. Which of the following is the best paraphrase of the quotation?
       a. The study of language is unique.
       b. Through a study of language, we can learn about what makes humans different from other living things.
       c. We need to know more about the unique nature of human language, the human essence, and the human mind.

4. Look carefully at the first and last sentences of paragraphs 1 and 2. (Do not read anything else.) Which sentence do you think probably best expresses the main idea of the entire selection?
    a. the first sentence in paragraph 1
    b. the last sentence in paragraph 1
    c. the first sentence in paragraph 2
    d. the last sentence in paragraph 2

5. A number of words throughout this selection have been printed in italic type. Look quickly for some of these words. They have been printed in italics for several reasons.
   A. Some of the words are in italics because they are the title of a book or other type of publication. Can you find an example of this use of italics?
   _____

   B. Some of the words are in italics because the authors use them as examples of language to demonstrate a general principle. Can you find an example?
   _____

   C. Other words have been printed in italics because the authors want to emphasize their meaning to the reader. Find an example of this use.
   _____

DIRECTIONS FOR READING

The reading for this chapter is taken from *An Introduction to Language* by Victoria Fromkin and Robert Rodman. The book is an introductory linguistics text used by undergraduate university students as part of their general education.

The previewing exercises you just completed gave you a general idea of the content and organization of the reading. You are now ready to read it carefully.

The selection has been divided into three parts. You will read each section quickly for general understanding and then examine each part more closely as you complete the study questions.

What Is Language?
Victoria Fromkin and Robert Rodman

> When we study human language, we are approaching what some might call the "human essence," the distinctive qualities of mind that are, so far as we know, unique to man.
>
> Noam Chomsky, *Language and Mind*

1   Whatever else people may do when they come together—whether they play, fight, make love, or make automobiles—they talk. We live in a world of words. We talk to our friends, our associates, our wives and husbands, our mothers and mothers-in-law; we talk to total strangers and to our adversaries. We talk face to face and over the telephone. And everyone responds to us with more talk. Television and radio further swell this torrent of words. As a result, hardly a moment of our waking lives is free from words. We talk even when there is no one to answer. We talk to our pets. We sometimes talk to ourselves. And we are the only animals that do this—that talk.

2   The possession of language, more than any other attribute, distinguishes humans from other animals. To understand our humanity one must understand the language that makes us human. According to the philosophy expressed in the myths and religions of many peoples, it is language which is the source of human life and power. To some people of Africa, a newborn child is a *kuntu*, a "thing," not yet a *muntu*, a "person." Only by the act of learning language does the child become a human being.[1] Thus according to this tradition, we all become "human" because we all know at least one language. But what is it that we know? What does it mean to "know" a language?

LINGUISTIC KNOWLEDGE

3   When you know a language, you can speak and be understood by others who know that language. This means you are able to produce sounds which signify certain meanings and to understand or interpret the sounds produced by others. We are referring here to normal-hearing individuals. Deaf persons produce and understand signs just as hearing persons produce and understand spoken language.

4   How is it possible for you to do this and is there anything more that you know when you have acquired knowledge of a language? Much of your knowledge is unconscious knowledge; you are not even aware of what you know when you know English, or French, or Japanese as a native speaker of these languages. We hope to convince you in this book that your knowledge is profound, and also hope to show you what this linguistic knowledge includes.

5   For one thing, if you know a language, you know, without being aware of it, which sounds are part of the language and which are not. This knowledge is often revealed by the way speakers of one language pronounce words from

---

[1]Diabate, Massa-Makan, "Oral Tradition and Mali Literature," in *The Republic of Mali* (Mali Information Center).

another language. If you speak only English, for example, you may (and usually do) substitute an English sound for a non-English sound when pronouncing "foreign" words. How many of you pronounce the name *Bach* with a final *k* sound? This is not the German pronunciation. The sound represented by the letters *ch* in German is not an English sound. If you pronounce it as the Germans do, you are using a sound outside of the English sound system. Have you noticed that French people speaking English often pronounce words like *this* and *that* as if they were spelled *zis* and *zat*? This is because the English sound which begins these words is not part of the French sound system, and the French mispronunciation reveals their unconscious knowledge of this fact.

6   Knowledge of a language also includes knowing which sounds may start a word, end a word, and follow each other. The name of the former president of Ghana was *Nkrumah*. Ghanaians pronounced this name with an initial sound identical to the sound ending the English word *sing* (for most Americans). But most English speakers, including radio announcers, would start the word with a short vowel before the *n* sound, or insert a short vowel after the *n*. We would predict that you would do this also, and would probably similarly pronounce the name *Ngaio Marsh*, the mystery story writer. The reason for this is that in English no word may begin with the *ng* sound. As children, when we learn English, we learn or discover this fact about our language, just as Ghanaians learn that words may begin with the *ng* sound.

7   Knowledge of the sounds and sound patterns in one's language constitutes just part of our linguistic knowledge. The most important aspect of knowing a language is knowing that certain sounds or sound sequences signify or represent different concepts or "meanings." Knowing a language is therefore knowing the system which relates sounds and meanings. When you don't know a language, the sounds spoken to you in this foreign tongue mean nothing to you. You can't even figure out by any logical or rational process what the speaker's message is. This is because the relationship between speech sounds and the meanings they represent is, for the most part, an **arbitrary** relationship. You have to learn (when you are acquiring the language) that the sounds represented by the letters *house* (in the written form of the language) signify the

concept ⌂ ; if you know French, this same concept is represented by *maison*;

if you know Twi, it is represented by *ɔdaŋ*; if you know Russian, by *dom*; if you know Spanish, by *casa*.

8   Similarly, the concept ✋ is represented by *hand* in English, *main* in French, *nsa* in Twi, and *ruka* in Russian.

9   The following are words with definite meanings in some different languages. How many of them can you understand?

   a. kyinii   d. asubuhi   g. wartawan
   b. doakam   e. toowq   h. inaminatu
   c. odun   f. bolna   i. yawwa

If you don't know the languages from which these words are taken, you undoubtedly don't know that they mean the following:

   a. a large parasol (in a Ghanaian language, Twi)
   b. living creature (in an American Indian language, Papago)
   c. bridge (in Turkish)
   d. morning (in Swahili)

       e. is seeing (in a California Indian language, Luiseño)
       f. to speak (in a Pakistani language, Urdu); ache (in Russian)
       g. reporter (in Indonesian)
       h. teacher (in a Venezuelan Indian language, Warao)
       i. right on! (in a Nigerian language, Hausa)

10   These different words show that the sounds of words are only given meaning by the language in which they occur. The idea that something is called X because it looks like X or called Y because it sounds like Y was satirized by Mark Twain in his book *Eve's Diary*:

> The minute I set eyes on an animal I know what it is. I don't have to reflect a moment; the right name comes out instantly. . . . I seem to know just by the shape of the creature and the way it acts what animal it is. When the dodo came along he [Adam] thought it was a wildcat. . . . But I saved him. . . . I just spoke up in a quite natural way . . . and said "Well, I do declare if there isn't the dodo!"

11   There is some "sound symbolism" in language. That is, there are words whose pronunciation suggests the meaning. A small group of words in the vocabulary of most languages is "onomatopoeic"—the sounds of the words "imitate" the sounds of "nature." Even here, the sounds differ from one language to another, reflecting the particular sound system of the language. In English we say *cockadoodledoo* and in Russian they say *kukuriku* to represent the rooster's crow.

12   One also finds particular sound sequences which seem to relate to a particular concept. In English many of the words beginning with *gl* have to do with sight, such as *glare, glint, gleam, glitter, glossy, glaze, glance, glimmer, glimpse*, and *glisten*. Many rhyming word pairs begin with *h: hoity-toity, harum-scarum, hotsy-totsy, higgledy-piggledy*. But these are a very small part of any language, and *gl* may have nothing to do with "sight" words in another language.

13   When you know English you know these *gl* words, the onomatopoeic words, and all the words in the basic vocabulary of the language. You know their sounds and you know their meanings. It's extremely unlikely, of course, that there are any speakers of English who know the 450,000 words listed in *Webster's Third New International Dictionary*. But even if they did, and that was all they knew, they would not know English. Imagine trying to learn a foreign language by buying a dictionary and memorizing words. No matter how many words you learned, you would not be able to form the simplest phrases or sentences in the language or understand what was said by a native speaker. No one speaks in isolated words. (Of course you could search in your traveler's dictionary for individual words to find out how to say something like "car—gas—where?" After many tries, a native might understand this question and then point in the direction of a gas station. If she answered you in a sentence, however, it is highly probable that you would be unable to understand her or even look up what she said in your dictionary, since you would not know where one word ended and another began.)

14   Your knowledge of a language enables you to combine words to form phrases, and phrases to form sentences. Unfortunately, you can't buy a dictionary with all the sentences in any language, since no dictionary can list all the *possible* sentences. This is because knowing a language means being able to produce new sentences never spoken before and to understand sentences never heard before. The linguist Noam Chomsky refers to this ability as part of

the "creative aspect" of language use. This doesn't mean that every speaker of a language can create great literature, but it does mean that you, and all persons who know a language, can and often do "create" new sentences every time you speak and are able to understand new sentences "created" by others. This is because language use is not limited to stimulus-response behavior. We are "free" from the constraints of either internal or external events or states. If someone steps on our toes we will "automatically" respond with a scream or gasp or grunt. These sounds are really not part of language; they are involuntary reactions to stimuli. After we automatically cry out, however, we can say "That was some clumsy act, you big oaf" or "Thank you very much for stepping on my toe because I was afraid I had elephantiasis and now that I can feel it hurt I know it isn't so," or any one of an infinite number of sentences, since the particular sentence we produce is not controlled by any stimulus. Of course knowing a language also means knowing what sentences are appropriate in various situations; saying "Hamburger costs 98 cents a pound" after someone has just stepped on your toe during a discussion on the weather in Britain would hardly be an appropriate response, but it would be possible.

15   Consider, for example, the following sentence:

> Daniel Boone decided to become a pioneer because he dreamed of pigeon-toed giraffes and cross-eyed elephants dancing in pink skirts and green berets on the wind-swept plains of the Midwest.

You might not believe the sentence; you might question its logic; you might even understand it to mean different things; but you can understand the sentence, although it is very doubtful that you have heard or read it before now.

16   It is obvious, then, that when you know a language you can recognize and understand and produce new sentences. All of them do not have to be as "wild" as the Daniel Boone sentence. In fact if you go through this book counting the number of sentences you have ever seen or heard before, we predict the number would be very small. Next time you write an essay or an exam or a letter see how many of your sentences are new. It can't be that all possible sentences are stored in your brain and that when you speak you pull out a sentence which seems to fit the situation, or that when you hear a sentence you match it with some sentence already stored. How can one have in his or her memory a totally novel sentence never heard before?

17   In fact, it can be shown that simple memorization of all the possible sentences in a language is impossible *in principle*. If for every sentence in the language one can form a longer sentence, then there is no limit on the length of any sentence and no limit on the number of sentences. We can illustrate this by a well-known example in English. When you know the language, you know you can say:

This is the house.
or
This is the house that Jack built.
or
This is the mat that lay in the house that Jack built.
or
This is the dog that chased the cat that killed the rat that ate the mat that lay in the house that Jack built.

18   And one needn't stop there. How long, then, is the longest sentence? One can also say:

The old man came.
or
The old, old, old, old, old man came.

How many "old's" are too many? Seven? Twenty-three?

19   We will not deny that the longer these sentences become, the less likely one would be to hear or to say them. A sentence with 276 occurrences of "old" would be highly unlikely in either speech or writing, even to describe Methuselah. But such a sentence is *theoretically* possible. That is, if you know English, you have the knowledge to add any number of adjectives as modifiers to a noun, as in:

The beautiful, rich, snobbish, stubborn, blond, blue-eyed princess married the hunchbacked, gnarled, lame, dirty old man.

20   To memorize and store an infinite set of sentences would require an infinite storage capacity. But the brain is finite, and even if it were not we could not store totally novel sentences.

21   But when you learn a language you must learn something, and that something must be finite. The vocabulary is finite (however large it may be), and that can be stored. If sentences in a language were formed by putting one word after another in any order, then one's knowledge of a language could be described simply by a list of words. That this is not the case can be seen by examining the following strings of words:

(1) a. John kissed the little old lady who owned the shaggy dog.
    b. Who owned the shaggy dog John kissed the little old lady.
    c. John is difficult to love.
    d. It is difficult to love John.
    e. John is anxious to go.
    f. It is anxious to go John.
    g. John who was a student flunked his exams.
    h. Exams his flunked student a was who John.

22   If you were asked to put a star or asterisk before the sentences that seemed "funny" or "no good" to you, which ones would you "star?"[2] Our "intuitive" knowledge about what "is" or "is not" a sentence in English convinces us to "star" sentences *b,f*, and *h*. Which ones did you "star?"

23   Would you agree with our judgments about the following sentences?

(2) a. What he did was climb a tree.
    b. *What he thought was want a sports car.
    c. Drink your beer and go home!
    d. *What are you drinking and go home?
    e. I expect them to arrive a week from next Thursday.
    f. *I expect a week from next Thursday to arrive them.

[2]It has become customary in presenting linguistic examples to use the asterisk before any of them which speakers reject for one reason or another. We shall use this notation throughout [this selection].

g. Linus lost his security blanket.
h. *Lost Linus security blanket his.

24 If you "starred" the same sentences we did, then it is clear that not all strings of words constitute sentences in a language, and our knowledge of the language determines which do and which do not. Therefore, in addition to knowing the words of the language you must know some "rules" to form the sentences and to make the judgments that you made about the examples in (1) and (2). These rules must be finite in length and finite in number so they can be stored in our finite brains. Yet they must permit us to form and understand an infinite set of new sentences as was discussed above. How this is possible will be discussed in Chapter 8. It is one of the most interesting properties of human language.

25 We can say then that a language consists of all the sounds, words, and possible sentences. And when you know a language you know the sounds, the words, and the rules for their combination.

WHAT YOU KNOW AND WHAT YOU DO: LINGUISTIC COMPETENCE AND PERFORMANCE

"What's one and one and one and one and one and one and one and one and one and one?"
"I don't know," said Alice. "I lost count."
"She can't do Addition," the Red Queen interrupted.

Lewis Carroll, *Through the Looking-Glass*

26 We have mentioned some aspects of a speaker's linguistic knowledge. We said, for example, that our linguistic ability permits us to form longer and longer sentences, illustrating this by showing how we can keep piling up adjectives as modifiers of a noun. We pointed out that this is theoretically, if not practically, possible. That is, whether one limits the number of adjectives to three, five, or eighteen in speaking, one cannot limit the number of adjectives which one *could* add if one wanted to. This demonstrates that there is a difference between having the necessary knowledge to produce such sentences and the way we use this knowledge when we are performing linguistically. It is a difference between what one *knows*, which linguists refer to as one's linguistic **competence**, and how one *uses* this knowledge in actual behavior, which is called linguistic **performance**.

27 You have the competence to understand or produce an infinitely long sentence. But when you attempt to use that knowledge—when you perform linguistically—there are physiological and psychological reasons why you cut off the number of adjectives, adverbs, clauses, and so on. You may run out of breath; your audience may leave; you may lose track of what has been said if the sentence is too long; and of course you don't live forever.

28 In discussing what you know—your linguistic competence—we are not talking about your conscious knowledge. We learn the rules of the language without anyone teaching them to us and without being aware that we are learning such rules. That this knowledge is learned is clear from the fact that you use it to speak, to understand, and to make judgments about sentences.

29 The fact that linguistic competence and performance are not identical and that "knowing" something is not the same as "doing" something is not unique to language knowledge and behavior. The quote from *Through the Looking-*

Glass at the beginning of this section illustrates this difference. Alice could count up the "ones" if they were written down on paper. She knew the rules of addition. She had the competence, but her performance was impeded by the limitations of her short-term memory.

30   Lewis Carroll was intrigued with the difference between competence and performance in linguistic matters as well, as is shown by the following excerpt from *Alice's Adventures in Wonderland*:

> "I quite agree with you," said the Duchess, "and the moral of that is—'Be what you seem to be'—or, if you'd like it put more simply—'Never imagine yourself not to be otherwise than what it might appear to others that what you were or might have been was not otherwise than what you had been would have appeared to them to be otherwise.'"
>
> "I think I should understand that better," Alice said very politely, "if I had it written down: but I'm afraid I can't quite follow it as you say it."
>
> "That's nothing to what I could say if I chose," the duchess replied, in a pleased tone.

The Duchess and Alice were both correct. The Duchess had the knowledge to go on indefinitely, and Alice would have understood the sentence better, if not entirely, had it been written down.

31   To see why this is so, try the following. Combine sentence *a* with sentence *b* to form one sentence.

a. The girl milked the cow.
b. The cow was brown.

You might have come up with sentence *c, d,* or *e*.[3]

c. The girl milked the cow and the cow was brown.
d. The girl milked the cow that was brown.
e. The cow the girl milked was brown.

Now add sentence *f*.

f. The boy kissed the girl.

If you used the same "combining rule" as was used to form sentence *c*, you would get:

g. The boy kissed the girl and the girl milked the cow and the cow was brown.

If you used the rule which formed sentence *d*, you would get:

h. The boy kissed the girl who milked the cow that was brown.

And if you followed the pattern of sentence *e*, you would get:

i. The cow the girl the boy kissed milked was brown.

---

[3]There are, of course, other ways to combine these sentences; for example, *The girl milked the brown cow*. The particular "conjoining rules" illustrated are used to make a specific point.

32 Even when "written down," sentence *i* is not an easy one to understand. But knowing the rule—and you must know it if you could undertand sentence *e*—you could work out the meaning and even produce such a "crazy" sentence. You have the competence to do so. Sometimes when we use this competence in forming and understanding sentences we get "performance-blocked."

33 Another example of the difference between competence and performance is illustrated in a quote from the nineteenth-century *Mathematical Gazette* (Vol. 12) attributed to a certain Mrs. La Touche:

> I do hate sums. There is no greater mistake than to call arithmetic an exact science. There are permutations and aberrations discernible to minds entirely noble like mine; subtle variations which it requires a mind like mine to perceive. For instance, if you add a sum from the bottom up, and then again from the top down, the result is always different.

In using our knowledge of the rules of arithmetic we can make mistakes, as did Mrs. La Touche.

34 In using our knowledge of language in speaking we also make mistakes—slips of the tongue, false starts, and so on. But this doesn't mean that we can't recognize errors—we have the knowledge to do so.

35 The word "spoonerism" was invented to describe a common type of error made famous by an eminent don of Oxford University. When the Reverend Spooner said "You have hissed my mystery lecture—you have tasted the whole worm" instead of "You have missed my history lecture—you have wasted the whole term," or when he mistakenly called a prominent member of the royal family "queer old dean" instead of "dear old queen," he was making performance errors. He knew what he wanted to say, but his tongue "slipped."

36 Someone may say, "Well, like, man, I mean—uh—like, you know the—uh—girl like—er—is—you know—going," but that same person would probably not accept that as an "unstarred" sentence of English. His linguistic competence, his knowledge of the language, tells him it isn't proper. His performance could have been the result of a number of factors, mostly nonlinguistic in nature.

37 If someone is riding a bicycle and falls off, that does not mean she doesn't know how to ride the bicycle. Or if she gets tired in fifteen minutes and stops to rest, it doesn't mean she hasn't the knowledge to ride the bicycle continually for a month, or a year, or forever, if she lived that long. She might not be able to tell you the physical laws she is obeying to maintain her balance, but she knows how to ride the bike. Similarly, you may not be able to state the linguistic "laws" (rules) which account for your knowledge, but these rules make it possible for you to produce and understand an unlimited number of unfamiliar utterances.

PART 1: STUDY QUESTIONS
(Paragraphs 1 and 2)

Read paragraphs 1 and 2 quickly for general understanding. Then refer to the selection to answer the following study questions.

1. Read paragraph 1 again carefully.
   A. What is the main idea of this paragraph?
      a. Language is an extremely important aspect of our lives.
      b. In general, people talk more than they should.
      c. Most people like to talk, even if there is no one to talk to.
   B. Sentence 6 states, "Television and radio further swell this torrent of words." Which of the following statements best paraphrases this sentence?
      a. Television and radio operate almost twenty-four hours a day.
      b. Television and radio add to the large amount of language around us.
      c. Television and radio are different from other types of communication because we listen but do not talk.
   C. In this paragraph, what do the authors suggest is unique to humans?
   _____

2. Read paragraph 2 again carefully.
   A. According to this paragraph, in some areas of Africa, when does a child cease to be considered a *kuntu* (thing) and begin to be considered a *muntu* (person)?
   _____

   _____ _____
   What general idea does this specific example support?
      a. Myths vary from one culture to another.
      b. All children learn language.
      c. Language makes us human.
   B. What is the purpose of the last two sentences in this paragraph? (Think about where you would look to find the answers to the questions in these sentences.)
   _____

   _____

   _____

PART 2: STUDY QUESTIONS
(Paragraphs 3–25)

Directions: Read paragraphs 3–25 quickly for general understanding. Then refer to the reading to answer the following study questions.

1. Read paragraph 3 again carefully.
   A. What is the relationship between the first two sentences?
      a. Sentence 2 restates sentence 1, but in more detail.
      b. Sentence 2 gives an example of the general statement in sentence 1.
      c. Sentence 2 explains the result of a cause stated in sentence 1.
   B. What is the main idea of this paragraph?
      a. Knowing a language means being able to communicate in that language.

Language

242

      b. There is no significant difference between normal-hearing and deaf persons in knowing a language.
      c. The sign language used by deaf persons is fundamentally different from spoken language.

2. Read paragraph 4 again carefully.
   A. In the first sentence, to what does the word *this* refer?

   _____

   B. According to this paragraph, which of the following is true?
      a. We are aware of most of what we know about our own language.
      b. English speakers have little conscious knowledge of Japanese or French.
      c. We are unaware of much of what we know about our own language.
   C. Which of the following is a synonym for the word *profound* in the last sentence?
      a. deep
      b. limited
      c. native
   D. According to the last sentence, what is the authors' goal in this book?

   _____

   _____

3. Read the first sentence in paragraph 5, the first sentence in paragraph 6, and the first two sentences in paragraph 7. Each of these paragraphs discusses one aspect of what it means to know a language. In a short phrase, list the aspect discussed in each paragraph.
      a. paragraph 5: _____
      b. paragraph 6: _____
      c. paragraph 7: _____

4. Now read all of paragraph 5 again carefully.
   A. What is the main idea of this paragraph?

   _____

   B. What two examples are given to help you understand the main idea?

     example 1: _____

     example 2: _____

   C. Sentences 4 and 8 are in question form. Do the authors give the answers to these questions? What is the purpose of these questions?

   _____

   _____

5. Read paragraph 6 again carefully.
   A. Which of the following is the main idea of this paragraph?

What Is Language?

243

   a. Americans have trouble pronouncing the sound at the end of the word *sing* if it occurs at the beginning of a word.
   b. Knowing the possible patterns of sounds is part of our knowledge of a language.
   c. We learn what we know about our language when we are children.
B. List three or four English words that you have difficulty pronouncing correctly. Are these words difficult for you because they include sounds that do not normally occur in your native language? Are they difficult because they include sounds that your native language normally restricts to other positions within a word?

_____
_____
_____
_____

6. Read paragraphs 7 and 8 again carefully.
   A. What is the purpose of the first sentence in paragraph 7? (Does it point back to the previous paragraph or ahead?)

   _____
   _____

   B. The second sentence in paragraph 7 expresses the main idea of the paragraph. Which of the following statements best paraphrases that sentence?
      a. Understanding the meaning of words as they are spoken is the most important part of knowing a language.
      b. The relationship between sounds and sound sequences is an important part of our linguistic knowledge.
      c. Different sounds have different meanings in different languages.
   C. Why is the word *arbitrary* in boldface type in the sixth sentence in paragraph 7?

   _____

   What does *arbitrary* mean here?
      a. not fixed by rules
      b. unconscious; not aware
      c. learned; fixed by rules
   What do the authors mean when they state that the relationship between the sounds of words and the meaning of the words is arbitrary?

   _____
   _____

   D. Why are there pictures of a house and a hand in paragraphs 7 and 8? Why didn't the authors simply use the words *house* and *hand*?

   _____
   _____

7. Read paragraphs 9 and 10 carefully.
   A. Paragraph 9 lists a number of words in different languages. Do you think the authors want you to learn these words? Why or why not?

   _____
   _____

Language

   B. The first sentence in paragraph 10 explains the purpose of the examples in paragraph 9. What concept are the authors trying to convey?
      a. Knowing words in several different languages will give you a better sense of how sounds relate to meaning.
      b. Languages will permit sounds to occur only in certain sequences or patterns.
      c. The relationship between words and their meanings is arbitrary and makes sense only within a particular language.
   In paragraph 10, the authors provide a short excerpt from the book *Eve's Diary* by Mark Twain. Do you think that Twain was being serious when he wrote this? Explain your answer.

   _____
   _____

   The purpose of the quotation from *Eve's Diary* is to support the idea that the relationship between the sounds of words and their meanings is arbitrary. Do you think that the quotation is helpful to the reader? Why or why not?

   _____
   _____

8. Read paragraphs 11 and 12 carefully.
   A. What is the topic of these two paragraphs?
      a. pronunciation
      b. sound symbolism
      c. sound sequences
   B. In your own words, what do the authors mean by *sound symbolism*?
      _____
      _____

   C. What does *onomatopoeic* mean?
      _____
      _____

   What example of an onomatopoeic word is given?
      _____

   Can you think of other examples of onomatopoeic language, either in English or in your native language?
      _____

   D. According to paragraph 12, what is the significance of the letters *gl* at the beginning of words in English?
      a. Many English words that begin with *gl* are rhyming words.
      b. Most English words have something to do with sight.
      c. Many English words that begin with *gl* involve the concept of seeing.
   E. Do you think that the "sound symbolism" discussed in these paragraphs can be of great help to someone learning English as a foreign or second language? Why or why not?
      _____
      _____

What Is Language?

245

9. Read paragraph 13 carefully.
   A. This paragraph acts as a transition between ideas. That is, it points both backward *and* forward. Which sentences in this paragraph point backward to summarize ideas presented in the preceding paragraphs?
      a. sentence 1 only
      b. sentences 1 and 2
      c. sentences 1, 2, and 3
   B. What general idea does this paragraph point forward to?
      a. Studying a dictionary is not an effective way to learn a language.
      b. Even native speakers of a language do not know all the words in that language.
      c. Knowing a language is more than knowing its words and sounds.
   C. What do you expect the rest of this section, paragraphs 14–25, to discuss?
      a. what is necessary in order to know a language, besides knowing words and sounds
      b. what it means to know the sound system of a language
      c. how it is possible to use a dictionary in order to speak a foreign language well

10. Read paragraph 14 carefully.
    A. According to this paragraph, when you know a language, you can use it "creatively." What do the authors means by the "creative aspect" of language use?

    _____

    _____

    What sentence defines the "creative aspect" of language use? (More than one choice may be correct.)
       a. sentence 3
       b. sentence 4
       c. sentence 5
       d. sentence 6
    B. According to the authors, is language use limited to stimulus-response behavior?

    _____

    C. Read the last sentence in this paragraph. What is another aspect of knowing a language?

    _____

11. Read paragraph 15 carefully.
    A. This paragraph gives an example of a sentence that does not make sense. Is the sentence *grammatically* correct? _____
    B. What point are the authors trying to make with this example?
       a. Some sentences are not believable even if they make sense.
       b. We can create nonsense sentences that are logical and have several different meanings.
       c. We can understand sentences we have never seen or heard before, even if they do not make sense.

12. Read paragraph 16 carefully. The authors restate the idea that individuals can both understand and create new sentences that have never been heard before. What support do they offer in proof of this? Summarize their argument.

    _____

    _____

    _____

Language

246

13. Read paragraphs 17–20 carefully. These paragraphs give further support for the argument that all the possible sentences in a language cannot be stored in the brain. Fill in the blanks in the following paragraph to summarize the authors' argument.

There is no _____ on the length of a sentence, and there are an _____ number of possible sentences. Any sentence can be made _____ by adding another word to it. In order to memorize all sentences in a language, our brains would have to have an infinite _____. However, the brain is _____, so it is impossible for it to store all sentences.

14. Read paragraphs 21–25 carefully.
    A. Which of the following is true according to paragraph 21?
       a. Although there are an unlimited number of possible sentences in a language, what we learn about the language must be limited.
       b. Sentences in a language can be formed by placing one word after another in any order.
       c. Our knowledge of a language can be described simply by a list of words in that language.
    B. What is the purpose of the list of sentences given in paragraph 21?
       _____
       _____

    C. Paragraph 24 states that, in addition to knowing the words of a language, we must also know some "rules." According to the authors, what two things must be true about these rules?
       a. _____
       b. _____
    D. Fill in the blanks in the following paragraph to summarize the main idea of paragraph 24.

    Words must be arranged in a certain order to be meaningful. Speakers of a language must know some _____ that allow them to determine if a group of words make up a sentence. Because our brains have a limited storage capacity, these rules must be _____ in length and finite in _____. Although these rules are finite, they allow us to create and to understand an _____ number of sentences.

PART 2: COMPREHENSION EXERCISES
(Paragraphs 3–25)

Exercise 1

The following statements are either *true* or *false* according to paragraphs 3–25 of the reading. Write either T or F in the space before each one.

1. _____ Almost all of your knowledge of your native language is conscious; that is, you are aware of your knowledge.

2. _____ English speakers tend to pronounce the German name *Bach* incorrectly because English does not include the German sound signified by the letters *ch*.

3. _____ Young children must be taught in school which sounds are part of their native language and which are not.

4. _____ For most words, the relationship between sound and meaning is arbitrary.

5. _____ Knowing the vocabulary of a language is sufficient to be able to communicate in that language.

6. _____ We are all able to create and understand sentences that are completely new and that have never been spoken or heard before.

7. _____ We are able to memorize virtually all the possible sentences in a language.

8. _____ Native speakers of a language have difficulty agreeing whether or not a particular string of words makes an acceptable sentence in that language.

9. _____ Knowing a language includes knowing some "rules" for combining words and phrases.

Exercise 2

Complete the following summary of paragraphs 3–25 by filling in the blanks with an appropriate word or phrase.

Knowing a language means being able to _____ and to be _____ by other people who know that language. However, much of our knowledge of a language is _____; that is, we are not aware of what we know.

When we know a language, we know about the _____ system of the language. This fact is demonstrated when we try to pronounce words in another language that contain sounds not found in _____. For example, speakers of English have difficulty pronouncing the German sound represented by the final two letters in the name *Bach* because that sound does not exist in English. Another part of our knowledge of a language is what _____ of sounds are possible. Thus, knowing a language also includes knowing which sounds can start a word, end a word, and follow each other.

Probably the most important part of knowing a language is the knowledge of which sounds or sequences of sounds represent which _____. In other words, we know the _____ of the language. It is important to realize that the relationship between sound and meaning in a language is _____ _____; there is no logical or rational relationship between the two. However, there is some _____ in language in words whose pronunciation suggests the _____. For example, the English word for the sound made by a rooster, *cockadoodledoo*, is similar to the actual sound made by the rooster.

Language

248

Even when you know the sound system of a language, the possible sequencing of sounds, and the basic vocabulary, you need to know more in order to communicate. Words must be placed in a certain _____ to make meaningful sentences. Our knowledge of a language includes rules that allow us to do this. The linguist Noam Chomsky states that the _____ aspect of language is the ability to speak and understand sentences we have never heard before. Thus, there is an _____ number of possible sentences in any language. Obviously, we cannot memorize an unlimited number of sentences because the capacity of our brains to store information is _____. So the rules we need in order to form sentences must be finite in _____ and finite in _____.

Exercise 3

Look back at questions 1, 2, 3, and 4 in the Warmup section at the beginning of the chapter. Now that you have read Part 2 of "What Is Language?" which of these questions might you answer differently? Which would you answer in the same way?

PART 3: STUDY QUESTIONS
(Paragraphs 26–38)

Directions: Part 2 of "What Is Language?" discussed the knowledge involved in knowing a language. Part 3 examines how we use this knowledge to communicate in the language. Read paragraphs 26–38 quickly for general understanding. Then refer to the reading to answer the following study questions.

1. Look carefully at the heading for this section, above paragraph 26.
   A. How many subsections do you think this section contains? _____
      What do you think these subsections are?

      a. _____

      b. _____

   B. Without referring to paragraph 26, can you provide general, informal definitions of *linguistic competence* and *linguistic performance*?

      a. linguistic competence: _____

      b. linguistic performance: _____

2. Read paragraph 26 again carefully.
   A. According to this paragraph, what is linguistic competence?

      What is linguistic performance?

      Were your definitions of these terms in question 1 correct?

B. In the second sentence of paragraph 26, to what does the word *this* refer?
_____
_____

C. Look at the phrase *piling up* in the second sentence. What do you think the general meaning of this phrase is?
    a. to use again and again
    b. to understand
    c. to add one item on top of another
What is the specific meaning of *piling up* in this paragraph?
_____
_____

D. The quotation below the heading for Part 3 is from a famous English children's story called *Through the Looking-Glass*. What do you think the quotation means? Now find the first place in the text where *Through the Looking-Glass* is mentioned. What is the paragraph number and sentence number?
_____

Carefully read the paragraph you just identified. In your own words, explain why the authors began the section with this dialogue between Alice and the Red Queen.
_____
_____
_____

3. Read paragraph 27 again carefully.
   A. According to this paragraph, what two types of reasons explain why our linguistic performance is not always the same as our competence?

      a. _____
      b. _____

   B. Four examples of such reasons are listed. Indicate whether each is type a or type b.

      a. "run out of breath" _____
      b. "audience may leave" _____
      c. "lose track of what has been said" _____
      d. "you don't live forever" _____

4. Read paragraph 28 again carefully. Which of the following gives the main idea of this paragraph?
    a. Linguistic competence helps us to speak and understand.
    b. Linguistic competence is learned, but unconscious.
    c. No one can teach us the rules of a language.

5. Read paragraph 29 again carefully.
   A. Which of the following is an accurate paraphrase of the first sentence in this paragraph?
      a. The ideas of competence and performance are unique to language.
      b. It is difficult to distinguish competence from performance.
      c. The distinction between competence and performance can be applied to behavior other than language.

Language

250

    B. Try to paraphrase the last sentence in this paragraph (which refers to the quotation from *Through the Looking-Glass*).

    _____

    _____

6. Read paragraphs 30, 31, and 32 carefully.
    A. What is the overall purpose of these three paragraphs?
        a. They demonstrate that the Red Queen's competence was superior to Alice's performance.
        b. They demonstrate that it is important to study the rules for forming relative clauses because they can become very long and complex.
        c. They demonstrate that although sentences can become very long and complex, we have the competence to understand them.
    B. Read the last sentence in paragraph 30. Paraphrase this part of the sentence: "Alice would have understood the sentence better . . . had it been written down."

    _____

    _____

    C. Refer to paragraph 31. Read the following statements, and write *yes* or *no* in the space next to each.

        a. _____ Sentence *e* is an acceptable sentence.

        b. _____ Sentence *i* follows the same pattern as sentence *e*.

        c. _____ Sentence *i* is grammatically correct because it follows the same pattern as sentence *e*.

        d. _____ Sentence *i* is easy to understand.

        e. _____ Sentence *i* is not easy to understand because of a competence problem.

        f. _____ Sentence *i* is not easy to understand because of a performance problem.

    D. To what does *do so* refer in the third sentence of paragraph 32?
        a. understanding sentence *i* and making up similar sentences
        b. knowing the rule and understanding sentence *e*
        c. writing down sentences such as *e* and *i*
    E. What does *performance-blocked* mean in paragraph 32?

    _____

    _____

7. Read paragraph 33 again carefully.
    A. What is Mrs. La Touche's problem?
        a. She thinks her mind is too noble for an exact science like arithmetic.
        b. She gets different answers each time she adds a list of numbers.
        c. She does not know the rules of arithmetic well enough to add a list of numbers.
    B. What general idea does the example of Mrs. La Touche illustrate?

    _____

    _____

What Is Language?

251

8. Read paragraphs 34, 35, and 36 again carefully.
   A. These paragraphs discuss slips of the tongue and false starts. Are these performance mistakes or competence mistakes?

   _____

   B. What do the authors mean by *slip of the tongue*?

   _____
   _____

9. Read paragraph 37 again carefully.
   A. Why do the authors write about riding a bicycle?

   _____
   _____

   B. The example about the bicycle in this paragraph is called an *analogy*. Study this example carefully. Then, without consulting a dictionary, write your own definition of *analogy*.

   _____
   _____

   C. Indicate whether each of the following statements is *true* or *false* according to the analogy presented in this paragraph.

   a. _____ Falling off a bicycle is similar to a performance mistake in speaking.

   b. _____ Becoming tired of riding a bicycle and stopping to rest may be compared to a linguistic competence problem.

   c. _____ The inability to explain the physical laws involved in riding a bicycle is similar to the unconscious nature of our knowledge of language.

COMPREHENSION EXERCISES
(Paragraphs 26–38)

Exercise 1

The following statements are either *true* or *false* according to paragraphs 26–38 of the reading. Write either T or F in the space before each one.

1. _____ Linguistic performance allows a speaker to understand and produce an infinitely long sentence.
2. _____ Linguistic competence can be defined as "what you know."
3. _____ The reasons why performance might be blocked are almost always physiological.
4. _____ The competence/performance distinction can be applied to other types of behavior besides language.
5. _____ A spoonerism is an example of a performance mistake.
6. _____ Linguistic competence represents conscious knowledge about one's language.
7. _____ Our linguistic competence allows us to guess the meaning of words we have never heard before.
8. _____ If we make performance mistakes while speaking, we are not able to recognize them as mistakes.

Language

Exercise 2

Complete the following summary of paragraphs 26–38 by filling in each blank with an appropriate word or phrase.

There is a difference between our unconscious knowledge of a language and the way we use this knowledge when we speak. Linguists refer to the former as our _____ _____ and the latter as our _____. For example, we have the *ability* to create and understand infinitely long sentences, but we may not actually be able to do so for a number of different reasons. That is, our linguistic _____ _____ may be limited due to _____ factors (we run out of breath) or to _____ factors (we lose track of what we are saying).

The distinction between _____ and _____ _____ can be applied to other types of behavior. Thus, the knowledge of simple arithmetic may be distinguished from the ability to apply this knowledge in specific circumstances. When an individual has the competence to do something, but cannot because of physiological or psychological limitations, we say that the individual is _____ _____.

Sometimes, we make performance errors when we speak, such as _____ _____ and _____. One type of performance error, confusing the first letters of different words in a phrase, is called a _____.

Exercise 3

Look back at questions 5, 6, and 8 in the Warmup section at the beginning of this chapter. Now that you have read Part 3 of "What Is Language?" which of these questions might you answer differently? Which would you answer in the same way?

CHAPTER 14

Acquisition and Learning

WARMUP QUESTIONS

The selection in this chapter, "Acquisition and Learning," comes from a book titled *The Natural Approach* by Steven Krashen and Tracy Terrell. It examines the concept of language from the point of view of an adult learning a second language.

How do we learn languages as adults? Should we study grammar? Should we memorize lists of vocabulary? How important is it to speak the language with others? Before you read the selection, consider the following statements, and indicate whether you *agree* or *disagree* with each one. Discuss your opinions with your classmates.

1. _____ Children can learn a second language only if they are taught the grammar rules for that language.
2. _____ Adults learn a second language more easily if they are able to use it naturally in communicative situations.
3. _____ Learners of a second language use their conscious knowledge of grammar rules at all times when speaking the language.
4. _____ When individuals begin to learn a second language, it is important for them always to speak in grammatically correct sentences.
5. _____ Conscious knowledge of the rules of a language can help learners of a second language to write more effectively.

The following questions are about learning a second language—specifically, about your learning English as a second language. Answer the questions with your own ideas and from your own experiences, and then discuss your answers with your classmates.

a. What has been the most difficult part of learning English for you?

_____

Language

b. How can your English teachers best help you to improve your English?

_____

_____

c. Rate how well you use English in each of the following situations:
   Speaking to American friends
       very good   good   fair   poor
   Listening to American television and radio
       very good   good   fair   poor
   Writing an essay examination or a paper for an academic class
       very good   good   fair   poor
   Reading an English textbook
       very good   good   fair   poor

DIRECTIONS FOR READING

Before you read this selection, first scan it quickly. Read the first sentence of each paragraph, and note the words that are highlighted. Then read the entire selection quickly for general understanding and turn to the study questions that follow.

Acquisition and Learning
Steven Krashen and Tracy Terrell

1. The most important and useful theoretical point is the *acquisition-learning* distinction, the hypothesis that adult language students have two distinct ways of developing skills and knowledge in a second language. Simply, **acquiring a** language is "picking it up," i.e., developing ability in a language by using it in natural, communicative situations. Children acquire their first language, and most probably, second languages as well. As we shall see in Chapter Two, adults also can acquire: they do not usually do it quite as well as children, but it appears that language acquisition is the central, most important means for gaining linguistic skills even for an adult.

2. Language **learning** is different from acquisition. Language learning is "knowing the rules," having a conscious knowledge about grammar. According to recent research, it appears that formal language learning is not nearly as important in developing communicative ability in second languages as previously thought. Many researchers now believe that language acquisition is responsible for the ability to understand and speak second languages easily and well. Language learning may only be useful as an editor, which we will call a **Monitor**. We use acquisition when we initiate sentences in second languages, and bring in learning only as a kind of after-thought to make alterations and corrections.

3. Conscious rules have therefore a limited function in second language use; we refer to conscious grammar rules only to make changes, hopefully corrections. These changes can come before the sentence is actually spoken or written, or they can come after (self-correction). The function of conscious learning seems even more limited when we consider that in order to Monitor our speech successfully, that is, in order to make corrections, several conditions have to be met: (1) the second language user has to have *time* to inspect the utterance before it is spoken, (2) the speaker has to be consciously concerned about **correctness**, and (3) he has to **know** the rule. In natural conversation, all of these conditions are rarely met. Normal conversation tends to be quite rapid, and the speaker's attention is usually on **what** is being said, not **how** it is being said. In addition, our conscious knowledge of grammar covers only a small portion of the rules of a language. On the other hand, all three conditions are met quite well on grammar tests. These are usually written rather than oral and are designed to make students think about language form and not the message; they usually focus almost exclusively on rules that have just been taught in the classroom. In this situation knowledge which has been learned is, of course, of great help.

4. Knowledge of conscious rules can be helpful in situations other than formal grammar exams. In writing and in prepared speech, performers do have time to apply conscious knowledge of the second language and can use this knowledge to improve the form of their output by Monitoring. Ideally, learning will supplement acquired competence in such cases, performers using learning to supply aspects of language that have not yet been acquired. Such items may not add much to the communicative value of the output, but they may give a more polished, a more "educated" look. In writing, learning may also be useful for some spelling and punctuation problems.

5   Difficulties arise when performers, especially beginners, become over-concerned with correctness in communicative situations, trying to check their output against conscious rules at all times. This overuse of the Monitor results in hesitancy and subsequent difficulty in participating in conversation. Ideal or optimal use of the Monitor occurs when second language speakers use the rules they have learned without interfering with communication.

STUDY QUESTIONS

Directions: Refer to the reading to answer the following study questions.

1. Read paragraph 1 again carefully.
   A. What are the two basic means of developing skills and knowledge in a second language?
      a. _____
      b. _____
      Is this distinction considered to be a scientific fact? How do you know?
      _____
      _____

   B. In your own words, define *acquiring a language* as it is explained in this paragraph.
      _____
      _____

   C. According to this paragraph, how do child language learners and adult language learners differ?
      _____
      _____

2. Read paragraph 2 again carefully.
   A. In this paragraph, the authors define *language learning* (as it differs from *language acquisition*). Paraphrase the authors' definition.
      _____
      _____

   B. Which of the following can you infer from this paragraph?
      a. Adults cannot master a second language completely unless they study its grammar.
      b. Adults cannot speak a second language easily and well unless they *acquire* it.
      c. *Learning* is the same as having an unconscious knowledge about grammar.

   C. Which do many researchers now think is more important in mastering a second language, acquisition or learning?
      _____

   D. What word in this paragraph means the same as *editor*?
      _____
      What is the function of the editor?
      a. to begin sentences
      b. to make changes
      c. to acquire language

3. Read paragraph 3 again carefully.
   A. Which do you think is the topic sentence of this paragraph?
      a. sentence 1
      b. sentences 1 and 2 together
      c. sentence 3
      d. the last sentence

Language

258

B. Does the first sentence in this paragraph introduce a new idea, or does it restate a previous idea?

_____

C. According to this paragraph, when do we refer to our conscious grammar rules? (More than one answer may be correct.)
   a. to make changes
   b. to correct our mistakes
   c. to help on written grammar tests

D. What are the three conditions for editing or monitoring language use?

   a. _____

   b. _____

   c. _____

   In what type of situation are these conditions *not* usually met?

   _____

4. Read paragraphs 4 and 5 again carefully.
   A. Which of the following statements is true, according to these paragraphs?
      a. People may be able to understand your writing even if it contains grammar or spelling errors.
      b. Frequent use of the Monitor will help you to participate normally in everyday conversation.
      c. Conscious knowledge of formal rules helps only when you are taking examinations.
   B. Which of the following has the same meaning as "the communicative value of the output" in the fourth sentence of paragraph 4?
      a. how much a speaker says about a certain topic
      b. the speaker's message and how well it is supported
      c. how much of what the speaker says is understood by others
   C. Which of the following is true, according to paragraph 4?
      a. Conscious knowledge of grammar rules can greatly improve the communicative value of the output.
      b. Conscious knowledge of grammar rules can improve the form, or polish, of the output.
      c. Conscious knowledge of grammar rules can take the place of acquisition.
   D. What is the main idea of paragraph 5?
      a. Learners should use conscious rules to check their output at all times.
      b. Difficulties arise when beginners are not concerned enough about correctness.
      c. Learners should use the Monitor only if it does not interfere with what they are trying to say.
   E. Patrick, an American student who is living in France for a year, is studying comparative literature. The following is a list of things that Patrick does in order to improve his French.

      Put an *L* next to the items that you think are examples of *learning*. Put an *A* next to the items that you think are examples of *acquisition*. Be prepared to explain your choices.

      _____ Listen to the news on the radio

      _____ Watch TV shows that have been dubbed so that the actors are speaking French

      _____ Spend time with his friend Nicole, whose first language is French

_____ Meet with his American friends to discuss difficult points of French grammar
_____ Take a course in "Vocabulary of Business French"
_____ Make a list of difficult words, with their meanings translated into English, and memorize them
_____ Frequently visit parts of the city where tourists do not go

INTEGRATION QUESTIONS FOR DISCUSSION AND WRITING

Directions: The following questions ask you to find relationships among the ideas in the first two selections in this unit: "What Is Language?" (Chapter 13) and "Acquisition and Learning" (Chapter 14). Discuss your answers with your classmates.

1. "What Is Language?" is written for American students and discusses what it means for native speakers to know a language. "Acquisition and Learning" was written for people who teach a second language to adults and discusses what it means to know a second language.

    Consider both reading selections. What is the difference between competence in a first language and competence in a second language? How is competence attained in each situation?

2. Consider the following quotations from "What Is Language?":
    "You have the competence to understand or produce an infinitely long sentence."
    "In using our knowledge of language in speaking we also make mistakes. . . . But this doesn't mean that we can't recognize errors."
    "Sometimes when we use this competence in forming and understanding sentences, we get 'performance blocked.'"
What is the relationship between competence and acquisition, as it is defined by Krashen and Terrell in "Acquisition and Learning"? What is the relationship between competence and learning?

CHAPTER 15

Child Language Acquisition

WARMUP QUESTIONS

The selection in this chapter is taken from *Child Psychology: A Contemporary Viewpoint* by E. Marvis Hetherington and Ross D. Parke. It approaches the topic of language from the point of view of how children learn to speak.

How do children learn their native language? Is it a process of repeating what adults around them say? Do young children use a grammatical rule system when they speak? Do they learn certain words before others? Before you read the selection, consider the following statements, and indicate whether you *agree* or *disagree* with each one. Discuss your opinions with your classmates.

1. _____ The first words that children learn are those they hear spoken most often by the adults around them.
2. _____ Young children sometimes use one word to express an idea that an adult would express in a complete sentence.
3. _____ When children learn their first language, they learn grammar, vocabulary, and communication skills separately.
4. _____ Children raised in different cultures with different languages learn language in different ways.
5. _____ When a child speaks a two-word phrase such as "Mommy book," it may have various meanings, for example, "Mommy is reading a book" or "That is Mommy's book."

The following questions concern how children learn their first language. Answer the questions with your own ideas and from your own experiences, and then discuss your answers with your classmates.

a. List several words that you think are learned earliest by children.

_____

_____

b. What types of words have you listed? What parts of speech are they? What aspect of a child's life do they involve? Why do you think a child would learn these words before other words?

_____

_____

_____

_____

DIRECTIONS FOR READING

Before you read this selection, first scan it quickly. Read the first sentence in each paragraph, note the headings, and look carefully at the illustrations. Then read the entire selection quickly for general understanding, and turn to the study questions that follow.

Child Language Acquisition
E. Marvis Hetherington and Ross D. Parke

ONE WORD AT A TIME

1   The title of this section, which is also a title of a book (Bloom, 1973), reflects our continuing fascination with the young child's first halting steps on the road to language mastery, namely, her early one-word utterances. Between 10 and 13 months, the child speaks her first word (McCarthy, 1954), and for the next few months language occurs "one word at a time." In a recent study of the first fifty words, Nelson (1973) classified words into six categories. Figure 15-1 illustrates the different kinds of words used by young children. Children show considerable uniformity in their early vocabulary, but early words are still highly selective. Children learn words that represent objects that they can act on and that produce a change or movement. For example, the words "shoes," "socks," and "toys" are more common than words denoting objects that are just "there," such as "tables," "stove," and "trees." Language—from the first words onward—is always closely linked to function. The child learns those words which are perceptually salient and meaningful in terms of her own world, for these words are most important for identifying objects that she may wish to interact with.

2   However, children use words differently than adults. Children may use a word in a highly restricted and individualistic way. A child may only use the word "car" when she sees her father's yellow Porsche and call all other automobiles trucks. Or later children overgeneralize; everyone has heard a young child term horses, cows, and other four-legged animals, "doggie." The child is not just making an error; he or she is trying to find the relationship between a linguistic form and an element of experience. As Bloom notes:

> It seems entirely reasonable for the child to use an available word to represent different but related objects—it is almost as if the child were

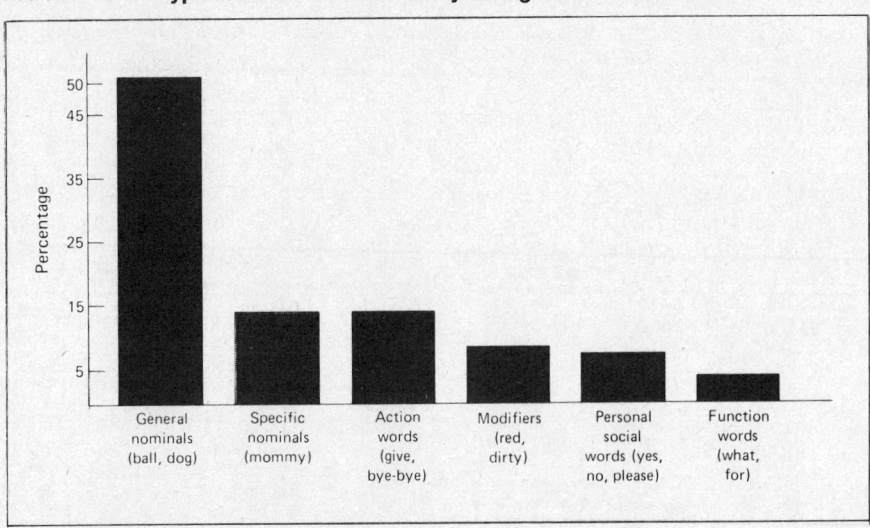

FIGURE 15-1 Types of First Words Used by Young Infants and Children.

SOURCE: Based on data from Nelson, 1973.

reasoning, "I know about dogs, that thing is not a dog, I don't know what to call it, but it is like a dog." (1977, p. 23)

For the child, applying words in different contexts is a type of hypothesis testing, a process that will continue throughout childhood. This process manifests itself particularly in the first three years when the process of relating the word form with the object begins (Bloom, 1973, 1976). Gradually as the child's discriminations improve and their conceptual categories become more stable, the child's accuracy in the use of words increases. But are they just single words?

3   When a young child points to a toy airplane on a high shelf and says "down" or when he takes a spoon from his mother and says "me," is there more than meets the ear? In the first case, the child may be requesting that the toy be taken down off the shelf, or in our second example, the child may be saying "I want to do it myself." As Dale notes:

> First words seem to be more than single words. They appear to be attempts to express complex ideas, ideas that would be expressed in sentences by an adult. The term "holophrastic speech" is often used to capture this idea of "words that are sentences." (1976, p. 13)

Whether or not children are really expressing sentences in a word remains more an intriguing idea than a proven fact at this point.

4   These early observations do underline one of the important insights about language development: children do not acquire different skills—grammar, meaning, and communication skills—separately. Rather there is a constant interplay among these three faces of language. Well before children can formulate the correct grammatical form, they are actively trying to communicate to others around them and to indicate what they mean. It is out of these early attempts to make themselves and their wishes understood and meaningful for others that their grasp of grammar gradually emerges. The next step is from one word to two words.

BEYOND SINGLE WORDS

5   The next important step in language development is the use of not just a single word but two words together. Children generally take this step around 18 to 20 months of age. At this point, language is still simpler than adult language and more selective since although nouns, verbs, and adjectives are generally present, others, such as articles, prepositions, etc., are often absent. However, the child's speech is still novel and creative and not merely a copy of adult language. Table 15-1 shows some of the kinds of two-word sentences used by young children not only in English, but in other cultures as well. Notice the high degree of similarity of the semantic relations of the two-word sentences used by children in cultures as different as Finnish, English, and Samoan. As Slobin observed:

> If you ignore word order and read through transcriptions of two word utterances in the various languages we have studied, the utterances read like direct translations of one another. (1970, p. 177)

6   Why are the early utterances of children similar? Language can be viewed as a way of expressing what one understands about the world at a particular

TABLE 15-1 Some Semantic Relations in Stage I Speech from Several Languages

Relation	English	German	Russian	Finnish	Luo	Samoan
Recurrence	more milk	mehr Milch (more milk)	yesche moloka (more milk)	lisaa kakkua (more cake)		
Attributive	big boat	Milch heiss (milk hot)	papa bol-shoy (papa big)	rikki auto (broken car)	piypiy kech (pepper hot)	fa'ali'i pepe (headstrong baby)
Possessive	mama dress	Mamas Hut (mama's hat)	mami chashka (mama's cup)	tati auto (aunt car)	kom baba (chair father)	paluni mama (balloon mama)
Action-locative	walk street	Sofa sitzen (sofa sit)		viedaan kauppa (take store)	odhi skul (he-went school)	tu'u lala (put down)
Agent-action	Bambi go	Puppe kommt (doll comes)	mama prua (mama walk)	Seppo putoo (Seppo fall)	chungu biro (European comes)	pa'u pepe (fall doll)
Action-object	hit ball		nasbla yaechko (found egg)	ajaa bmbm (drives car)	omoyo oduma (she dries maize)	
Question	where ball	wo Ball (where ball)	gdu papa (where papa)	missa pallo (where ball)		fea Pupafu (where Pupafu)

SOURCE: Adapted from Table 1 of D. I. Slobin, Universals of grammatical development in children. In G. B. Flores d'Arcais and W. J. M. Levelt (Eds.), *Advances in psycholinguistics*, Amsterdam: North-Holland, 1970, pp. 178–179.

age. The content of what children say is closely related to their general level of intellectual functioning at any given stage in development. Children who are beginning to speak are also beginning to understand various environmental relationships, such as self-other distinctions, primitive concepts of causality, and notions about the permance of objects. Therefore, beginning speakers all over the world use similar types of relations in their early speech, such as agent-action relations, possessives, disappearance, and reappearance. This is presumably because these particular relations are significant in the children's cognitive processes at that time. That is, semantic development and cognitive or intellectual development are probably closely related (Bloom, 1970; Nelson, 1973).

7   These early utterances of children cannot easily be understood by an examination of the syntax or grammatical relations alone. A knowledge of the context in which early speech occurs is critical for capturing the child's meaning. For instance, 21-month-old Kathryn, who was studied by Bloom (1970), was observed to say "Mommy sock" in two separate contexts: when Kathryn picked up her mother's sock, and when mother was putting Kathryn's sock on Kathryn. In the first context Kathryn was probably describing the sock as belonging to Mommy, whereas in the second context she probably meant that Mommy was doing something involving a sock. Theoretically, "Mommy sock" might express many things, including "Mommy is that a sock?" "Mommy, give me the sock," or perhaps even "Mommy, go sock Daddy!" As another example, Bloom (1970) has pointed out that the observed negative sentence "No dirty soap" could be interpreted in at least four ways: There is no dirty soap; the soap isn't dirty; that isn't dirty *soap*; and I don't want the dirty soap.

8   Since the meaning is ambiguous from word order alone, Bloom has made the important suggestion that the child's immediate behavior and the context in which the language occurs be carefully recorded and evaluated as a clue to the meaning. She sees this as necessary in studying the child's progress in expressing meaning syntactically. Even as children move from words to sentences, in order to understand language the context in which it occurs must be considered. In the next section, we watch the children's grammatical skills unfold as they begin to move from words to sentences.

REFERENCES

Bloom, L. *Language and development: Form and function in emerging grammars.* Cambridge, Mass.: M.I.T. Press, 1970.

Bloom, L. *One word at a time.* The Hague: Mouton, 1973.

Bloom, L. An interactive perspective on language development. Keynote address, Child Language Research Forum, Stanford University, 1976.

Bloom, L. The integration of form, content and use in language development. Unpublished manuscript, Columbia University, 1977.

Dale, P. S. *Language development: Structure and function* (2nd ed.). New York: Holt, 1976.

McCarthy, D. Language development in children: In L. Carmichael (ed.), *Manual of child psychology.* New York: Wiley, 1954, pp. 452–630.

Nelson, K., Carskaddon, G., and Bonvillian, J. D. Syntax acquisition: Impact of experimental variation in adult verbal interaction with the child. *Child Development*, 1973, *44*, 497–504.

Slobin, D. I. Universals of grammatical development in children. In G. B. Flores d'Arcais and J. M. Levelt (eds.), *Advances in Psycholinguistics.* New York: American Elsevier, 1970, pp. 174–184.

STUDY QUESTIONS

Directions: Refer to the reading to answer the following study questions.

1. Read paragraph 1 again, and examine Figure 15-1 carefully.
   A. According to the information in this paragraph, which of the following is true?
      a. Children first learn function words, such as *what* and *for*.
      b. Children first learn words that will allow them to communicate what is important to them.
      c. Children between the ages of 10 and 13 months learn one word at a time, but often use several words together in a phrase.
   B. Refer to the ideas presented in the paragraph. Which of the following sets of words do you think children would learn first?
      a. *go, read, house, with*
      b. *desk, blue, fall down, John*
      c. *cat, book, truck, spoon*

2. Read paragraph 2 again carefully.
   A. Which of the following is an example of overgeneralization of a word by a young child?
      a. The child calls all men *Daddy*.
      b. The child calls her father a *man*, but all other men *boys*.
      c. The child calls all dogs *doggies*.
   B. What is one reason that children become more accurate in using words as they become older?
      a. They become better at seeing the differences between objects.
      b. They begin to enjoy testing hypotheses more.
      c. They start to use several words together to express their meaning.

3. Read paragraph 3 again carefully.
   A. What is the main idea of this paragraph?
      a. The term *holophrastic speech* is used to describe single-word speech.
      b. Young children will point and say *down* when they want something on a high shelf.
      c. Young children may express a full-sentence idea in a single word.
   B. Is the concept of holophrastic speech considered to be a scientific fact? Explain your answer.

   _____

   _____

4. Read paragraph 4 again carefully.
   A. What are the "three faces of language" to which the authors refer?

      a. _____

      b. _____

      c. _____
   B. Which of the following is true, according to this paragraph?
      a. In most cases, children learn grammar before they learn communication skills.
      b. Children can communicate effectively only if they have already mastered the grammar of a language.
      c. Children gradually learn the grammar of a language by trying to communicate their ideas.

Language

268

5. Read paragraph 5 again carefully and examine Table 15-1.
   A. According to this paragraph, what is the second stage of first-language acquisition?

   _____

   How is language at this stage different from adult language?

   _____

   _____

   How is language at this stage similar to adult language?

   _____

   _____

   B. What do you think the authors mean by *semantic relations* of two-word sentences?
      a. the relationship between the meanings of words
      b. the relationship between the sounds of words
      c. the relationship between words in different languages
   C. Table 15-1 lists seven different semantic relations that are commonly found in the two-word stage of child speech. List these relations, and indicate what you think each means.

      a. _____

      b. _____

      c. _____

      d. _____

      e. _____

      f. _____

      g. _____

   D. What type of semantic relation do the following child sentences display: "Big boat," "Milk hot," "Broken car"?
      a. causality
      b. attribution
      c. possession

6. Read paragraph 6 carefully.
   A. Why does the speech of same-aged children all over the world show similar semantic relationships?
      a. Certain types of relationships are significant to children at certain ages.
      b. All parents attempt to teach their children similar types of language.
      c. Certain relationships are easier for children to express in language than others.
   B. According to this paragraph, what two aspects of a child's development influence each other?

      _____ and _____

7. Read paragraphs 7 and 8 again carefully.
   A. What is the main idea of paragraph 7?
      a. Negative sentences can have a variety of different meanings.
      b. In order to understand children's early speech, it is necessary to examine its syntax, or grammatical relations.
      c. Children's early speech can sometimes be interpreted in several different ways.

B. What are some possible meanings of this child sentence: "Daddy go"? (Use your imagination.)

_____

_____

_____

C. Why is it suggested that researchers record children's behavior as well as their words when studying child language?
   a. Children can express meaning through action before they can express the same meaning through words.
   b. How children act is as important as what they say.
   c. Children's behavior can help clarify the meaning of their words.

INTEGRATION QUESTIONS FOR DISCUSSION AND WRITING

Directions: The following questions ask you to find relationships among the ideas in the three selections in this unit on language: "What Is Language?" (Chapter 13), "Acquisition and Learning" (Chapter 14), and "Child Language Acquisition" (Chapter 15). Discuss your answers with your classmates.

1. "What Is Language?" discusses what it means to use language creatively (see paragraph 14). Do you think it is possible for a child in the two-word stage of language development to use language in a creative way? Why or why not?

2. "What Is Language?" defines *competence* and *performance*. Is a child of 20 months limited to two-word sentences by competence or performance? Explain your answer.

3. According to "What Is Language?" knowing a language means knowing (unconsciously) the rules for combining words into sentences. Do you think a child in the two-word stage possesses such "grammar" rules? If so, are they the same rules that an adult possesses?

4. According to "Acquisition and Learning," an adult can either learn or acquire a second language, but children only acquire their first language. Does "Child Language Acquisition" support or disprove Krashen and Terrell's theory? Explain your answer.

UNIT

VI

Fiber Optics

CHAPTER 16

The Global Telecommunications Revolution

WARMUP QUESTIONS

The readings in this unit explain how lasers or other specialized light sources can be used in communication. Thin glass wires (fibers) are used together with lasers to transmit large amounts of complex information more quickly and efficiently than normal metal wires.

This combination of glass wires and laser light is called *fiber optics*. It can be used for telephone signals, television, and computer data. How does this new technology work? How can it be used to improve our communications systems? And what effect will it have on our lives?

The first reading in this unit is by Robert Jastrow, an astronomer, physicist, and science writer. It originally appeared in the March 1984 issue of *Science Digest*, a magazine designed to inform the general public about new developments in science and technology.

Before you read the selection, consider the following statements and indicate whether you *agree* or *disagree* with each one. Then discuss your opinions with your classmates.

1. _____ Glass is not a suitable material for making wires because it is expensive and can break easily.
2. _____ The light from a laser can travel very long distances.
3. _____ Telephone companies are interested in conducting research about new ways to send information from one place to another, especially if they can improve speed and accuracy.
4. _____ It is technically possible to send high-quality television pictures over the same wires that now carry telephone conversations.
5. _____ Telephone lines are not suitable for sending large amounts of computer data from one place to another.
6. _____ In the future, many workers will stay at home and do their work by computer, rather than go to an office.

Fiber Optics

What do you already know about lasers? In the following space, make some notes concerning what you know about lasers—especially how they work and what they are used for.

_____
_____
_____

Now write three things that you would like to know about lasers, laser communication, or fiber optics. (See the preceding definition of *fiber optics*.)

_____
_____
_____

DIRECTIONS FOR READING

Before you begin this reading, skim it quickly. Read the first sentence of every paragraph, and note the headings. Scan quickly for numbers, statistics, words in italics, and words or phrases that are frequently repeated. Then read the entire selection quickly for general understanding, and turn to the study questions that follow.

The Global Telecommunications Revolution
Robert Jastrow

1. American revolutions come once in a century. The first one got rid of George III; that was in 1776. The second one started 100 years later, at the end of the nineteenth century. It emptied the farms into the cities, transformed America from an agricultural to an industrial economy and propelled us into the age of the automobile and the highway. The telephone and the radio completed the transformation.

2. The third revolution has just begun, right on schedule. This one moves on highways of glass wire called fiber optics. Fiber optics means a pair of wires—each the thickness of a horsehair, made from glass of a purity never dreamed of prior to a few years ago—that carry tiny pulses, or flashes, of laser light at the rate of hundreds of millions of pulses a second. AT&T has learned how to cram thousands of telephone conversations—each broken down into a series of minute flashes of light—into one pair of glass wires. Glass wires are cheaper for the telephone company than copper wires and make the old-style copper telephone cables obsolete. That is bad news for the copper-mining companies, which have been selling a large fraction of their output to AT&T, but it is good news for the telephone company's customers.

3. How can a glass wire carry a telephone conversation? Here is the way it works. When you speak into a telephone connected to a fiber-optic network, electronic equipment breaks up your voice into many short electrical pulses. Then other equipment converts the pulses of electricity into little pulses, or flashes, of light and sends the light flashes through AT&T's network of glass wires. At the receiving end, another piece of equipment converts the flashes of light into electrical pulses, then converts them back again into the original words of the speaker.

4. Two bits of technical wizardry are necessary for this process. First, the light has to be the special kind produced by a laser; ordinary light will not do. The reason is that ordinary light is usually a jumble of many different wavelengths, which travel through the glass at different speeds. Consequently, as a pulse of light travels along the glass wire, the slower-moving wavelengths lag behind and the faster-moving ones get ahead, so that the pulse, which was sharply defined at the start, gradually spreads out and becomes blurred. In fact, after a while it becomes so blurred that it is not recognizable as a pulse at all. This means that if you were to try to transmit the human voice as a series of ordinary light pulses, when you converted the light pulses back into sound, the sound would be unintelligible.

5. The light in a laser beam, however, is very pure; it has only one wavelength. Therefore, a laser pulse that starts out sharply defined remains sharp, even after it has traveled hundreds of miles along the glass wire.

6. The second bit of technical magic involves the manufacture of the glass in the wire. This glass has to be incredibly pure and transparent—so transparent that the light can travel through it for many miles without growing appreciably weaker; yet, paradoxically, the light must stay inside the glass and not leak out. The threadlike glass wires used by AT&T are so ingeniously constructed that if a ray of light inside a wire starts to get out, it is curved around and bent back toward the wire's center. The result is that the light flows through the glass wires

like water through a pipe; none escapes. Even if you bend the wire and tie it into knots, the light will still go around the bends without leaking out.

240,000 CALLS AT ONCE

7   Tests using the glass wires and laser light to transmit conversations have been so successful that AT&T has started to install telephone cables made of bundles of glass wires on the main trunk line between New York City and Washington, D.C. A bundle of glass wires no thicker than a finger can carry 240,000 telephone conversations at one time.

8   But glass wires can do more than carry telephone conversations. They can transmit *television* conversations as well. This is not possible with the ordinary copper wires that carry telephone conversations because a television picture has so much detail. Each television image is made up of about 100,000 distinct little picture elements, which must be transmitted at the rate of 16 full pictures a second to give the illusion of movement on the TV screen. That means that a copper wire carrying this series of images would have to transmit 1.6 million electrical pulses a second. That is impossible. If a million electrical pulses were compressed into one second and sent through a copper wire, they would run together into a continuous stream of electricity, blurring and destroying the TV picture. But a million pulses of light can easily be sent through a glass wire in one second without running together, because the wavelength of light is so short. Television images, converted to sharp little flashes of light, can be transmitted across a continent by glass wire, with no appreciable loss of detail.

TWO-WAY TV CONVERSATIONS

9   This means that when all the homes and businesses in the United States are connected by a network of glass wires, people will easily be able to have two-way television conversations. When I was working for NASA in New York City, once in a while my boss would call up from Washington to say that he was cutting our budget. Well, my first reaction was to pick up a spear and plunge it through his heart. But I didn't. Instead, I got on a plane to go down to Washington and reason with him. If we'd been able to sit around the table electronically and discuss the matter by two-way TV transmission, that would have been just as good. Looking at the other fellow's electronic persona, each of us could have been able to tell when the other was holding something back—the blush, the twitch, the bead of sweat, the shifty eye, the gaze averted to the ceiling. The voice carries only part of the message; body English carries the rest.

10   This kind of television will be quite different from the TV programs that come into your home today, over the air or by cable. A TV program is a one-way street; you see the program, but it doesn't see you. There is no dialogue. But when the glass wires are installed in home and office and are used to transmit private two-way TV signals, they will bring you into contact with friend, business partner, boss or employee—in living color, anywhere in the world.

TRAVEL: JUST FOR FUN

11   The glass wires will eliminate most business travel, a development with staggering implications for the airlines. But the savings to the country as a

whole will be great. American business spends upward of $700 billion a year on people-related travel and communications. Nearly all that expense can be wiped out by fiber optics. And the productivity gains to a company through savings in the time and energy of high-priced executives will be even greater than the direct savings in travel costs. People will never again go anywhere unless they want to climb a mountain, catch some salt air or see loved ones in the flesh.

12   When will it happen? Corporations have already started to hold teleconferences, but the transmissions usually go via satellite, and they're expensive. Only a large and rich corporation can afford them. The point of fiber optics is that it can reduce the cost of a two-way TV conversation to the cost of a telephone call, so that anyone can dial up the man or woman he wants to see for a quarter. It will be some years before you can make a television call for 25 cents. But one generation—about 20 years—will probably suffice to change the country over from copper to glass.

13   At some point during that period, the big cities will start to disappear. This is beginning to happen already; some people work at home in the suburbs or the country, with their computers and word processors, and send their output to the office over a phone line. The AFL-CIO calls this trend the "computer cottage" and says it is thinking of organizing a computer-cottage union. When glass-wire hookups give the dweller in the computer cottage a video link to the outside world, he or she will never have to leave the house at all, and the computer cottage will become the "electronic cottage." Then big companies can move their headquarters out of the cities. Many New York City companies have done that, but some have come back because they could not find the labor they needed in the suburbs. But when everyone does piecework in his electronic cottage, a company can tap the entire continent for its staff. The congeries of lawyers and corporate executives will disperse to the clean countryside, taking their video links with them.

The Global Telecommunications Revolution

279

STUDY QUESTIONS

Directions: Refer to the reading to answer the following study questions.

1. Look carefully at paragraphs 1 and 2.
    A. The author refers to fiber optics as being part of "the third revolution." According to paragraph 1, what were the first two revolutions?

    _____

    _____

    B. According to paragraph 2, how many telephone calls can a pair of glass wires transmit at one time?
       a. hundreds of millions
       b. thousands
    C. According to paragraph 2, why are the glass wires used in fiber optics so special? (Circle all that apply.)
       a. Because they have an unusually small diameter.
       b. Because they are made of glass that is extremely pure.
       c. Because they can carry large amounts of information.
       d. Because they can carry phone conversations.
    D. What must be done to a telephone conversation in order for it to be sent over a glass wire?

    _____

    _____

    E. Why do you think glass wires are "good news for the telephone company's customers"?

    _____

    _____

2. Carefully reread paragraphs 3, 4, and 5.
    A. Paragraph 3 explains how a glass wire can carry a telephone conversation. According to the paragraph, this process has four main steps. Use no more than three or four words to describe each of these four steps.

       a. _____
       b. _____
       c. _____
       d. _____
    B. According to paragraph 4, why can ordinary light not be used for fiber optics? (More than one answer may be correct.)
       a. Ordinary light has too many wavelengths.
       b. Ordinary light moves through the fiber at different speeds.
       c. The human voice cannot be converted into ordinary light.
       d. Ordinary light begins as sharply defined but ends up unclear.
    C. According to paragraph 5, why is laser light able to travel hundreds of miles without losing its sharpness?

    _____

Fiber Optics

280

3. Read paragraph 6 again carefully.
   A. Compare the first sentences of paragraphs 4 and 6. What word in the first sentence of paragraph 4 means the same as *magic* in the first sentence of paragraph 6?

   _____

   B. What is the relationship between paragraphs 4 and 5, and paragraph 6?
      a. Main idea—Supporting point
      b. General topic—Specific example
      c. First supporting idea—Second supporting idea
      d. Hypothesis—Conclusion
   C. Summarize the paradox, or seeming contradiction, mentioned in paragraph 6 by filling in the blanks in the following sentence.

   The glass must be_____; however,

   _____.

   D. Which of the following sentences are *true*, according to paragraph 6?
      a. Any light that starts to escape the fiber is curved back toward the center.
      b. The light can travel around very sharp corners and over long distances through the fiber.
      c. None of the light leaks out.
      d. The wires are coated with an incredibly pure type of glass.

4. Look carefully at paragraphs 7 and 8.
   A. Why is the statistic about the number of telephone conversations possible at one time with glass wires (paragraph 7) different from the number given in paragraph 2?

   _____

   B. According to paragraph 8, what is the main difference between a telephone signal and a television signal?

   _____

   C. According to paragraph 8, why can copper not be used to transmit television pictures?
      a. The wavelength of copper is too short.
      b. Copper wire is too expensive.
      c. Electricity moves too slowly through copper wire.

5. Look again at paragraphs 9 and 10.
   A. According to paragraph 9, what is the main advantage of two-way television conversations?
      a. They save on the cost of air transportation.
      b. They provide better service for the same cost.
      c. Picture and voice together carry more information than just voice by itself.
   B. How will television be different once optical fibers are in common use (paragraph 10)?

   _____

6. Look again at paragraphs 11 and 12.
   A. To what does *it* refer in the first sentence of paragraph 12?
      a. climbing a mountain or going to the ocean
      b. spending $700 billion a year on travel and communications
      c. more energy for high-priced executives
      d. significant reduction in business travel
   B. According to paragraph 12, which of the following will be true 20 years from now?
      a. There will be more copper than glass.

The Global Telecommunications Revolution

281

      b. A telephone call will cost 25 cents.
      c. Fiber optics will make television conferences more affordable.
      d. There will be teleconferencing via satellite.

7. Reread paragraphs 13 and 14.
    A. According to the author, why will the cities start to disappear?

_____

_____

8. Take a moment to look back at the Warmup Questions at the beginning of this chapter. Which of these questions would you answer differently now? Why?

_____

_____

_____

_____

CHAPTER 17

Laser Communication

WARMUP QUESTIONS

Before you begin the second reading in this unit about fiber optics, consider the following statements, and indicate whether you *agree* or *disagree* with each one. Then discuss your answers with your classmates.

1. _____ The idea of communicating with light waves is a relatively new invention.
2. _____ The current means of transmitting information (telephone, radio, television) will be able to take care of our electronic communication needs for many years to come.
3. _____ Light waves can travel long distances through the atmosphere without losing their strength or intensity.
4. _____ Lasers are very expensive and require a great deal of electricity.

What is your opinion about the type of telephone service currently available in terms of cost, reliability, and so on? What kinds of improvements would you like to see in telephone service?

_____

_____

_____

Look back to the Warmup Questions at the beginning of the previous chapter. Do you have any remaining questions about what lasers are and how they work? List your remaining questions here; the following reading goes into much greater detail about lasers and fiber optics.

_____

_____

Laser Communication

283

PREVIEWING

1. The reading in this chapter has been taken from a book entitled *Lasers: Supertools of the 1980's*. What do you think the authors mean by the word *supertool*?
   _____

2. Look through the reading quickly. How many paragraphs does it contain? _____
   How many pages long is the reading? _____

3. Before you begin reading carefully, you should get an idea of the overall organization of the reading.
   In the following spaces, list the titles of the seven sections of the reading and the paragraphs that each includes.

   Introduction _____   Paragraphs 1–5 _____
   _____   _____
   _____   _____
   _____   _____
   _____   _____
   _____   _____

4. On the basis of the titles you listed in question 3, predict what each section of the reading will be about. Discuss your predictions with your classmates.

5. Figure 17-2 consists of a box containing an illustration and several paragraphs of text. What is the title of this figure?
   _____

6. In addition to the illustration in Figure 17-2, the reading contains one additional illustration. On what page is this illustration located? _____
   In no more than three words, identify the subject of this illustration.
   _____
   _____

7. Look through the reading at the words that appear in italics. Why have most of these words been printed in italics?
   a. They describe unusual or surprising ideas.
   b. They give the titles of books or magazines.
   c. They are important words that are defined or explained in the text.
   d. They are Latin and Greek words.
   e. They are abbreviations.

Fiber Optics

DIRECTIONS FOR READING

The selection for this chapter comes from *Lasers: Supertools of the 1980's* by Jeff Hecht and Dick Teresi. The book is written for a general, nontechnical audience.

The previewing exercises you just completed gave you a general idea of the content and organization of the selection. You are now ready to read it carefully.

The selection has been divided into three parts. You will read each section quickly for general understanding and then examine each part more closely as you complete the study questions.

Laser Communication: Toward the Fibered Society

Jeff Hecht and Dick Teresi

1. Long before people learned how to use electricity, long-distance communication was by light: by signal fires, smoke signals, or semaphores on hilltops. The invention of the telegraph did not kill the idea of optical communication. A century ago, Alexander Graham Bell turned his attention to transmitting voices over beams of light. However, it was an earlier invention of Bell's, the telephone, that has set the tone of communications for the past century.

2. For the last two centuries, people have been developing ways of sending more and more information faster and faster. The telephone transmits voices, which, from the standpoint of the communications scientist, represent more information per unit time than telegraph signals, which carry, at best, a few letters per second. A television signal, in turn, carries more than a thousand times as much information as a telephone line.

3. It all adds up to a lot of information being transmitted, and that presents a problem. The amount of information that can be carried by an electromagnetic wave depends on its frequency—the higher the frequency, the more information can be transmitted. But the amount of information to be transmitted has increased faster than the available ways to transmit it, creating a bottleneck.

4. Communication by light offers a way around this problem. Voice frequencies transmitted by telephone are a mere 1,000 to 4,000 cycles per second, or hertz. Television signals have frequencies of around 50 million hertz. The frequencies of light waves, on the other hand, are around 800 *trillion* hertz.

5. The theory behind transmitting information by light was around for years before there was a way to put it into practice. The first requirement was a suitable light source, which had to await the development of the laser. The second requirement was a suitable way to transmit the light, which emerged a decade ago in the form of the *optical fiber*, a hair-thin strand of glass that guides light along its length. The combination of laser, fiber-optic, and computer technology could revolutionize the way in which we communicate with other people in the coming decades, by interconnecting homes, businesses, and government to form a "fibered society."

THE OPTICAL TELEGRAPH AND THE PHOTOPHONE

6. The science of rapid long-distance communications began nearly two centuries ago with the optical telegraph. This was the brainchild of Claude Chappe, a French engineer who was trying to meet his country's need for fast and reliable communications during the turbulent early 1790s. His system was a simple one: a series of hilltop towers, to which vertical posts carrying moveable wooden beams were attached. The beams served as a semaphore; each letter of the alphabet was represented by a different semaphore position. A man sat in each tower and watched for signals from the adjacent towers, which had to be visible. The system eventually grew to over 500 towers stretching over 3,000 miles.

7   The optical telegraph was labor-intensive, and even in that era of cheap labor, it was expensive to operate. However, it remained by far the best means of communication available until the electrical telegraph replaced it around 1850.

8   The idea of communication by light was resurrected a quarter of a century later by Alexander Graham Bell, who turned his attention to finding a way to transmit conversations using light shortly after he developed the telephone. In 1880, he demonstrated what he is said to have considered his most important invention—the photophone.

9   The photophone transmitted voices—and voices only—by using the sound waves to vibrate a thin, flexible mirror. The vibrations altered the direction in which the mirror reflected sunlight, causing some of the light to miss the remote receiver, thereby modulating the light with the voice signal. The hardest part was converting the modulated light into an electrical current (done by a primitive ancestor of today's photocells), so that the photophone could use the same type of earpiece that Bell had used for the telephone.

10   Bell and his assistant Sumner Tainter performed their first successful photophone experiments on February 19, 1880, in Washington, D.C. More experiments followed, but although Bell refined the hardware, the photophone wasn't practical. Clouds could block the sun, and even with artificial light sources, rain, snow, or fog could block the beams of light.

11   Shortly after his first experiments, Bell put his original photophone into storage at the Smithsonian Institution. There it remained for nearly a century, virtually forgotten.

12   In the intervening years, there were a few attempts to use optical communications, but little came of them until lasers and fiber optics arrived on the scene. These two new technologies revived interest in optical communications, particularly at Bell Labs, which has one of the world's largest research programs in the field. As a result, Bell's original photophone was retrieved from storage, and on February 19, 1980, his original experiments were reenacted at the site of his Washington lab (now a parking lot) by representatives of Bell Labs, the National Geographic Society, and the Smithsonian, along with Forrest M. Mims III, a San Marcos, Texas, inventor and writer, who was a driving force behind the photophone centennial. (Ironically, Mims was also involved at the time in a dispute with Bell Labs over rights to an invention.)

ENTER THE LASER

13   Scientists were quick to realize the potential of the laser for communications. Even before the first laser was demonstrated, people who understood the concept were suggesting its use in communications. Others followed soon after the laser was actually invented in 1960.

14   By August 1962 Isaac Asimov was writing about the potential of optical communications in his monthly column in *The Magazine of Fantasy and Science Fiction*. He ran through some calculations that indicated that, in theory, the visible portion of the spectrum could be used to transmit up to 100 million television channels, while the ultraviolet region could be used to transmit six billion additional channels. Then he thought about the low quality of television programming: "Imagine what the keen minds of our entertainment industry could do if they realized that they had a hundred million channels into which they could funnel new and undreamed-of varieties of trash. Maybe we ought to stop right now!"

15   Scientists rarely heed warnings to stop, and the developers of optical communication systems were no exception. They set up lasers in their laborato-

Laser Communication

ries and began rediscovering what Alexander Graham Bell had learned eighty years earlier—that the atmosphere isn't a very good medium for transmitting light.

16 Researchers at Bell Labs soon turned to an idea that goes back to a patent issued in 1934 to Norman R. French—the light pipe. In its simplest form the light pipe is literally that—a pipe with a reflective inner surface. If the surface reflects a large enough fraction of light, a beam shone down the tube will keep on going, although with small losses. More refined versions were soon proposed, such as pipes containing a vacuum to prevent light absorption by the air, and pipes containing a series of lenses to refocus the beam and make certain it follows the desired path.

17 Meanwhile other researchers looked upward to space, where there is no air to absorb or scatter light. The National Aeronautics and Space Administration studied the prospects for communication from ground to satellites and between satellites. Military planners were interested in the same ideas, largely because the narrow beam from a laser would provide much more secure transmission than radio waves, which radiate in all directions. The hottest current military project is the development of a system that would use blue-green lasers to relay signals from satellites to submerged submarines.

DAWN OF THE FIBER ERA

18 We ordinarily think of light as traveling in a straight line. It's possible, however, to make thin fibers of glass that can carry light signals around corners and bends, in a way that is superficially similar to the way copper wires carry electricity. These optical fibers rely on a phenomenon known as total internal reflection (see Figure 17-1).

19 This means that when light traveling through a dense material (say, glass) strikes an interface with a less dense material (say, air) at a low, glancing angle, all of the light can be reflected back into the denser medium. What this means in practice is that you can make an optical fiber out of two types of glass: a dense glass for the core, and a less dense glass for the outer cladding. The light will travel in straight lines through the core until it hits the interface with the

FIGURE 17-1 Optical fibers rely on a principle called *total internal reflection*. All this means is that when light traveling through a dense material strikes the interface with a less dense material at a small angle, as shown, all of the light can be reflected back into the denser medium. In practice, an optical fiber is made of two types of glass: a dense glass for the core and a less dense glass for the outer cladding. If light in the core hits the interface with the cladding at a small enough angle, it will bounce back into the denser core and keep on going through the fiber, even around bends. If the angle is too large, however, the light passes through the cladding and is absorbed by the jacket on the cable or is simply lost from the fiber.

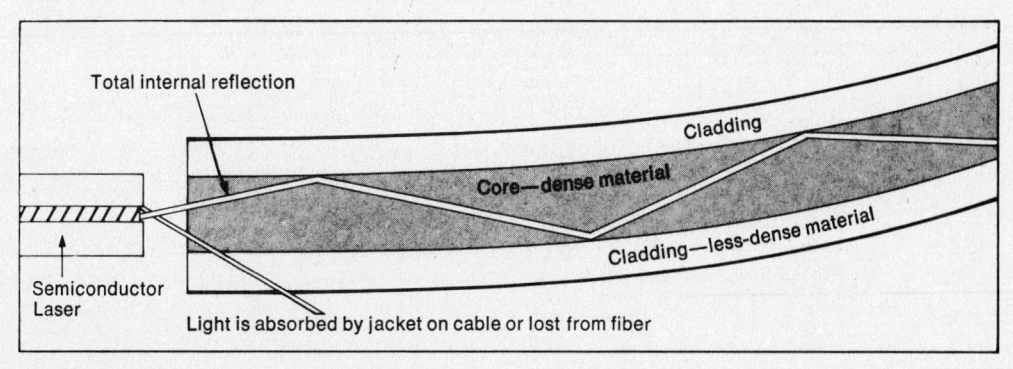

cladding. If the light hits at a gentle enough angle, it will bounce back into the denser core and keep on going through the fiber, even around bends.

20   A century ago, British physicist John Tyndall demonstrated the concept with water flowing out of a tank. In the 1950s, the American Optical Corporation developed light-transmitting fibers made of two types of glass. These early fibers could carry light around corners, but not very far—no more than tens of meters (or yards).

21   It wasn't until 1970 that the first long-distance fiber was made, by Robert Maurer at the Corning Glass Works. Maurer was inspired by research into the absorption of light by ultrapure glass by Charles Kao and George Hockham at Standard Telecommunication Laboratories, a British subsidiary of the International Telephone and Telegraph Corporation. In 1966 Kao and Hockham predicted that glass fibers should be able to transmit light well over a kilometer (or even a mile). As it turned out, their optimism was well justified.

22   Some numbers will give you an idea of how far the technology has come. In the mid-1960s, the best commercial fibers absorbed about 90 percent of the light that entered them within only 10 m (about 11 yd). This distance was increased to 500 m (about 550 yd) with Maurer's first low-loss fibers. Today, the best fiber fabricated in a laboratory can transmit light for well over 30 km (about 20 miles) before 90 percent of the input light is absorbed. All these distances are for the wavelengths where absorption is the lowest—in current fibers, about 1.3 to 1.5 micrometers, in the infrared region, about twice the wavelength of visible light.

PRINCIPLES OF FIBER OPTICS

23   Fiber-optic communication is somewhat analogous to electronic communication, except that the signal takes the form of light. A light source, or transmitter, generates light that has had a signal superimposed on it through a process called *modulation*. The light signal is transmitted through an optical fiber, which, in practice, is encased in a cable that from the outside looks like an ordinary (though small in diameter) electrical cable. At the end of the fiber is a receiver that "catches," or detects, the optical signal, decodes the information (*demodulates* it from the light), and amplifies the resulting electrical signal for the next stage in the communications network.

24   Two types of light sources are used. One is the semiconductor laser: a crystal no bigger than a grain of salt that contains a tiny laser resonator and emits a beam that is recognizably a laser beam, although it spreads out more rapidly than the beam from other kinds of lasers. The other is the *light-emitting diode*, or *LED*, a semiconductor crystal that is similar to a semiconductor laser except that it doesn't contain a laser resonator and emits a broader beam. (Most fiber-optic light sources actually emit infrared, and strictly speaking are *IREDs* —*infrared-emitting diodes*—but we'll go along with the vast majority of engineers who just call them LEDs anyway.)

25   When an electrical current that exceeds a certain *threshold* value is passed through a laser or an LED, the semiconductor chip emits light. Once you exceed the threshold current, the amount of light is proportional to the current passing through the chip: increase the current and you increase the light. Thus, variations in the current show up as variations in the light—or modulation of the beam. So the light beam can carry the same information as the electrical signal driving the laser or the LED. The modulated beam travels through the fiber and is caught by a receiver at the other end. In the receiver, a semiconductor device called a *detector* produces an electrical signal proportional to the amount of light that strikes it.

26	From the standpoint of the receiver, it doesn't matter if the light source is a laser or an LED. In fact, that distinction is important only to the engineer designing a fiber-optic system. For that reason, we're going to change our focus for the rest of this chapter and talk about fiber optics rather than about lasers *per se*. Although lasers are not used in every single fiber-optic communication system, fiber optics is an exciting technology whose growth has been stimulated by the laser.

27	Lasers are likely to always play a role in some fiber-optic communications, but how large that role will be is unclear. LEDs are giving lasers a run for the money, because LEDs are less expensive and last longer. The main advantages of lasers are that they emit more light and can be modulated faster. At the moment, a rough rule of thumb is that lasers are used to transmit information rapidly over distances of 1 km (0.6 mile) or more, whereas LEDs are used for transmission at lower speeds and over shorter distances. Advances in LED and laser technology may change that, but you'd never notice the difference.

SQUEEZING IN INFORMATION

28	If fiber optics were only able to do as much as electronic communications, there wouldn't be much use for fibers. But they can do much more. Fibers can break the information bottleneck, because they can transmit much more information in a given amount of time than wires. A single fiber, for example, can carry the equivalent of over a thousand telephone conversations.

29	This greater capacity is critical. Everything that is communicated can be looked upon as information, whether it's music, a television program, a series of telegraphic dots and dashes, or digital data for a computer. The rate at which information can be transmitted has traditionally been a major limitation on communications.

30	Fiber optics may be the answer. The difference between wires and fiber optics is dramatic. Ordinary telephone conversations in *analog format* (see Figure 17-2) have a *bandwidth* of 3,000 cycles per second, or hertz. (Bandwidth, measured in hertz, is one indication of how much information can be transmitted.) High-fidelity music has a bandwidth of about 20,000 hertz. Television signals have a bandwidth of about 6 million hertz (6 megahertz). The transmission capacity of optical fibers, on the other hand, has now surpassed 1 *billion* hertz in laboratory demonstrations.

31	These values are all for the analog format, which is used in most existing communications equipment. Optical fibers themselves operate quite happily in analog format. However, there is a problem with lasers—they distort analog signals. And LEDs have a different limitation—they can't operate as rapidly as lasers and hence can't transmit information as fast.

32	Fortunately, there's a way around this problem—shifting to *digital* transmission, in which information is encoded as a series of zeroes and ones (see Figure 17-2). These *bits* of information can be electronically decoded to generate a signal in analog format, such as high-fidelity music. Lasers, LEDs, fibers, and detectors all handle digital signals without difficulty.

LONG-DISTANCE TRANSMISSION

33	There's a second major advantage to fiber optics. Not only do fibers transmit information faster than wires, they can also transmit it farther. The key breakthrough that made fiber-optic communications possible was a dramatic reduction in the amount of signal lost in the fiber—corresponding to a dramatic

FIGURE 17-2 Analog and Digital Communications

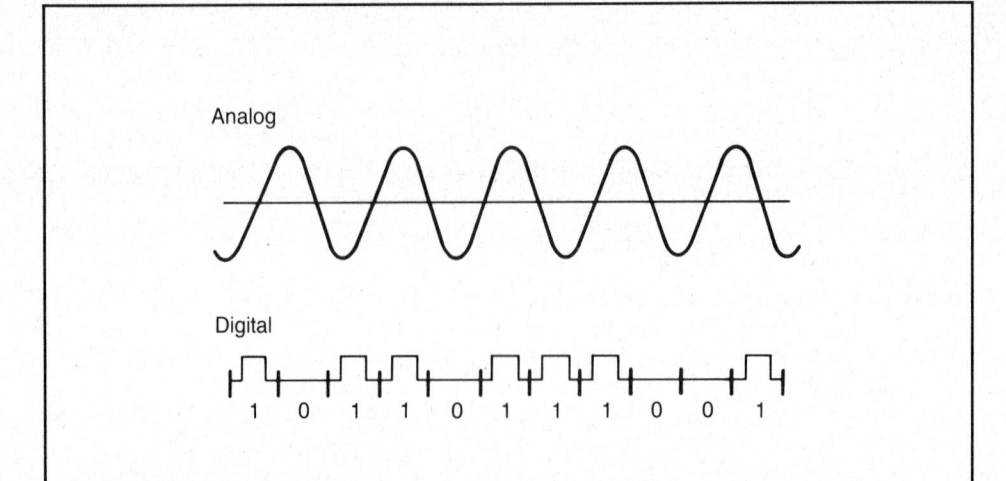

1. Information can be transmitted in either of two formats: *analog* or *digital*. An analog signal is one that varies in amplitude continuously, such as sound. Almost all home electronics that reproduce sound or television signals use analog format.
2. In digital transmission, information is encoded as a series of zeroes and ones (see diagram). Digital format was originally developed for numerical information, and pocket calculators and computers use it.
3. Any information in one format can be translated into the other and back again. This can be done repeatedly, and it sometimes happens in the telephone network. The need for conversion arises because rapid advances in digital electronics have pushed it far beyond older analog electronics; thus, the new digital equipment that telephone companies are installing must be compatible with the billions of dollars worth of existing analog hardware. Besides offering higher-fidelity reproduction (as in many modern sound studios), the digital format permits computer processing and switching of information—a feature particularly important in telecommunications.

increase in the transparency of the glass used. Researchers have kept on going. Now fibers that transmit signals much farther than ordinary wires are mass-produced.

34 To understand the importance of this breakthrough, let's look briefly at how a long-distance communication system works. A signal is transmitted as far as it will go along a wire, optical fiber, or some other transmission medium. The low-level signal at the end of the line is then amplified to produce a higher-level signal that can be fed into another length of transmission line. The thing that does the amplifying is called a *repeater*.

35 A repeater may sound simple, but in practice it can be a lot of trouble. As well as amplifying the low-level signal, a repeater has to make sure that the output signal looks like the signal fed into the original transmission line. Thus, repeaters are expensive to build, and they also have to be installed, often outdoors and sometimes in hard-to-reach locations. What's more, things can go wrong with them, requiring repairs that can be very difficult and costly if the repeaters are hard to reach.

36 Because of these problems, operators of communication systems would like to reduce the number of repeaters they use. Fiber optics can be a big help, particularly for the operators of the most pervasive communication system, the telephone network.

37 Telephone companies are most interested in fiber optics for the "trunk" lines that carry many telephone conversations simultaneously between central

offices. Metal-cable trunk lines connecting central offices require a repeater about every 1.6 km (1 mile) or so. Fiber-optic systems can easily operate with repeater spacings of 6 km (4 miles) or more—equivalent to the average spacing between central offices in urban and suburban areas. That's important, because a telephone office is a far more benign environment for a repeater than the bottom of a manhole or many of the other places where repeaters are housed. What's more, new developments in fiber optics are stretching repeater spacing up to as much as 20 km (12.5 miles).

PART 1: STUDY QUESTIONS
(Paragraphs 1–5)

Directions: Read paragraphs 1–5 quickly for general understanding. Then refer to the selection to answer the following study questions.

1. Look carefully at paragraphs 1 and 2 again.
   A. In the first sentence of paragraph 1, *signal fires*, *smoke signals*, and *semaphores* are all examples of
   _____

   B. Which of these phrases means the same thing as *optical communication* in the second sentence of paragraph 1?
      a. long-distance communication
      b. communication by light
   C. What phrase in the third sentence of paragraph 1 means the same as *optical communication*?
   _____

   D. What two ways of communicating by electricity are mentioned in paragraph 1?
   _____

   E. In paragraph 2, what do the authors say is the advantage of television over the telephone?
   _____

   F. According to paragraph 2, what is the advantage of the telephone over the telegraph?
   _____

2. Look carefully at paragraphs 3 and 4.
   A. What is the problem to which the first sentence of paragraph 3 refers? Why is this a problem?
   _____

   B. Look at the word *bottleneck* in the last sentence of paragraph 3. Read the paragraph carefully; then, without consulting a dictionary, give a general definition of this word. (In other words, give a definition of *bottleneck* that could apply to any situation, not just the one described in this reading.)
   _____
   _____

   C. In the first sentence of paragraph 4 to what does "this problem" refer?
   _____

   D. According to paragraph 4, what is the definition of *hertz*? (The paragraph provides a definition, so you do not need to consult a dictionary.)
   _____

   E. Paragraph 4 talks about *million* vs. *trillion*. To get some idea of how large these numbers are, do the following problem.

Fiber Optics

Suppose that you had one trillion dollars in one dollar bills, and you gave your friend the dollar bills at the rate of one dollar per second. How long (in days or years) would it take to give your friend one million dollars? One trillion dollars?

3. Carefully reread paragraph 5.
   A. According to paragraph 5, what two things are required for optical communications?

   B. Why was the theory of communicating by light around so long before it was put into practice?

   C. According to the last sentence of paragraph 5, what additional technology is required to build a practical optical communications system?

   D. The last sentence in paragraph 5 contains the word *interconnecting*. What do you think is the difference between *connect* and *interconnect*?

PART 2: STUDY QUESTIONS
(Paragraphs 6–22)

Directions: Read paragraphs 6–22 quickly for general understanding. Then refer to the selection to answer the following study questions.

1. Before you reread this section carefully, make sure you have an idea of what it is about.
   A. Paragraphs 6–22 contain many dates. Look for all the four-digit numbers, and count the number of times a specific year is mentioned in these paragraphs. How many dates did you find?
   B. In what order are the dates arranged?
      a. no special order
      b. from past to present
      c. from present to past
   C. What can you conclude about a group of paragraphs that contains many dates?
      a. It will give the history of the subject.
      b. The dates indicate that it is part of the introduction.
      c. It gives some general information.
      d. The dates have no special significance.

2. Look carefully at paragraphs 6 and 7.
   A. What is the main topic of these two paragraphs?
      a. the science of long-distance communication
      b. the optical telegraph
      c. the photophone
      d. Claude Chappe
   B. Test your knowledge of history. Why do the authors refer to the early 1790s in

France as "turbulent"? Why did the country need fast and reliable communications during that period?

___

C. After reading paragraph 6, explain in your own words the purpose of a semaphore, and how it works. Draw a simple diagram of the device.

___

D. What is the meaning of *labor-intensive* in the first sentence of paragraph 7? (Read the entire sentence before you answer.)
   a. The people who operated the optical telegraph were paid very high salaries.
   b. The people who operated the optical telegraph had a physically demanding job.
   c. The optical telegraph required a large number of people working many hours.

E. According to paragraph 7, what happened in 1850?

___

3. Carefully reread paragraphs 8–11.
   A. In the following space, write one word that identifies the main topic of paragraphs 8–11. ___
   B. What date do the authors mean when they say "a quarter of a century later" in the first line of paragraph 8?

   ___
   C. Who invented the photophone?

   ___
   For what other well-known invention is this individual responsible?

   ___
   D. Look at these two definitions of *photo*.
      1. picture taken with a camera; photograph
      2. light
   Which of these meanings is most closely related to the word *photophone* in paragraph 8? How do you know?

   ___
   E. After reading paragraph 9, look at Figure 17-3 on p. 296, which illustrates how a photophone works, and label the various parts.
   F. What is the main idea of paragraphs 10 and 11?
      a. Bell's photophone experiments were successful.
      b. The photophone was not practical, so no one pursued the idea.

Fiber Optics

FIGURE 17-3

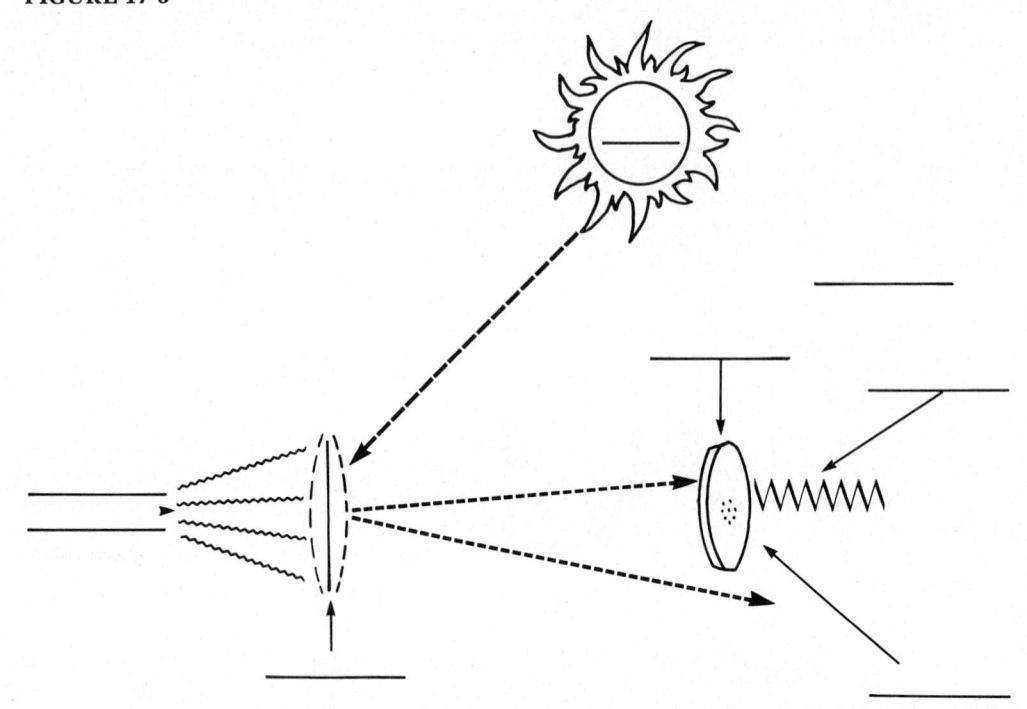

c. Clouds could block the sun; rain, snow, or fog could block artificial forms of light.
d. Bell put his original invention in the Smithsonian.

4. Carefully reread paragraph 12.
   Which of the following sentences is correct, according to paragraph 12?
   a. Because the original photophone was brought out of storage, research in optical communications increased.
   b. When Bell Labs began working with lasers and optical fibers, interest in Bell's original experiments revived.

5. Look again at paragraphs 13 and 14.
   A. Which of the following sentences best summarizes the main idea of paragraph 13?
   a. Starting around 1960, people began to develop theories about how to use lasers for communication.
   b. After building a working model of a laser, scientists began suggesting its use in communications.
   c. People understood the potential value of the laser in communications even before the first one had been invented.
   B. Assume for a moment that you are not sure about the meaning of the phrases *visible portion of the spectrum* and *ultraviolet region* in paragraph 14. According to your knowledge of the topic of this chapter, to what scientific idea are these phrases probably related?
   a. light
   b. sound
   c. electricity
   C. According to paragraph 14, what is the total number of television channels that could be transmitted using both visible and ultraviolet light?

Laser Communication

297

       Is this number an opinion or a fact?

   D. According to paragraph 14, what is Isaac Asimov's opinion of optical communications?

6. Carefully reread paragraphs 15 and 16.
   A. What is the main idea of paragraph 15?
      a. Scientists do not listen to warnings of danger.
      b. Bell Labs scientists were the exception to this.
      c. The earth's atmosphere cannot transmit light very well.
   B. What is the main topic of paragraph 16?

   C. When was the light pipe invented, and by whom?

   D. Although it is not directly stated, why do you think Bell Labs scientists were interested in light pipes?

   E. List the three kinds of light pipes described in paragraph 16.
      a. _____
      b. _____
      c. _____
   F. Why are the second and third kinds of light pipes superior to the original design?

7. Look again at paragraph 17.
   A. According to paragraph 17, why is space better for optical communications than the earth's atmosphere?

   B. Why would the military prefer lasers over radio waves?
      a. Lasers can be used over long distances.
      b. Radio waves need more electrical current than lasers.
      c. Radio waves do not scatter in the atmosphere.
      d. Lasers are easier to control, so it is easier to keep communications a secret.
   C. Why do you think the United States military is interested in the project described in the last sentence of paragraph 17?

8. Carefully reread paragraph 18.
   A. According to paragraph 18, how does light usually move from one place to another?

   B. What is the importance of the thin fibers of glass described in the same paragraph?

Fiber Optics

C. What is the meaning of *superficially similar* in the second sentence of paragraph 18?
   a. exactly similar
   b. not similar; different
   c. similar in some ways
   d. similar in many ways
D. What two things are "superficially similar"?

E. Which of the following words or phrases do you think best gives the meaning of the word *phenomenon* in the last sentence of paragraph 18?
   a. idea
   b. physical fact or property
   c. invention
   d. material or substance
F. According to paragraph 18, what is the name of the important concept explained in Figure 17-1?

9. Carefully reread paragraph 19. Look at Figure 17-1, and read the caption that accompanies it.
   A. To what does the word *this* refer in the first sentence of paragraph 19?
      a. light traveling in a straight line
      b. the similarity between glass fibers and copper wires
      c. total internal reflection
   B. According to paragraph 19, why is an optical fiber made of two types of glass?

   C. Compare paragraph 19 with the information in the caption accompanying Figure 17-1. On the basis of your comparison, which of the following statements is most nearly correct?
      a. Paragraph 19 gives exactly the same information as the caption.
      b. The caption explains a slightly different topic.
      c. The caption restates the ideas in paragraph 19, and gives a few additional facts as well.
      d. Paragraph 19 gives more information about the facts discussed in the caption.
   D. According to the caption accompanying Figure 17-1, how does light escape from the optical fiber?
      a. It hits the outer layer of glass (the cladding) at a large angle.
      b. It is absorbed by the outer layer of glass.
      c. It bounces back into the denser core.
      d. It hits the cladding at a very small angle.
   E. When light escapes from an optical fiber, is this good or bad? Explain your answer.

   F. What is the meaning of the word *interface* in sentences 1 and 3 of paragraph 19?
      a. a kind of computer hardware
      b. a certain kind of light from a laser
      c. the place where two things are connected
      d. a less dense material

10. Look again at paragraphs 20–22.
    A. Read paragraphs 20 and 21, and give the approximate date when each of the following took place.
       _____ demonstration of total internal reflection with water
       _____ development of short-distance fiber
       _____ prediction of long-distance fiber
       _____ development of first long-distance fiber
    B. What was the problem with the glass fibers made in the 1950s?
       _____
    C. According to paragraph 21, what was the prediction of Kao and Hockham? Does the paragraph say that this prediction came true?
       _____
       _____
    D. What is the main idea of paragraph 22?
       a. The technology has come a long way.
       b. The best commercial fibers in the 1960s absorbed 90 percent of the light.
       c. Current fibers use infrared light.
    E. For each type of optical fiber listed, give the distance (in meters or kilometers) that light can be transmitted before 90 percent of it is lost.

	Distance
Fibers in the 1960s	_____
First low-loss fibers	_____
Best fiber today	_____

PARTS 1 AND 2: COMPREHENSION EXERCISES
(Paragraphs 1–22)

Exercise 1

The following statements are either *true* or *false* according to paragraphs 1–22 of the reading. Write either T or F in the space before each statement.

1. _____ People had the idea of transmitting voices using beams of light many years before they had the technology to do so.
2. _____ One of the biggest benefits of optical communications is that more information can be transmitted more quickly.
3. _____ Using light for communications was not economical until the invention of the optical fiber.
4. _____ Scientists did not realize that the laser could be used in optical communications until a working laser had actually been built in the laboratory.
5. _____ Isaac Asimov believed that optical communications would improve the quality of television programs.

Fiber Optics

6._____ The first step toward the development of today's optical fibers was a simple pipe, with a covering inside that could reflect light.

7._____ According to the principle of *total internal reflection*, an optical fiber is covered with a material that is denser than the glass at the center of the fiber.

8._____ British physicist John Tyndall developed the first light-transmitting fibers in the early 1950s.

9._____ Twenty-five or thirty years ago, the farthest a message could be sent using a beam of light was only about 10 meters.

10._____ The development of optical communications was delayed because of the difficulties in transmitting light through the air.

Exercise 2

Complete the following summary of paragraphs 1–22 by filling in each blank with an appropriate word or phrase.

Long before people learned to use electricity for long-distance _____, light was used in such things as _____ and smoke signals. For the last two centuries, people have been learning to send _____ more quickly. Telephones can carry more information than the _____, and television signals can carry as much as _____ times more information than a telephone line.

Unfortunately, the amount of information that needs to be transmitted has _____ faster than the available technology. Communication by _____ may be the answer to this problem. Light waves have a much higher _____ than telephone or television signals.

One of the first methods of long-distance communication was invented by _____ _____ in the 1790s. His invention, called the _____, used a series of semaphore towers that transmitted messages one _____ at a time. Around 1850, his invention was _____ by the electric telegraph.

In 1880, Alexander Graham Bell invented the _____, which used _____ to transmit information. The light was _____ to electricity and the electricity to sound. The invention worked, but it was not _____ _____. Clouds could block the sun; rain, fog, or snow could _____ artificially produced light beams.

Scientists were quick to _____ the potential of lasers. In August 1962, for example, Isaac Asimov _____ that light could be used to transmit about _____ billion television channels. Bell Labs scientists began investigating the _____ and laser communications in space to get around the problem of transmitting light in the _____.

Laser Communication

301

Finally, an optical fiber was designed for transmitting light long distances and around corners. The fiber contains two types of _____ and works on a principle called _____. The light travels in the center of the fiber. When it strikes the _____ between the _____ and the dense core, it bounces back toward the center and continues on its way.

The first optical fibers could transmit light a distance of only _____, but today's best fibers can transmit light about 30 kilometers before _____ percent of the light is absorbed.

Exercise 3

Look back at the Warmup Questions at the beginning of Chapters 16 and 17. Which of these questions apply to the information you have just read? Which questions would you answer differently? Which would you answer in the same way?

PART 3: STUDY QUESTIONS
(Paragraphs 23–37)

Directions: The first two parts of this reading discussed the history of optical communications and the discoveries that led up to the development of fiber optics. This section is concerned with how fiber optics works and the advantages of optical fibers over traditional wires.

Read paragraphs 23–37 and Figure 17-2 (Analog and Digital Communications) quickly for general understanding. Then refer to the reading to answer the following study questions.

1. Reread paragraph 23 carefully.
   A. Read the first three sentences of paragraph 23. Then fill in the blanks in the following paragraph, which compares fiber-optic communication and electronic communication. You may have to supply some of the information from your own knowledge.

   In fiber-optic communication, the signal, or means of communication, is _____, which is sent from one place to another through _____ fibers. In electronic communication, the means of communication is _____, which is sent from one place to another through wires made of _____.

   B. Paragraph 23 describes the components of a typical fiber-optic communications system. Label the parts of Figure 17-4 (see p. 302) based on the description in paragraph 23. Note that some parts have more than one name. The names of the parts are as follows: *electrical signal (in and out), modulator/transmitter/light source, modulated light, optical fiber, demodulator/receiver.*
   C. Which sentence in paragraph 23 gives the definition of *modulation*?
      a. the second sentence
      b. the third sentence
   D. To help you understand exactly how *modulation* is used in this reading, look carefully at the following dictionary definitions of *modulate* (the verb form of the noun *modulation*).

Fiber Optics

FIGURE 17-4

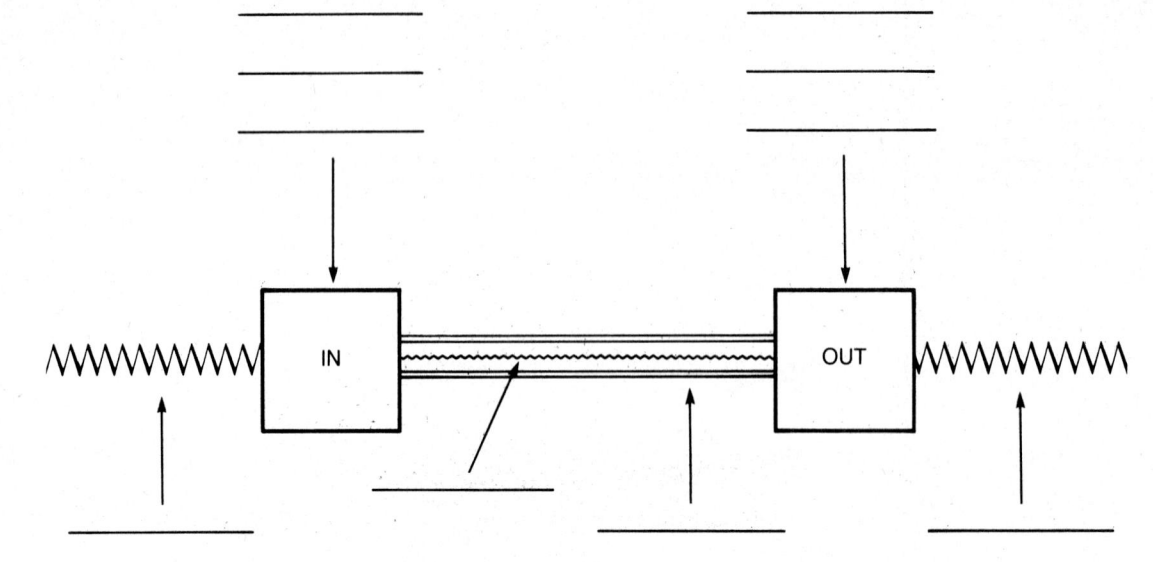

a. to regulate, adjust, or adapt
b. to vary the pitch or intensity of the voice
c. to sing
d. in music, to change to another key
e. in electronics, to produce a variation in the frequency of (for example) a radio wave by combining it with some other signal, impulse, or wave

Now that you have some idea of the possible meanings of *modulate*, answer the following question, which pertains specifically to this chapter. How does fiber-optic communication use light to send a message from one place to another?
a. by turning the light off and on very rapidly
b. by quickly changing the light from very bright to very weak and back again

2. Carefully reread paragraph 24.
   A. What two important technical terms are defined in paragraph 24?

   _____

   _____

   B. Complete the following chart, which is based on the information in paragraph 24.

Semiconductor Laser	Light-emitting Diode (LED)
crystal	semiconductor crystal
	no resonator
narrow laser beam	

3. Carefully reread paragraph 25.
   A. Which of the diagrams in Figure 17-5 best expresses the main idea of the first three sentences in paragraph 25? _____
   B. What is the best meaning for the phrase *threshold value* (paragraph 25, sentences 1 and 2)?
      a. maximum value

Laser Communication
303

FIGURE 17-5

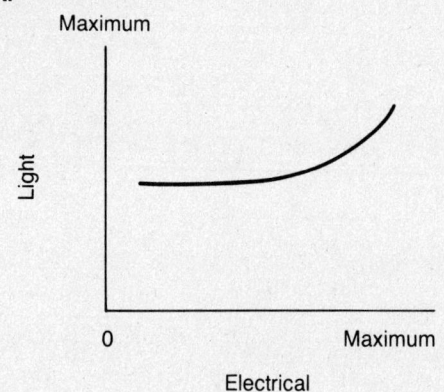

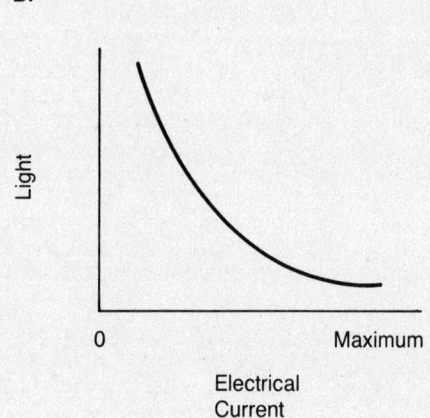

A.

[Graph: Light vs Electrical Current, curve starts flat then rises sharply near maximum]

B.

[Graph: Light vs Electrical Current, curve starts high and decays downward]

C.

[Graph: Light vs Electrical Current, curve rises gradually from low to maximum]

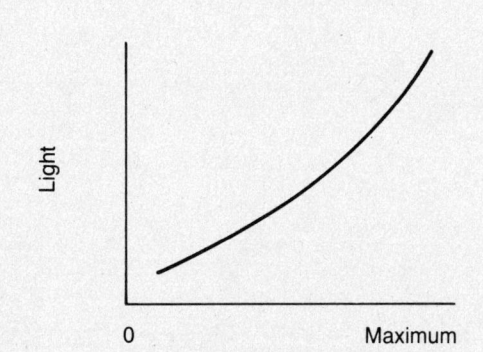

D.

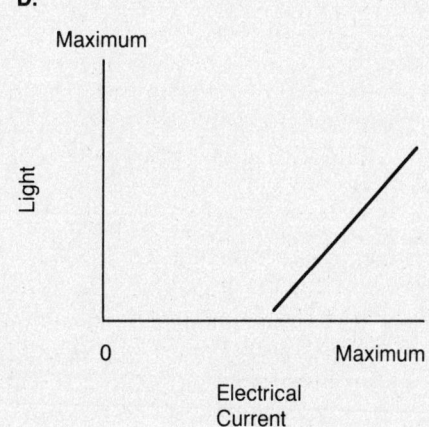

[Graph: Light vs Electrical Current, linear line rising from mid-x to maximum]

      b. minimum value
      c. value beyond which some change occurs
      d. electrical charge
      e. amount of light
  C. Which of the following phrases means the same as *modulation of the beam* in sentence 3 of paragraph 25?
      a. variations in the current
      b. variations in the light
  D. What is the function of the *detector*?
      a. turn light into electricity
      b. turn electricity into light

4. Look again at paragraph 26.
    Which of the following is the main idea of paragraph 26?
      a. The distinction between a laser and an LED is important to the engineer.
      b. The principles of fiber optics are the same in both laser and LED systems.
      c. Lasers are not used in every fiber-optic system.
      d. The development of fiber optics is closely tied to the development of lasers.

Fiber Optics

5. Complete the following table with information from paragraph 27.

	Lasers	LEDs
Uses	_____	_____
	_____	_____
Advantages	_____	_____
	_____	_____

6. Before you read the last two sections of the reading, try to get some idea of what they are about.
    Look at the section titles that precede paragraphs 28 and 33, and quickly reread these two paragraphs. What two advantages of optical fibers will be discussed?
    _____
    _____

7. Read paragraphs 28 and 29 again carefully.
    A. Paragraph 28 contains one general idea and one example of that idea. Express these two concepts in your own words.
    Main idea of paragraph 28:
    _____
    Example:
    _____

    B. What is the meaning of *critical* in the first sentence of paragraph 29?
        a. difficult
        b. negative
        c. important
        d. theoretical
    C. According to paragraph 29, what has been one of the major technological limits on modern communications?
    _____
    _____

8. Carefully reread paragraph 30.
    A. What is the main idea of paragraph 30?
        a. Fiber optics may be the answer.
        b. There is a great difference between wires and optical fibers.
        c. Bandwidth is a measurement of how much information can be transmitted.
        d. Optical fibers have a capacity of 1 billion hertz.

    B. Complete the following chart with statistics from paragraph 30.

Method of Communication	Bandwidth (in hertz)
Telephone	3000
_____	_____
Optical fibers	_____

C. What is the purpose of the statistics you listed in question B? What general idea do they support?

_____

_____

9. Look again at Figure 17-2, Analog and Digital Communications.
   A. What type of information format is defined in paragraph 1?
      a. analog
      b. digital
      c. both
   B. In the second sentence of paragraph 1, *amplitude* means the same as
      a. strength.
      b. amount of information.
      c. voltage.
      d. numerical sequence.
   C. What is the purpose (function) of the second paragraph?

   _____

   D. Write the word *analog* or *digital* next to each of the following devices.
      a. Computer   _____
      b. Telephone   _____
      c. Calculator   _____
      d. Television   _____
   E. List the two advantages of the digital format given in paragraph 3.

   _____

   _____

   F. Can a device that uses digital information communicate with a device that uses analog information?

   _____

10. Carefully reread paragraphs 31 and 32.
    A. What is the relationship between the ideas in paragraphs 31 and 32?
       a. General idea—Specific example
       b. Cause—Effect
       c. Argument—Opposing argument
       d. Problem—Solution
    B. The main purpose of paragraph 31 is to discuss the
       a. advantages
       b. disadvantages
       of
       a. analog format.
       b. optical fibers.
       c. digital format.
       d. lasers and LEDs.
    C. The main purpose of paragraph 32 is to discuss the
       a. advantages
       b. disadvantages
       of
       a. analog format.

Fiber Optics

306

      b. optical fibers.
      c. digital format.
      d. lasers and LEDs.

11. Look carefully at paragraph 33, which begins the final section of the reading. This section discusses the advantages of optical fibers for long-distance communication.
    A. What are the two major advantages of fiber optics, as summarized in paragraph 33?

    _____

    B. According to this paragraph, what caused the decrease in the amount of signal lost?

    _____

12. Read paragraph 34 again carefully.
    A. According to the first sentence, this paragraph will mainly discuss
        a. the importance of long-distance communication.
        b. how long-distance communication works.
    B. What is the function of a *repeater* (sentence 4)? (Circle all that apply.)
        a. to amplify the signal
        b. to reflect the light back into the fiber
        c. to repeat the signal
        d. to change the low-level signal to a high-level signal
        e. to bend the light around a corner
    C. Fill in the blanks in the following sentence, which explains why repeaters are required.

        Repeaters are needed in an optical-fiber system because the light can

        only _____ a certain _____ before all of it

        _____.

13. Carefully reread paragraphs 35 and 36, which continue the discussion of repeaters.
    A. Which of the following sentences best restates the main idea of the first sentence of paragraph 35?
        a. The fact that repeaters are complex leads to certain problems.
        b. Repeaters are expensive to build.
        c. Repeaters are difficult and costly to repair.
    B. What is the function of the second sentence in paragraph 35?
        a. It explains how a repeater works.
        b. It identifies an advantage of repeaters.
        c. It identifies a disadvantage of repeaters.
    C. What is the function of the third sentence in paragraph 35?
        a. It explains how a repeater works.
        b. It identifies an advantage of repeaters.
        c. It identifies a disadvantage of repeaters.
    D. What is the function of the fourth sentence in paragraph 35?
        a. It explains how a repeater works.
        b. It identifies an advantage of repeaters.
        c. It identifies a disadvantage of repeaters.
    E. According to paragraph 36, what will be the biggest advantage of fiber optics for operators of communication systems?
        a. It will decrease the number of repeaters.

Laser Communication

307

      b. It will establish a communication network.
      c. No reason is given.
  F. Although it is not stated directly, *why* will the advantage you chose in question E help communication systems operators?

_____

_____

14. Look carefully at paragraph 37 again.
    A. Fill in the blanks in the following sentence.

        Metal wires require a repeater every _____ kilometers, whereas fiber-optic cables require a repeater every _____ kilometers.

    B. What example of a "benign environment for a repeater" is given in the fourth sentence of paragraph 37?

_____

    What example is given of an environment that is not benign?

    C. To show that you understand the meaning of *benign*, give an example of a place that would be a benign environment for a human being. Then give an example of a place that would not be a benign environment for a human being.

_____

_____

_____

    D. Can optical fibers carry a light beam 20 kilometers before it must be amplified?

_____

PART 3: COMPREHENSION EXERCISES
(Paragraphs 23–37)

Exercise 1

The following statements are either *true* or *false* according to paragraphs 23–37 of the reading. Write either T or F in the space before each statement.

1. _____ In the typical fiber-optic communication system, it does not matter if the light source is an LED or a laser.
2. _____ A fiber-optic system sends messages by changing the amount of electricity that goes to the LED or laser, thereby changing the amount of light that goes through the optical fiber.
3. _____ Lasers are better than LEDs for high-speed, long-distance communication.
4. _____ A single optical fiber can carry the same amount of information as is contained in about a thousand telephone conversations.
5. _____ While optical fibers can be used to carry information in analog format, it is not very practical at this time.

Fiber Optics

6. _____ Most televisions and stereos use the analog format for transmitting information.
7. _____ Scientists have still not been able to produce high-quality optical fibers in large quantities.
8. _____ Telephone companies are most interested in optical fibers for their ability to transmit information over very long distances, such as from one coast of the United States to the other.
9. _____ Most telephone companies would prefer to build fewer repeaters.

Exercise 2

Complete the following summary of paragraphs 23–37 by filling in each blank with the appropriate word or phrase.

Fiber optics is somewhat like _____ communication. A light source, or _____, is converted into a signal by means of a process called _____. The signal is sent through an _____, and the information is caught and interpreted by a _____.

Two types of light sources are used in optical communication: _____ and _____. When a certain amount of _____ is passed through a laser or LED, it will emit light. The point at which the object begins to emit light is called the _____. Once that point is exceeded, the amount of light _____ by the laser or LED is _____ to the amount of _____ that is passing through it.

Although both LEDs and lasers can be used for optical communication, _____ emit more light and can be _____ faster. LEDs are mostly used for _____ speed communication over _____ distances.

Optical communication has two advantages over ordinary communication: it is capable of sending _____ information over _____ distances. Traditionally, the _____ at which information could be transmitted has been a major _____ in communications. Whereas telephones can transmit information at a rate of _____ hertz, and television at the rate of _____ hertz, fiber optics can break the communications _____ by transmitting information at a speed of more than 1 billion hertz.

The problem with sending _____ this fast is that lasers and LEDs have a tendency to distort _____ signals. The solution to this problem is to use a _____ format for the data. This will allow communication at _____ speeds without difficulty.

Optical communication can be used for longer distances because there has been a dramatic _____ in the amount of signal that is _____ when sent over an optical fiber. Increasing the distance that the signal can be transmitted means that users of fiber optics (such as _____ companies) will have to build fewer _____. Since these are expensive to build and maintain, the _____ _____ distance between them is an _____. Ordinary _____ _____ telephone lines require a repeater every mile or so. Fiber-optic systems need a repeater every _____. Soon there will be optical fibers that can transmit signals as much as _____ without the use of a _____.

Exercise 3

Look back at the Warmup Questions at the beginning of Chapters 16 and 17. Which of these questions apply to the information you have just read? Now that you have finished the entire reading, which questions would you answer differently? Which would you answer in the same way?

INTEGRATION QUESTIONS FOR DISCUSSION AND WRITING

Directions: The following questions ask you to find relationships among the ideas in the first two readings in this unit: "The Global Telecommunications Revolution" (Chapter 16) and "Laser Communication" (Chapter 17). Discuss your answers with your classmates.

1. Find the places in "Laser Communication" that explain the same fiber-optics principles discussed in Jastrow's "The Global Telecommunications Revolution" (especially paragraphs 4–9). Compare Jastrow's explanation with that of Hecht and Teresi. In your comparison, include the following points:

    Does Jastrow disagree with or contradict any of the points in the Hecht and Teresi reading? Has he left out any important information?

    Which of the explanations is more detailed? Which is easier to understand?

    How much of the differences between the two readings can be accounted for by the fact that these readings were intended for different audiences, and written for different purposes?

    Support your comparison with specific examples from both of the readings.

2. Do you think Hecht and Teresi would agree with Jastrow that fiber optics will completely change the way people live within the next twenty years?

3. In paragraphs 13 and 14 of "The Global Telecommunications Revolution," Jastrow presents some of the arguments for and against his belief that the cities will begin to disappear within twenty years. Do you think Jastrow is correct? Why or why not?

4. Do you think that fiber optics will have other, more important effects on society than the ones Jastrow has mentioned?

QUESTIONS FOR FURTHER RESEARCH

1. Because the reading in this chapter was published in 1982, some of the information may no longer be current. Locate some of the more important statistics in the reading and verify that those statistics are still accurate. For example, what is the farthest distance today that a laser signal can be transmitted without the use of a repeater (paragraph 37)?

2. Music has become increasingly available on what are known as *digital audio discs*. These are plastic discs on which music is stored in a digital format. The machines used to play digital discs contain a laser for reading the information and converting it to music.

    Find out more about the technical aspects of digital discs. How are they different from the familiar phonograph records and cassette tapes? Why does music from a digital disc have such improved sound quality?

CHAPTER 18

Fiber-Optics Applications

WARMUP QUESTIONS

The last reading in this unit on fiber optics is also taken from Jeff Hecht and Dick Teresi's *Lasers: Supertools of the 1980's*. In this reading, the authors discuss some of the optical-fiber installations that were being built or were in the planning stages at the time the book was written.

Before you begin the reading, discuss the following questions with your classmates.

1. Would you be interested in a product that was a combination of a telephone and a television? How would you use such a product? Would a combination telephone/television have any disadvantages?

2. Would you like to have a combination computer terminal/television screen in your home through which you could request any movie you wanted, twenty-four hours a day? Would this product have any disadvantages?

3. Would you like to be able to use a computer terminal/television screen to shop for food, clothes, and luxury items from your home? Why or why not?

4. Do you think that you could get an advanced education from courses over a computer terminal/television screen in your home, instead of going to college? Why or why not?
   This reading discusses some of the applications of the optical-fiber technology you read about in the preceding two chapters.
   What uses of optical fibers do you know about already, or can you imagine?
   _____
   _____

   What questions do you have about the practical uses of optical fibers?
   _____
   _____

DIRECTIONS FOR READING

Before you read this selection, first skim it quickly. Look at the section headings, and read the first sentence of each paragraph. Then read the entire selection quickly for general understanding.

Fiber-Optics Applications
Jeff Hecht and Dick Teresi

JAPAN'S FIBERED CITY

1   Over the past decade, Japan has made tremendous strides in commercial electronics, particularly in consumer products. The progress has been so rapid that many U.S. electronics companies are running scared. Since about 1975, Japan has been making a similar push in fiber optics and, as a result, has become the world leader in many areas of optical-fiber and semiconductor-laser technology. Japan was also the first to demonstrate broadband fiber-optic communications to homes, on July 18, 1978, in Higashi Ikoma. At this writing, that experiment is continuing.

2   It's called HI-OVIS, for Highly Interactive Optical Visual Information System, and serves 158 homes. Its exact cost hasn't been disclosed, but around 1980 knowledgeable estimates ran in the $25- to $40-million range. Most of the money has come from Japan's powerful Ministry for International Trade and Industry.

3   The goals for HI-OVIS include evaluating fiber-optics technology and helping Japan develop a fiber-optics industry. But the most interesting part of the experiment involves the four major *social* goals of the program:

- Establishing a new community of people linked together by HI-OVIS—a sort of video neighborhood.
- Making educational courses available in the home.
- Developing a "safe local-welfare society" by encouraging people to help each other and by helping deliver medical, police, and fire-protection services over the communications network.
- Making subscribers actively select a source of information rather than passively watch broadcast television.

4   The central element of this social experiment is an interactive television channel. Technically, the transmission originates at a studio in HI-OVIS headquarters. However, the subscribers have television cameras and microphones in their homes, which they can use to send homemade programs to the studio—much in the way people use telephones to participate in radio talk shows. Engineers at the studio can select a signal from the studio or one from a subscriber's home to send to all homes watching the program.

5   Programs on the interactive channel are designed to encourage participation. Some programs feature discussions of political issues. In others, subscribers share experiences. One example is a cooking program that encourages viewers to show others how they make their favorite recipes in their own kitchens.

6   HI-OVIS also functions as a cable-television system, retransmitting television signals from remote stations to subscribers' homes. Subscribers can use their home control consoles to request that one of a handful of videotapes in a small library be played especially for them. That library once included children's programs, but the children became such enthusiastic users of the service that no one else could use it—and in the process they wore out some of the videotapes by playing them more than 500 times. Viewers can also request displays

of still pictures, including frequently updated information, such as train and plane schedules.

7   The Japanese seem to be satisfied with the initial results. "HI-OVIS has become a part of the lives of [subscribers]," a preliminary report concludes. The next step under consideration is expansion to create HI-OVIS II, which would serve a few thousand homes and probably cost over $100 million. If it gets the go-ahead HI-OVIS II could be in operation by 1985.

FIBERED FARMS—THE CANADIAN VERSION

8   A somewhat less ambitious—and much less expensive—test of fiber-optic service to homes was to begin in rural Manitoba in September 1981. This system is to serve about 150 homes: 50 each in the villages of Elie and St. Eustache and 50 farms between the two. It's intended as a step toward Canada's goal of providing rural communities with telecommunication services equal to, or better than, those enjoyed by urban residents, according to Brian B. McCallum, who helped organize the test. Canada's interest in improving the quality of rural life reflects the importance of agriculture to the country's economy.

9   The cost is about $6.3 million, only about one-fifth that of HI-OVIS, but the services are similar except for the absence of an interactive channel. The Manitoba subscribers can pick two channels at a time out of nine available; each HI-OVIS subscriber can receive only one channel at a time (meaning that all television sets in the house must be tuned in to that one channel). Canadian subscribers can choose from among seven stereophonic music signals, a service not available from HI-OVIS. The optical fibers also provide telephone service in the Canadian system (but not in the Japanese system); many of the Manitoba subscribers are getting single-party telephone service for the first time in their lives. In fact, some of them only recently had the number of parties sharing their telephone lines reduced to four. The Manitoba subscribers also have a channel for communicating with a computer, but they cannot request specific video programs from a stored library.

FRANCE'S VISION OF THE FUTURE

10   At this writing, the latest and most ambitious vision of the fibered future to be translated into hardware is in France. The French Directorate of Telecommunications, which operates the country's telecommunications network, is spending about $100 million to install a fiber-optic system connecting some 4,500 homes in the resort city of Biarritz. Current plans call for service to the first 1,500 homes to begin in early 1983. The system is part of an effort to push technological development in France.

11   Biarritz is the first project to include videophone service. The idea is similar to the Bell System's Picturephone, which never really got off the ground in the United States. However, the French system may have a better chance, because its technology is more advanced. It uses the full resolution of a European television screen, which has about 20 percent more lines than a U.S. screen, in contrast to the much lower resolution used in Picturephone. Because the videophone service is not expected to be much more expensive than regular French telephone service, planners of the Biarritz system hope to avoid another deterrent to Picturephone use—its high cost.

12   Each Biarritz subscriber will receive a color television set and a black-and-white television camera. Although the videophone service can operate with

color-television cameras, there aren't any French-made color-television cameras that can compensate for home-to-home variations in lighting. Rather than importing cameras, the French government decided to supply French-made black-and-white cameras only. Users can add their own color-television cameras if they wish.

13   In addition to videophones, the system will provide a choice among five color-television channels, three in French and two in Spanish (because Biarritz is near the Spanish border). Videotapes and local broadcasts will be added to make at least fifteen television channels available. One possibility might be continuous monitoring of the surf on the resort city's beaches with a remote television camera, according to Alain Bernard, Directorate engineer responsible for the project. Subscribers will also have their choice of five channels of stereophonic music.

STUDY QUESTIONS

Directions: Refer to the reading to answer the following study questions.

1. This reading discusses fiber-optics applications in three countries. In the following spaces, identify the three countries, and the locations within those countries, that have set up fiber-optics experiments.

    CountryLocation

    _____

    _____

    _____

2. Carefully reread paragraphs 1 and 2.
    A. According to paragraph 1, Japan was the first country to develop
        a. commercial electronics.
        b. consumer products.
        c. semiconductor-laser technology.
        d. optical communications to homes.
    B. Fill in the following blanks with information from paragraph 2 about the Japanese fiber-optics project.

        Name: _____

        Size: _____

        Cost: _____

        Sponsoring agency: _____

3. Look again at paragraph 3.
    A. According to this paragraph, what was HI-OVIS supposed to help develop? (Circle all that apply).
        a. fiber-optics technology
        b. additional export income
        c. industry and manufacturing
        d. social progress
        e. better relations with industrialized nations
    B. What is a "video neighborhood"?

        _____

    C. What is a "local-welfare society"?
        a. a society in which the government pays for education and medicine
        b. a society in which people help their neighbors
        c. services on a communications network

4. Carefully reread paragraphs 4 and 5.
    A. According to paragraph 4, where do the HI-OVIS programs come from?
        a. HI-OVIS headquarters
        b. subscribers' homes
        c. both a and b
    B. List the types of interactive programs discussed in paragraph 5.

        _____

        _____

Fiber Optics

5. Look again at paragraphs 6 and 7.
   A. Which of the following are true statements, according to paragraph 6? (Circle all that apply).
      a. The HI-OVIS system is used to send ordinary television programs into subscribers' homes.
      b. Subscribers can request information about the arrival and departure of airplane flights.
      c. Children can no longer request frequently updated information.
   B. Which of the following statements is correct, according to paragraph 7?
      a. The government has decided not to continue with the project until further studies are made.
      b. The government plans to spend at least twice as much on HI-OVIS II as on the initial project.
      c. The authors think the Japanese are not really satisfied with the project.
      d. The second phase of the project will definitely be completed by January 1986.

6. Carefully reread paragraph 8.
   A. Which of the following ideas can be concluded from the first sentence of paragraph 8? (Circle all that apply.)
      a. HI-OVIS was a very expensive project.
      b. The Canadian project was inferior to HI-OVIS.
      c. More money was spent in Japan than in Canada.
   B. According to paragraph 8, why does the Canadian government want to improve telecommunications services in farming areas?

      _____
      _____

7. Look again at paragraph 9. The purpose of this paragraph is to compare the features of HI-OVIS with those of the Canadian project. Use the information in paragraph 9 to complete the following lists.
      HI-OVIS features not included in the Canadian project:

      a. _____
      b. _____
      Features of the Canadian system not included in HI-OVIS:

      a. _____
      b. _____
      c. _____
      d. _____

8. Read paragraph 10 carefully again.
   Compare and contrast the French project with HI-OVIS in terms of cost and number of homes served.

      _____
      _____

9. Carefully reread paragraphs 11 and 12.
   A. Paragraph 11 says that videophone service was not expected to be much more expensive than regular telephone service, and paragraph 12 says that every home in

the French system was to have its own television camera. From these facts, can you guess what a *videophone* is?

_____

_____

B. According to paragraph 11, what were the two main disadvantages of the Picturephone, which was developed by the Bell System in the United States?

_____

_____

How did the French system propose to solve these problems?

_____

_____

C. According to paragraph 12, why did the French engineers decide to use black-and-white television cameras?
   a. The technology was superior.
   b. The system uses black-and-white television.
   c. Videophones cannot operate with color television cameras.
   d. The government wanted to use French-made hardware.
D. According to paragraphs 10–13, how is the French system different from the Japanese and Canadian projects? How is it similar?

_____

_____

_____

_____

INTEGRATION QUESTIONS FOR DISCUSSION AND WRITING

Directions: The following questions ask you to find relationships among the ideas in the three readings in this unit: "The Global Telecommunications Revolution" (Chapter 16), "Laser Communication" (Chapter 17), and "Fiber-Optics Applications" (Chapter 18).

1. According to paragraph 14 of "Laser Communication," optical fibers could theoretically be used to transmit more than six billion television channels. Do you think this many television channels will ever be needed? Why or why not?

2. a. According to "Fiber-Optics Applications," two of the systems proposed or in development involved the installation of a television camera in subscribers' homes. Critics of this kind of system say that having a camera in a person's home—especially if that camera is hooked up to a system run by the government—is a potential invasion of privacy. Do you agree or disagree?
   b. Other critics of the kind of interactive systems described in this reading say that those who run the system can keep track of which television programs you watch, and how often you watch them. Would you feel uncomfortable in this kind of situation?

3. Could the three projects described in "Fiber-Optics Applications" have been completed using regular wire or cable? Did the services described in the reading *require* the use of fiber optics? Support your answer with specific information from the reading.

Fiber Optics

4. In Columbus, Ohio, in the early 1980s, the Warner Cable Company started an experimental cable service in which viewers could respond to questions on their television screen by pressing buttons on a special box attached to their television. Viewers could request special programs, participate in game shows or public opinion surveys, or ask for more information about a particular program they were watching. (Viewers watching a cooking show, for example, could press a button and the cable company would send them a copy of the recipe.)

After several years, however, the interactive part of the cable service was discontinued. Warner Cable continues to send cable television channels into subscribers' homes, but viewers at home can no longer communicate with the computer in the company's headquarters.

Why do you think this service failed? Was it because of the technology? (The system used ordinary copper wires rather than fiber optics.) Was it because of the cost? Was it because of the likes and dislikes of the viewers? Discuss your answers with your classmates.

QUESTIONS FOR FURTHER RESEARCH

1. Since the book from which the final two readings in the unit were taken was published in 1982, some of the information discussed (especially in the second of the two readings) may no longer be current. Consult the *Readers' Guide to Periodical Literature* to find more-recent articles about HI-OVIS or one of the other projects discussed. In particular, try to find out if these experimental systems were successful, and if they are still being developed or expanded.

2. Look for recent articles that discuss new developments in fiber-optics technology or report on other cases in which a small fiber-optics system was installed as an experiment. Compare your findings with the information presented in the readings in this unit.

Acknowledgments (continued)

"Controversies over Artificial Intelligence" by Nancy B. Stern from Stern/Stern, *Computers in Society,* © 1983, pp. 331–334. Reprinted by permission of Prentice-Hall, Englewood Cliffs, NJ.

"Populations, the Environment, and Humans," including Figures 7-1 to 7-5, from pp. 525–531, 533–535, 537–538 in *The Human Side of Biology* by William H. Mason and Norton L. Marshall. Copyright © 1983 by William H. Mason and Norton L. Marshall. Reprinted by permission of Harper & Row, Publishers, Inc.

"Factors Limiting Growth" and Figures 8-1 to 8-3 from *Biology Today,* third edition, by David L. Kirk. Copyright © 1980 by Random House, Inc. Reprinted by permission of the publisher.

"Population and Natural Resources" from *The Main Issues in Bioethics,* pp. 20–22. Andrew C. Varga. © 1980 Paulist Press. Reprinted by permission of the publisher.

"Social Relations" in *Psychology: An Introduction,* p. 600–608. A. F. Willig and G. Williams. © 1984 McGraw-Hill Book Company. Reprinted by permission of the publisher.

"Some Conditions of Obedience and Disobedience to Authority" reprinted by permission from *Social Psychology: Concepts and Applications* by Louis A. Penner; Copyright © 1986 by West Publishing Company. All rights reserved.

"Experiments in Conformity" and Figure 12-1 from *Psychology Today: An Introduction,* fifth edition, by Richard Bootzin, Elizabeth F. Loftus, and Robert B. Zajonc. Copyright © 1980 by Random House, Inc. Reprinted by permission of the publisher.

"What Is Language?" from *An Introduction to Language,* 2d ed., by Victoria Fromkin and Robert Rodman. Copyright © 1978, 1974 by Holt, Rinehart and Winston. Reprinted by permission of CBS College Publishing.

"Acquisition and Learning" from *The Natural Approach* by Krashen and Terrell; Hayward, California, Alemany Press, 1983; pages 118–119. Reprinted by permission of the publisher.

"Child Language Acquisition" from *Child Psychology,* second edition, by E. M. Hetherington and R. D. Parke. © 1979 McGraw-Hill Book Company. Reprinted by permission of the publisher.

Table 15-1 from "Universals of Grammatical Development in Children," D. I. Slobin, as printed in *Advances in Psycholinguistics,* G. B. Flores d'Arcais and W. J. M. Levelt, eds. Reprinted by permission of North-Holland Publishing Company. © 1970.

"The Global Telecommunications Revolution" by Robert Jastrow, first appeared in *Science Digest,* March 1984. © Robert Jastrow. Reprinted by permission.

"Laser Communication: Toward the Fibered Society" and "Fiber-Optics Applications" from *Lasers: Supertools of the 1980's* by Jeff Hecht and Dick Teresi. Originally published by Ticknor & Fields Publishers. Copyright © 1982 by Jeff Hecht and Dick Teresi. Reprinted by permission.

Index

"Acquisition and Learning" (Krashen and Terrell), 255–256
Affixes, 11
Ambiguity, 8–9
Arguments, reconstructing of, 15–16

Boone, Louis E., "Consumer Behavior: Basic Concepts" (with Kurtz), 25–35
Boorstin, Daniel J., 14–15
Bootzin, Richard R., "Experiments in Conformity" (with Loftus, Zajonc, and Braun), 217–219
Braun, Jay, "Experiments in Conformity" (with Bootzin, Loftus, and Zajonc), 217–219

"Child Language Acquisition" (Hetherington and Parke), 263–265
"Computers, Programs, and Programming Languages" (Kelley), 81–88
Concepts
 applying, 16–17
 summarizing, 17–18
"Consumer Behavior: Basic Concepts" (Kurtz and Boone), 25–35
Context, meaning and, 10–11
"Controversies over Artificial Intelligence" (Stern), 115–117
Critical readers, 2

"Experiments in Conformity" (Bootzin, Loftus, Zajonc, and Braun), 217–219

"Factors Limiting Growth" (Kirk), 157–260
"Fiber-Optics Applications" (Hecht and Teresi), 313–315
Fromkin, Victoria, "What Is Language?" (with Rodman), 233–240

"Global Telecommunications Revolution, The" (Jastrow), 275–277
Good readers, 1–2

Headings, scanning of, 2–3
Hecht, Jeff
 "Fiber-Optics Applications" (with Teresi), 313–315
 "Laser Communication: Toward the Fibered Society" (with Teresi), 285–291
Hetherington, E. Marvis, "Child Language Acquisition" (with Parke), 263–265

Illustrations, examining, 3

Jastrow, Robert, "The Global Telecommunications Revolution," 275–277

Kelley, J. Patrick, "Computers, Programs, and Programming Languages," 81–88
"Key Business Decisions" (Marcus et al.), 55–58
Kirk, David L., "Factors Limiting Growth," 157–160
Kolter, Philip, "Market Targeting," 67–70

Krashen, Steven, "Acquisition and Learning" (with Terrell), 255–256
Kurtz, David L., "Consumer Behavior: Basic Concepts" (with Boone), 25–35

Lahey, Benjamin B., "Vision: Your Human Camera," 5–8
"Laser Communication: Toward the Fibered Society" (Hecht and Teresi), 285–291
Loftus, Elizabeth F., "Experiments in Conformity" (with Bootzin, Zajonc, and Braun), 217–219

Main ideas, 11–15
 identification of, 11–12
 relationship between, 12–13
 summarizing, 17–18
 supporting details and, 13–15
Marcus, Burton, "Key Business Decisions," 55–58
"Market Targeting" (Kolter), 67–70
Marshall, Norton L., "Populations, the Environment, and Humans" (with Mason), 129–138
Mason, William H., "Populations, the Environment, and Humans" (with Marshall), 129–138
Meaning
 affixes and roots and, 11
 context and, 10–11
 of paragraphs, 9

323

Index

Notes, 17–18

Outlines, 18

Paragraphs
  main ideas of, 11–15
    relationship between, 12–13
    supporting details, 13–15
  meaning of, 9
  relationship between, 12–13
Parke, Ross D., "Child Language Acquisition" (with Hetherington), 263–265
Penner, Louis, "Some Conditions of Obedience and Disobedience to Authority," 209–210
Phrases and words
  definitions of, 10
  highlighted, 3
Poor readers, 1
"Population and Natural Resources" (Varga), 167–168
"Populations, the Environment, and Humans" (Mason and Marshall), 129–138
Prefixes, 11
Procedures, reconstructing of, 15–16

Reading, process of, 1–2
Reading strategies, 2–3, 8–18
  ambiguity and, 8–9
  concepts and, 16–17
  main ideas, 11–15
    identifying, 11–12
    relationship between, 12–13
    supporting details, 13–15
  preview selections, 2
  reconstructing arguments, procedures, or related sequences of ideas, 15–16
  rereading, 9
  scanning of, 2–3
    headings and subheadings, 2–3
    illustrations, 3
    words or phrases, 3
  summarizing as, 17–18
  topics and
    meaning related to, 9
    new information, 18
    recalling information, 2
  vocabulary and
    affixes and roots, 11
    contextual meaning, 10–11
    inessential, 9
Rereading, 9
Rodman, Robert, "What Is Language?" (with Fromkin), 233–40
Roots, of words, 11

Scanning material, 2–3
"Social Relations" (Wittig and Williams), 179–184
"Some Conditions of Obedience and Disobedience to Authority" (Penner), 209–210
Stern, Nancy B., "Controversies over Artificial Intelligence," 115–117
Subheadings, scanning of, 2–3
Summarizing
  after reading, 17–18
  sections of material, 17
Supporting details, 13–15

Teresi, Dick
  "Fiber-Optics Applications" (with Hecht), 313–315
  "Laser Communication: Toward the Fibered Society" (with Hecht), 285–291
Terrell, Tracy, "Acquisition and Learning" (with Krashen), 255–256
Thornburg, David D., "Thought, Creativity and the Computer," 107–108
"Thought, Creativity and the Computer" (Thornburg), 107–108
Topic
  meaning related to, 9
  post-reading review of, 18
  recalling information about, 2, 3

Varga, Andrew C., "Population and Natural Resources," 167–168
"Vision: Your Human Camera" (Lahey), 5–8
Vocabulary
  affixes of, 11
  contextual meaning of, 10–11
  inessential, 9

"What Is Language?" (Fromkin and Rodman), 233–240
Williams, Gurney, III, "Social Relations" (with Wittig), 179–184
Wittig, Arno F., "Social Relations" (with Williams), 179–184
Words and phrases
  definitions of, 10
  highlighted, 3

Zajonc, Robert B., "Experiments in Conformity" (with Bootzin, Loftus, and Braun), 217–219